*L*OOK AT CHRIST'S CHURCH AS YOU SEE HER VISIBLY IN the world, and I ask you, brethren, though she has much about her that is admirable, whether there is not much that might cause her Lord to cast her away. Even in her regenerate state, she speaks truly when she says, "she is black as the tents of Kedar". Mark the hypocrites that come into the Christian Church and that mar her purity.—Observe even the true saints—how unbelieving, how carnally-minded often, how childish, how ready to murmur against God. How few of them are fathers in Israel. When they ought to be teachers they have need to be instructed in the first elements of the faith. What heresies come into the Church, and how many unstable minds are carried away with them.

And yet you see, dear friends, it is written that Christ loved his Church and gave himself for it. I think I see it—a piece of ground untilled; neither hedged, nor walled, not covered with vines, nor redolent with the perfume of sweet flowers, but it is a spot in the wilderness, filled with thorn, and the thistle, and the brier; her hedges are broken down; the stones of her wall are scattered; the wild boar out of the wood wasteth her; all kinds of unclean creatures lurk among her weeds and brambles. Oh, how is it, thou Lord of glory, that thou couldst buy, at the price of thy heart's blood, such a waste piece of ground as that? What couldst thou see in that garden that thou shouldst determine to make it the fairest spot of all the earth, that should yield thee the richest of all fruit?

C. H. Spurgeon. Cited from sermon No. 628 titled "A glorious Church".

Local Church Practice

Local Church Practice

Baruch Maoz
Erroll Hulse
Herbert Carson
Dic Eccles
Colin Richards
Keith Davies
Ian Tait
John Davison

I am the true vine

John 15 v1

Carey Publications
5 Fairford Close
Haywards Heath Sussex

First printed 1978

ISBN 085479 6819

Design   Cover design—Lawrence Evans

Printed by Stanley L. Hunt (Printers) Ltd
Midland Road, Rushden, Northants

Contents

Introduction

The origin of the chapters of this book is described below. It is immediately apparent that most of the material is the result of the annual Carey Conference for ministers. Three chapters are taken from the bi-monthly magazine *Reformation Today*.

* These appeared in the book 'The Ideal Church' published by Carey Publications which is now no longer in print.

The titles of the chapters together with the sub-headings will give some indication as to their importance and relevance today. This is particularly the case with such obviously vital matters as church planting and missionary work (chapters 9 and 10). It seems strange that neglect to expound these fundamental subjects has prevailed for so long. The same can be said, although to a lesser degree, of chapters 6, 7 and 8.

Baruch Maoz's exposition puts the local church in the position designed for her by God. The call in chapter 1 for the work of the Gospel in all its ramifications to be church-based is followed in the next chapter by an exposition of what a local church is, the essential marks of a church being outlined.

The Charismatic challenge and how the church should live

The contemporary clamant Charismatic challenge of today is one that calls for a firm uncomprising authoritative repudiation based on Scripture. The challenge is simply that we ought to practise Christianity as it was practised in the apostolic era. At first sight that suggestion seems unanswerable and infallible. Who would dare to refute it? We contend that the Charismatic approach simply does not work. Yet it is not enough to argue from experience or to observe that the miracles and wonders of that extraordinary period have never been repeated in the apostolic fashion. No! We must have a solid biblical foundation for our belief that there is a difference between the extraordinary and temporary on the one hand and the ordinary and permanent on the other. This chapter is by no means a full apologetic for what we describe as Biblical Theology. However, it will show that we have a foundation for the way we conduct ourselves and that this is based on the Bible as a whole rather than on odd texts.

Chapters 4 and 5 on baptism!

Not infrequently Baptists are criticized for what is deemed their mistake of contending for *secondary* issues. Our critics feel that we would do well not to insist on believers' baptism as essential for church membership and that we should also leave the mode of baptism to the choice of the individual candidates. After all, they reason, we are living in times of constant pressure from the Ecumenical movement! Do we not do well to drop contention for *secondary* issues in the interests of evangelical unity?

In reply I would refer to the epistle of Jude. The key verse would seem to be that which says that churches had been infiltrated by evil people who were busy destroying the fabric from within (see Jude 4ff). Jude implies that in spite of such a terrible situation we should still contend for the faith. Under such circumstances believers should not despair.

Rather they should keep themselves in God's love, persevere in prayer and exercise discernment (verses 21, 22).

After expounding along these lines recently I received a telephone call from an experienced Christian who left Methodism and now worships in an Elim Pentecostal Church. He declared that he wholeheartedly agreed with my sermon. In his lifetime he had witnessed the destruction of Methodism. It had come about through lack of discipline. Most of the major denominations have been destroyed by the inclusion in their memberships of those who do not pass the test required for baptism, which according to its biblical mode signifies union with Christ.

It may be that, when the implications of baptism and the Lord's Supper are studied in more detail, our critics might be persuaded that more responsibility attaches to these commands of Christ than first meets the eye.

Unity among like-minded churches

The contributors to this volume do not agree on all details but all are committed to the necessity of church order and all are dedicated to the cause of evangelical unity. Not one would tolerate a sectarian or isola tionist attitude because of baptism or the Lord's table. I speak for all the contributors when I declare that we have a hearty respect for evangelical Presbyterian or Pentecostal churches which practise a different church order from our own. We respect them because they do maintain a discipline and know what they believe. Every local church has the right to maintain the church order it deems scriptural. It is the lack of discipline or church order in some quarters which is regrettable.

The subjects of worship, eldership and evangelism

These subjects form an important part of local church practice. Herbert Carson has given a paper on worship at the Carey Conference but feels that justice could not be done to that comprehensive theme in a few pages. He hopes to develop the subject into a book. Likewise the issue of eldership is one requiring extended treatment. I hope to gather up the articles which have appeared in *Reformation Today* and collate them in book form. Evangelism and the local church is not included because it forms part of the book, *The Way Ahead*, advertized on page 191.

The glory of a local church

All the matters treated in these pages have ultimately to do with the glory of the church. Would that the churches in all their worship and activity approximated to the description "fair as the moon, clear as the sun, and terrible as an army with banners" (Song 6:10). The distinction between basic and heightened glory is made in chapter 11. The important subject of revival is discussed before positive means of preserving the basic glory of a local church are outlined, as follows:

a. The importance of doctrinal instruction
b. The necessity of constant and genuine evangelism
c. Heresy and the glory of a church
d. Building according to the scriptural principles of 1 Corinthians 3:11-15

Even the architecture of a church contributes to her glory. Well-thought-out plans and aesthetic beauty show concern to honour the Lord in everything. Shabby or untidy premises hardly commend the Gospel. It is fitting that, having covered the internal spiritual issues, we should conclude with the outward fabric of the local sanctuary.

Names and illustrations

The publishers are indebted to pastor Don Elliot of Falmouth for the illustrations for chapter 9 and to Lawrence Evans for the cover designs and sketches on the back cover. If you are not sure about the one of Colin Richards there is a photo on page 93.

As for names, we spell Richard (Dick) Eccles as Dic, because he is at Hebden Bridge, Yorkshire. It is a Yorkshirism. When he is outside Yorkshire we spell it Dick!

The Publishers.

1

The Centrality of the Church in the work of the Gospel

by Baruch Maoz

MANY TODAY ARE SEEKING TO RE-EXAMINE THE PRINCIPLES UPON WHICH they have been operating in various areas of Christian endeavour. This is a very healthy tendency, so long as we steer clear of extreme positions and fashion our new ones with due recourse to the Holy Scriptures. Nor may we ignore the actual circumstances in which they must be applied. The fact that we are questioning things does not necessarily mean that we are suspicious of them. Nor does our insisting that we bring every concept to the bar of Holy Scripture necessarily imply that we reject concepts and patterns hammered out by previous generations. Rather, it is simply another way of asserting that it is our highest desire to do whatever God commands, and that we recognise that God commands us authoritatively nowhere but in the Holy Scriptures.

The thoughts offered here are the fruit of some years of thinking, reading and looking into the Scriptures, coupled with personal observations made in the course of nine years of missionary endeavour. However, I do not presume to have all the answers and would be grateful for criticisms and suggestions made by any of the brethren.

1. *The centrality of the church in God's purpose*

Ours is a time when there is a growing re-awakening to the doctrine of the church and a natural, as well as a necessary, desire to discover what practical implications are demanded by a more biblical view of the church. The church is God's major tool for the accomplishment of his will on earth. It is 'by the church' that God is to have glory 'throughout all ages, world without end' (Eph. 3:21). Hence the epistles of the New Testament were written almost exclusively to churches. It is *the church* that is the pillar and ground of the truth—not individuals. The Scriptures relate all Gospel work to churches and describe it as issuing therefrom. New Testament Gospel preaching had, as its purpose, not so much the salvation of individual human beings, but the creation by grace of a holy 'people, zealous of good works'.

In this the New Testament is in harmony with the Old. It is true that in both testaments there are cases when the ordinary way through which God works was substituted by him for another—such as in the cases of prophetesses such as Deborah. But even these were always carried out within the context of *a People* or *a Church*, either as their emissaries or on their behalf.

The church then, is the sphere of God's *evident* saving work. That is why the unity, welfare, purity and health of the church is so important. That is why Paul is so taken up by his concern for the church that he often seems quite literally carried away by it, ready to give his all if only the church might prosper. The examples of this are myriad and do not need proving.

2. *The work of the gospel issues out of the church*

Since the time in which the charismatic, extraordinary gifts ceased and the Apostles were taken from the church (they having heard the Word of God immediately, that is with no mediating instrument between them and God) it is to and through the church that God has granted his authority to teach, preach, comfort and rebuke men by the Gospel. Like the priesthood, none may legitimately take this office to himself unless it be given him by God—and God gives it through the church as his usual instrument of grace.

That is why Paul, after coming by the grace of God to know Jesus to be both Lord and Christ, returns to his own city until called to Antioch. That is why he does not depart from there until he is sent out by the church—and that is why it is to Antioch that he returns in order to render account. It is true that God had spoken to him through the mouth of Ananias (Acts 9:15-17) and also directly in a vision (Acts 22:21; 26:16-18). But Paul does not embark onto his divinely given calling until the Holy Spirit testifies to the truth of that calling by speaking to the church (Acts 13:2). Nor does Silas join him except with the approval and blessing of the church (ibid, 15:40).

It is clear from this that the Holy Scriptures teach that the source of every Gospel endeavour ought to be the church of God and not the desire or personal calling of individual men. Gospel work that follows the Scriptural pattern will issue out of the church, be subservient to its discipline and will be supported by its prayers and blessing.

In these modern days of heightened individualism, we must labour hard so as not to be influenced by the spirit of the age. Modern-day over-occupation with the individual is nothing short of an ungodly selfishness that sets itself over against the Holy Scriptures. We must constantly purge our minds from this kind of thinking if we are to live and to be according to God's good pleasure—and God's good pleasure is to raise up to himself Christian churches for the promotion of holiness, the spread of the Gospel, the encouragement and support of the weak, the rebuke of those that stray and the salvation of sinners to the glory of his own ever-blessed name. Even when John introduces us into heaven, we do not see every redeemed soul sitting on his private cloud singing his own little song before God. They are all singing together one glorious song of grace. That is how we must learn to live and think and labour.

There might be those who would support individualistic Gospel work by referring to the case of Paul, who engaged in Christian witness almost as soon as he was converted (Acts 9:20 and others). Our reply is firstly, that Paul was undergoing a process in which the light of revelation was becoming more and more clear to him. His later action shows that he awaited the call of the church and then engaged in Gospel work on an official basis. Secondly, what I have said is not to be misconstrued as if to say that no-one should be engaged in active witness except those officially recognised as messengers of the Gospel by their local church. All Christians are to be as lights in the world, holding forth the Word of Life. Those that were scattered in the persecution went about everywhere, bearing witness to the Saviour. What we are speaking of here is the office of an evangelist. That is, of one who devotes the whole or most of his time to the work of the Gospel. However, it must be said, that there are times when local churches might forbid an individual to engage in Christian witness until certain shortcomings in his life are corrected. This, not so much as a disciplinary measure, but as a means of protecting God's name from being blasphemed because of the evident disparity between the personal life of the individual and his verbal profession.

What we then learn from Paul's example in Acts 9 is that we should be constantly engaged in reforming our work so that its pattern will be brought ever closer to that revealed to us in the Holy Scriptures. This means, among other things, that we shall have to look into our present organisational settings in order to see whether or not they are in accordance with the Biblical pattern, and if not, seek to reform or to dismantle them. The point I am stressing is this: our present approach to the work of the Gospel is unbiblical. There is no biblical basis for Missionary Societies as we have them today. According to the Scriptures, it is the local church which initiates, commissions and supervises the Gospel work. It is from and by the local church that such a work is supported. Modern day practice represents a serious departure from the biblical pattern and, as such, carries within itself the seed of error with regard to the whole question of church life and the relation of the individual Christian to the church. Such a situation should surely alarm any who believe that a departure from the Scriptural pattern is a departure from the only right one, and that Christians owe the Holy Scriptures their undivided and unqualified obedience. It is our duty then, to seek God for the grace and wisdom needed to correct the situation—and the sooner we start, the better.

3. *Caution about dismantling societies*

A word of caution, however, is needed lest we hot-headedly rush to dismantle what most of us have had no part in building and what, under the hand of God, has served God for many years as a means of saving mercy to countless thousands in many parts of the world.

To start with, reformation does not necessarily have to be the work of a moment. Also we have to do some clear thinking as to what we intend to put in the place of the Missionary Organisations. We will do well to think some more on the subject before we take the axe to hand, lest, in cutting down the bad tree, we also damage that which is good.

I am not sure that the solution lies in leaving the Missions in order to join local churches (if we are not already members of such churches) even if they would thus become responsible for our work. In many cases the church in question does not really know us well, so that our joining is merely symbolic, void of any Scriptural content or substance. It is unlikely that such a church would be able to exercise true pastoral oversight over us. Nor will the church have necessarily commissioned us to the work which we have taken to hand; it is possible that we will have imposed upon them a situation not of their own choosing. For this reason, it seems that, in spite of all the appeal such a solution may hold, there are in it as many shortcomings as there are if we remain in the Missionary Societies and labour under their discipline for the establishment of local churches—to the which we may then submit our work. Either that or we must leave the work for a number of years, go to a country in which a church is to be found, join one, share in its life and labours, and then—if that church would separate us to the work of the Gospel, return to take up the work we left off, this time under the discipline and pastoral oversight of the church of which we have become members.

Perhaps there are cases in which it would be possible to formulate an 'adoption' of the individual by a church in such a way that the pastoral oversight would not be merely theoretical and the material support not the sole mode of support given. This could pertain until such a time when that work could be submitted to the oversight of a local church on the field itself. How this could be worked out in practice is something yet to be seen. I would be happy to have the opinions of others on this matter. It may be that there are no clear principles which may be applied here, and that the details will have to be worked out in the light of each particular case.

Nor is it any solution if we leave the Missionary Societies without joining a local church. We will have accomplished nothing by such a step. By no means would we get closer to the Scriptural pattern, for the Scriptures speak of Gospel work as subservient to the discipline of a local congregation; not of such a work free from Societies. Nor is it right to say that all forms of Missionary Societies are unbiblical, as I hope to show later. It is true that, as most Societies stand today, there is a conflict between conducting the work of the Gospel under *their* jurisdiction and under that of a church, but a situation in which we are not under the discipline of either Society or church is even worse, because it serves as a fruitful field for all kinds of aberrations similar to the ones with which I have become acquainted in my own country. We are over-run by freelancers who owe account to none. This is a state that encourages the natural sinful inclination of man, and will often lead to men doing little more than living around themselves.

We have in Israel a man who 'felt led by the Holy Spirit to preach the Gospel in Israel'. He forsook his wife and children in New York, 'trusting them to the Lord' (as he described it) with the full assurance that God would provide for them while he ran about in Israel doing all kinds of things in which there was little sense or value. But who is there to call such a man to account? To whom will he listen? How can he be controlled or corrected—and does any of us dare to think that we ourselves will never stand in need of correction? Nor will it do to say that the solution is that Christians supporting free-lance missionaries should only support men whom they are sure they can trust. How can anyone find out how much truth there is in reports that come to them from over the seas? It is the system that is corrupt—and a corrupt system is likely to corrupt the best among us.

4. *Co-operation among the churches*

There is another important factor which we must now consider—that of cooperation between churches. Often there are churches that are too small to allow themselves to support a messenger of the Gospel beyond their own pastor, and even that might be too heavy a financial burden. There are other cases in which the kind of work is such that, because of the sums involved, no one church could bear the burden alone.

It is not difficult to show that cooperation between churches is a Scriptural practice. Inter-church cooperation was an accepted thing in the New Testament churches. We find Jerusalem sending Barnabas to visit the congregations between that city and Antioch in Syria with a view to encouraging them in the Way. We find Barnabas later settling in Antioch after having brought Saul over with him from Tarsus (Acts 11:22-26). So too, although Paul had been set aside for the work of the Gospel in Antioch, he received financial support from Philippi (Phil. 4:10-17) and Timothy joins him, although he himself is not from Antioch but from Derbe (Acts 15:1-3). Later on we find others from various churches joining themselves to Paul. Paul's band actually developed into a cooperative effort on the part of many of the Asian and European churches in the work of the Gospel. The churches also joined together in sending relief to the 'poor saints which are at Jerusalem', and the gift is brought there by Paul who was accompanied by a group of believers who represented churches in various parts of the Roman Empire.

Further development of the subject by Mr. Maoz is anticipated.

The Welwyn Evangelical Church—
a good example of a missionary-minded people see chapter 10

5. *The Nature of Inter-church cooperation*

The Holy Scriptures clearly speak of inter-church cooperation. It should also be obvious that circumstances may arise in which such cooperation would be necessary. The question is, what is the Essential Nature of such cooperation? It is not denominational. There is no case in the New Testament in which denominations in any sense of the term are considered. The very concept of denominational church organisations is totally devoid of Scriptural support and should therefore be called into question. The term Church (ekklesia) refers in the New Testament to one of two realities: either a local organised body of Christians or the invisible universal Body of Christ in which all the regenerate take part from all generations and in every place in the universe, whether dead or living.

The only Scriptural reference to the term Church which may be claimed to denote a gathering of organised churches is found in Acts 9:31. However, as this text must be understood in the light of all others which bear upon the subject, denominationalists would be hard pressed to fit a whole denomination into this single, slender reference. The passage seems rather to speak of either the universal church (cf. Acts 9:4) or of the church of Jerusalem now scattered but still conceived of in terms of an organisational unity.

Inter-church cooperation in the New Testament is always described in terms of cooperation between local churches. Hence, any kind of organisation that would be determined upon in order to facilitate coopera-tion between churches must give adequate expression to the separate identi-

16

ty and independence of each local, organised church. Many such forms of organisation are possible, each having their strong and weak points. One such organisational form is that each individual church would be responsible for work in a certain area of the world or for a certain kind of work (such as publishing, radio broadcasts, loaning and selling recordings of sermons, theological education by extension and such like). All other churches would share in these various efforts by giving of their people or their financial resources to the work through that church.

Another possibility is to establish a representative body composed of member churches X, Y and Z. This body would be responsible for all types of work, including works X, Y, Z in which, under the other system, the respective churches would be engaged. Finances would be transferred through the representative body and decisions made through it—but these would first be hammered out in the local churches cooperating. If a problem arose, members of the representative body would confer, providing each other with the relevant information. They would then go back to their churches and lay the problem before them, where, depending on the nature of the problem, it would be discussed by the elders and deacons, or in the presence of the whole church body. Decisions would then be made in the representative body by the majority, just as if the question was dealt with by a single church.

In both cases outlined, the workers remain under the pastoral oversight of their respective mother churches, while the work itself is conducted by various churches being responsible for various fields of activity, or with overall responsibility through a representative body. Existing societies do not then have to dismantle, but merely to re-organise so that they become instruments of churches rather than the supra-church organisations of the contemporary christian scene.

6. *The nature of control exercised over the work*
It is important to clarify the kind of control exercised in the cases outlined. As a matter of fact, it is not so much control as cooperation, with the onus of responsibility and authority laid upon the shoulders of the individual worker on the field. It is high time churches sent their *best* men to the work of the Gospel, men whom they can trust and upon whose judgement they can rely. That is the Biblical pattern. Paul and Barnabas, and later Paul and his other co-workers, themselves decided where they should go, how long they should stay, what they should do and where they should go next. There is not the slightest hint that they leaned upon decisions made by the elders of sending churches. Theirs was the duty of faithfulness and of accounting for the work—*after* it had been carried out. That is not to say that there is no room for a missionary to seek advice or for a church to offer it, but the final decision must rest with the man on the field. This Biblical pattern is eminently practical because the man on the field is the only one who is thoroughly acquainted with the circumstances and

with those finer details of the work that cannot be described in a letter or comprehended during a brief periodic visit. Too many decisions are being made today with regard to missionary work by people who have little vital knowledge of the facts involved.

7. *Financial support*

Financial support would naturally come first from the sending church, although the New Testament shows other churches sharing that responsibility. Phillipi is one such case. We see Timothy and others joining a worker sent out by another church. This also probably implies a sharing of the financial responsibility. It unfortunately needs to be said that financial support is not enough. A deep, practical and personal involvement on the part of the sending or supporting churches is vital. The tendency to send a few dollars here and there, all over the world, borders on irresponsibility and might, in fact, indicate a lack of real concern for the holy work of the Gospel. It obviously lacks the heart-involvement that a real concern would breed. Nor is the habit of sending the missionary only used clothes, or giving him the *old* car necessarily indicative of a real concern for the work. Financial support must be accompanied by continuous, specific and consistent prayer, by moral support through correspondence, the sending of books, clothing and the such like and by sharing as much as is humanly possible in the work of the labourers on every human level as well as by prayer.

Missionaries should be supported so as to enable them to live honourably in the countries of their labour—not above the average of those among whom they work, nor below it. Standards and costs of living in each country are factors which should be taken into consideration when determining the monthly salary. There are messengers of the Gospel who are living very poorly because basic commodities cost a great deal more in the countries where they are labouring, or because the sending church is unwilling to make any real sacrifice. Why must sacrifice be limited to those on the field? A labourer is worthy of his hire. God has ordained that those who preach the Gospel should live by the Gospel. This is another area in which reformation is needed. It must also be said that there are some missionaries who live far above the average level of the countries in which they work. *This* is no better a witness to the Gospel than the other extreme. It is possible that it will be necessary to settle upon a salary that is much higher, or much lower, than that acceptable in the sending country. All depends on the country to which the missionary is being sent. Salaries must be revised periodically in the light of changes in rates of exchange. But they should always be ample. There is no reason why those who labour in the Word and in doctrine should be dependent upon the mercies of special help every time they need to buy the children shoes, go to the dentist or purchase another piece of furniture. Since the members of sending churches are not similarly dependent, there is no conceivable reason why such limitations should be imposed upon missionaries. Missionaries should be paid so that they are able to put aside some money for rainy days while still meeting all the needs of their families. After all, one who does not care for his own household is worse than an infidel: he has denied the faith. The best situation is probably one in which adequate salaries are paid and personal gifts beyond that forbidden—except on rare occasions or from close family and friends. Until then, it will, unfortunately be necessary to supplement the salaries of missionaries with periodic personal gifts.

In addition to regular monthly income, thought should be given to life and health insurance and to pension schemes. Account should also be taken of the fact that most missionary families usually have larger than normal expenses due to the fact that they are called upon to extend frequent hospitality and to share their material substance with others. Attention should also be given to their needs by way of books and cassettes. (This is equally relevant to the support of Pastors and ministers in the home countries, who often labour in adverse financial circumstances for which there is little justification.) The system of 'living by faith', as it is called, is nothing else but living by the faithfulness of others. It has nothing to commend it. It is a denial of the biblical principle that a labourer is worthy of his hire. It lacks any means whereby account can be made of what is done with the money and it encourages either embarrassment in talking about financial matters, or the need to try and make one's needs known without anyone noticing what you are doing, so long as they get the message. There is nothing in such a system that is good, or that is honouring to God. There are very few people in such a situation who have learned to be natural about financial and material matters.

8. *The Work of the Gospel and its Objective*

We have thought about the work of the Gospel in relation to the sending church and of some related practical issues. We must now consider the work of the Gospel with regard to its objective.

The end of all Gospel endeavour is not the salvation of men's souls; it is, the glory of God by raising up to him a 'people zealous of good works'. Gospel work must have the establishment of local churches as its goal. It is worthy of note that all too often radio, recording and correspondence ministries have become substitutes for proper church membership. This is especially common in the United States of America, where tape ministries and radio or TV broadcasts or setting up of Christian schools has taken the place of the church in many people's lives.

The purpose of our labours must be the establishment, edification and enlargement in grace of local Christian churches organised according to the Biblical pattern. Because that pattern includes the independence of churches from each other, the time must come when sending churches encourage the receiving church to stand on its own—and the sooner the

19

better. I fear that there is real substance in Ronald Allan's charge (*The Spontaneous Expansion of the Church and the causes which hinder it*) that the main reason for the evident reticence to carry this principle out into practice has, as its root, not a concern for the faith, but for *our version of it*; as if the truth has no effect of its own, or as if the Holy Spirit can work only through the instrumentality of the sending church.

Spiritual maturity and independent responsibility are two sides of the same coin and can by no means ever be separated. The New Testament teaches us that Paul and the other preachers of the Gospel of whose work we hear in the Scriptures committed their churches to the Holy Spirit and to the Word of God's grace in the confidence that he was indeed able to establish them in the truth and to ensure that they would partake of their inheritence together with all the saints. This they did in spite of their clear awareness of the dangers that hovered over the churches (Acts 20:1-36).

True, the severance was not immediate, nor ever absolute. We find Paul advising, comforting, rebuking and teaching the churches, even returning to visit them. Nevertheless (as the case in Corinth proves), their independence was very real and it undoubtedly served in the hand of God as an important tool to strengthen them in faith and in grace.

The process must, then, be gradual. It might not proceed with the same speed on all levels. Financial independence may well come before or after independence in other areas. In fact, if we conduct our work aright, it seems likely that one of the first responsibilities a new church should be able to bear is the financial—provided we have not encumbered them with commitments which they are not able to bear.

In closing I wish to make two short remarks.

First, the New Testament gives us at least one example of what is called today occupational missionary work. By this is meant missionaries who remove to another area or country with the primary view of labouring for the establishment of a local church, and who support themselves primarily or altogether by working in a secular profession. We will do well to give more attention to this efficient method of spreading the Gospel. It should be noted that, according to the Scriptures, this method is also to be subject to the pastoral oversight of a local church and to the call of the individual by the Holy Spirit through the church.

Secondly, the allergy that some of us have developed to deputational work is not necessarily an indication of spiritual health. It is difficult to conceive of any other way by which cooperating or supporting churches could be made effectively cognisant of the details of the work.

May God give us grace, and may it please him to use these thoughts in order to help us test our ways by the light of Holy Scriptures—and, if need be, to reform our ways so that they will accord with that good and perfect and acceptable will of God.

2

The
Ideal
Church

by Erroll Hulse

WHAT WOULD YOU REGARD AS THE IDEAL LOCAL CHURCH? WERE YOU TO move to another part of the country or across the seas to a land new to you and your family, what would you hope for by way of a local church? From the epistles of the New Testament and the letters to the churches recorded in the early chapters of Revelation we can get some idea of what the different churches were like. And from the New Testament we can establish what a local church ought to be like, this being the purpose of our study.

It is important to say that we are not dealing with any one particular church, or group of churches. With some there is the problem of *death*. Somes causes live more by tradition than by Scripture. As a consequence they are very dead, like the bones Ezekiel saw. (Ezek. 37). Some of the most vigorous and gifted men have been brought to despair in their efforts to revive dead causes. On the other hand there is the problem of *life*. How do you lead a number of converts, some with crazy ideas, some in their spiritual experience, like a yoyo, right up one week, rock bottom the next; others despising discipline as though it were an ugly, monstrous robot which threatens to crush their freedom to do as they please. No church this side of Heaven's border is ideal. If anyone reading this thinks that if he heads for Cuckfield he might find the golden pot that lies at the end of the rainbow, he is warned now! We have our own catalogue of sins, inconsistencies, weaknesses, disappointments and

21

inadequecies. And, if anyone thinks that reading this is going to solve the problems of his church he too will be disappointed. Most churches would need a volume of wisdom the size of John Flavel's six volume set to solve their perplexities! No, in these few pages the ideal will be be outlined. We will then stand back and say, "Well there it is, if that is truly Scriptural what kind of inward and outward surgery is needed for our church to be like that? What reformation is required?"

That we should be concerned about the church at all is interesting. We are living in an age of organizations. These have proliferated and the area of religion is not unaffected. Individuals who have no church connection and who themselves have never been subject to others in regard to spiritual discipline have set up organizations of all kinds. An organization has, for them, been a substitute for a church. As in the time of the Judges, every man is apt to do that which is right in his own eyes. To go back to the time before the Judges, to Moses and the children of Israel in the wilderness, can we imagine the confusion if over a thousand agencies registered themselves as authoritative organizations for hastening a quick and independent entry into Canaan? No! Either they did it together, God's way, or they did not get to Canaan at all. *The local church is God's way.*

There are some believers who are unlikely to read to the end of this article because they have picked up the popular notion of what a church should be. For them the ideal church is where they can take their relations and friends with the least embarrassment. There is some truth in this concept and we ought not to dismiss it. The popular idea is that services should be bright and attractive, the singing should be inspiring, the message short, to the point, always containing a brief, simple outline of how to be saved. The minister ought to be charming, well dressed, and preferably good looking. The decor ought to enhance the impression received by visitors. The people must be friendly. Well, it is obvious that there is no advantage in ghastly singing, an unkempt minister, uncomfortable seats, frigid people, or dull preaching. But it is superficial to stop with that which is mainly outward. The church has to do with the sanctification of believers and preparation for the world to come. If we read the book of Numbers we soon see the wide range of experience to which the church in the wilderness was subject. Gradually, a disorderly, rebellious mob was transformed. During forty years a change took place, until Joshua was able to lead a united people into the promised land.

What then does constitute an ideal church? The above-described popular notion is rejected as superficial, which idea often leads to a situation in which worship services are little more than services of entertainment.

A survey of Scripture and of literature on this subject would seem to confirm that all the essential features of an ideal church can be comprehended by an exposition of the following marks:

1. *Biblical preaching.*
2. *Scriptural church government.*
3. *The sacraments of baptism and the Lord's Supper.*
4. *Spiritual life evidenced by:*
   (*a*) *spiritual worship*　　(*b*) *holiness of life*
   (*c*) *brotherly love*　　(*d*) *evangelism and good works.*

1. Biblical Preaching

Biblical preaching is the first feature to be sought in a local church. If the preaching is truly Scriptural, edifying and inspiring it will make up for much else that might be imperfect. The Scriptures form the spring from which all life is derived by the Holy Spirit of God. All directives and all corrections stem from the Word of God.

As one fly in the apothecary's ointment maketh it to stink so it only needs one serious defect or eccentricity to spoil preaching. Preaching ought to be doctrinal, expository, evangelical, experimental, practical, applicatory and relevant in substance.[1] The delivery of the sermon should be characterized by sincerity, fervency and wisdom. The impression made upon young and old alike should be that a message from God has been heard. Hearers should come away not only having been taught some of the content and meaning of Scripture, but should be convicted of the imperative need to apply what they have heard to their everyday lives.

When I say that the preacher should be sincere I mean that it should be obvious that he has himself experienced the reality of the Christian Gospel and is fully aware that the eternal destiny of souls is involved as he addresses his congregation. By fervent I mean that he should be earnest, bold and affectionate in his preaching. A great deal is included in the word "wisdom". A wise preacher will not be too long, nor too short, nor too simple for the profound, nor too profound for the simple. He will avoid distasteful forms of speech, will be thoughtful in his use of illustrations, and, if possible, will seek by the help of the Holy Spirit to have a symmetry, beauty and proportion both in the content of his address and the style in which it is presented.

Let us never lose the sight of the primacy of preaching. Preaching is the means both by which souls are born again and by which they are built up in their most holy faith.

The systematic, expository method is important, if not vital, to a church. In this way all important subjects can be handled in a thorough way. Far more is learned and retained both by the preacher and by the congregation when a passage is fully opened up, the meaning explained, the doctrine drawn out, the teaching applied—than by the jumping about method. Great care has to be taken not to get bogged down when using the expository method. Happy preacher, he, who is skilful in the speed with which he travels down the straights and negotiates the corners of the expository track. To sustain the interest of the congregation is imperative. Each sermon should be complete in itself. Each should have a total impact of its own upon believer and unbeliever, young and old, educated and uneducated alike; yet each should interlock with the other expositions in the series.

Preaching of this order is the first mark that I would seek in a church. If the preacher's pantry is well stocked, if the diet is nourishing, balanced and well presented, then spiritual health is likely to result in every department of the Christian life. If the Scriptures are honestly, faithfully and fully expounded there will be light and direction for every subject and every situation.

How do we attain to preaching of the order just described? This leads us to consider the second mark:

2. Scriptural Church Government

It is difficult to know which should be placed first, preaching or Church Government. When we think of preaching we think of declaring all that is in the Scriptures—the whole counsel of God. But from where will such preachers come, and to whom are they responsible? Leadership is vital in every realm—civil government, the army, society and even a cricket team. Every aspect of a local church is affected by leadership which in the New Testament is synonymous with the eldership. (Heb. 13:7 and 17—"have the rule" could be translated "ones taking the lead").

The ideal church is a church in which elders have been appointed according to the requirements of Titus 1:5-9 and 1 Tim. 3:1-7. If this has been the case it is to be expected that the elders will feed the flock, which embraces the whole of the first point just outlined—i.e. Biblical Preaching. They will also shepherd, or pastor with diligence, the word "shepherd" being an ideal word because this term includes so much. The tasks of the shepherd are many and varied, but can all be summed up in the word "care". As in the New Testament deacons ought to relieve the elders of such matters as book-keeping, accounts, maintenance etc., so that they may give themselves to prayer, doctrine, and the nurture of souls.

For the fulfilment of their duties the elders have authority delegated to them by the Head of the church. All they do in His name should be reflected in their bearing, conversation, decisions and actions. Their responsibilities can be summed up under three heads as follows:—

24

(a) The ministry of the Word[2]

The church is described by Paul as "the pillar and ground of the truth". (2 Tim. 3:15). The value of truth can hardly be over-estimated in a world overrun with error. In each locality the Church must exhibit the truth as the columns of the Parthenon bore aloft the emblems of ancient Greek glory. So a reigning Christ, the Lamb once slain, able to save to the uttermost all who come God by Him, must be raised to view by means of truth. As the columns of the Parthenon were raised upon stable foundations so preaching must stem from solid doctrinal presuppositions. We should be concerned not only with the pillars but also with the foundations. Our heritage of Reformed truth should not only be taught, but means should be taken for its preservation for future generations. "The things which thou hast heard of me," said the apostle, "the same commit thou to faithful men, who shall be able to teach others also." Jude found it necessary to exhort the believers of his day to contend earnestly for the faith because false teachers were corrupting the Gospel. There is a constant tendency to compromise truth, especially truth which is distasteful to fallen human nature. The decrees of God, the fall of man, original sin, the bondage of the will, effectual calling and particular redemption are some doctrines of Scripture which we may be tempted to by-pass.

In most churches members are at different stages of doctrinal understanding and growth, but the elders should be mature men of experience who are zealous for the whole counsel of God, and diligent too, to ensure that our confessional standards are preserved and handed on to the children of the next generation. Spurgeon when he reprinted the 1689 Baptist Confession of Faith, and when he republished Thomas Watson's *Body of Divinity*, set a good example in this respect. A church is less than ideal if the elders fail in their concern for truth in this way, or if they are not zealous to maintain the highest standards in the pulpit. Watchfulness and oversight should extend to all meetings that are organized. Some churches find meetings in homes very effective as a means of Evangelism. The same high standards should be sought here as elsewhere. Oversight should pertain to young people's meetings where there is often a temptation to lower standards to accommodate the desires of young people who tend to over-simplify the Gospel, desire gimmicks, and seek worldly means to attract outsiders to the meetings.

(b) The personal application of the Word

It has been said that most believers retain less than twenty per cent of what they hear in the preaching. Some of the Puritans were noted for their efforts to conserve teaching by way of catechizing. After morning service the heads of families were encouraged to ask their children at the dinner table to repeat the main points of the sermon.

In an ideal church the teaching ministry ought to be followed up by the personal interest of the elders. They should not only pray for all the members but also try to maintain personal contact with them. Private devotion, family Bible reading, prayers and catechizing ought to be arranged for all the flock. Suitable books should be recommended as a further means of teaching and edification. The natural and spiritual gifts of members ought to be recognized. Such gifts are not privately owned, but are given by Christ for the blessing of the body. (1 Cor. 12. Rom. 12:3-8). Gifts ought, therefore, to be developed and put to use. Some who might think of themselves more highly than they ought, should be restrained. "Reprove, rebuke, exhort with all long-suffering and doctrine," wrote Paul to Timothy. It is in the field of personal application of the Word that there is widespread weakness today. Never was there a greater need for the restoration to the church of a plurality of ruling elders who will be diligent in the care of souls. The care of thirty people is about the maximum for any one elder if he is to be diligent. The elders should seek to review together all the members of the church at least once a month, if not more frequently.

(c) Discipline, admission to and exclusion from membership

An ideal church is one where discipline is maintained. If discipline breaks down a church can soon be overrun by unspiritual people and become the synagogue of Satan.

The elders are to present applicants for baptism and church membership to the church only after they have made a careful examination of their standing in Christ and after they are satisfied that the candidates understand the responsibilities which belong to them as believers.

The under-shepherds are also responsible to Christ and the church to attempt the recovery of any who are straying, either morally or spiritually, or who neglect their responsibilities as members of Christ's body. If such attempts fail then discipline must be enforced, either by exclusion from the Lord's Table or, in extreme cases, by excommunication.

Elders are to be watchful as to the timeliness of the appointment of additional elders or deacons according to 1 Tim. 3:1-13, the unanimity of the church being sought before such are set aside or ordained to office.

That services and the ordinances are carried out with order and reverence belongs also to the responsibility of the elders.

3. The Sacraments

What is a sacrament? It would be difficult to find a better definition than that found in the Larger Catechism which declares that, "a sacrament is an holy ordinance instituted by Christ in His Church, to signify, seal, and exhibit to those that are within the covenant of grace, the benefits of His mediation, to strengthen and increase their faith, and all other graces, to oblige them to obedience, to testify and cherish their love and communion one with another, and to distinguish them from those that are without." By this definition there can only be two sacraments, namely, Baptism and the Lord's Supper. We should not be afraid of the word "sacrament" even though it has been abused by the Roman Church which maintains that there are seven sacraments. The word ordinance which we commonly use is inadequate as it is a term used for more general use to describe that which has been ordained of God. Thus preaching is rightly termed an ordinance. The word "sacrament" is derived from the Latin *sacramentum*—an oath. Roman soldiers were bound by oath to Caesar. God by oath, and it is impossible for Him to lie, has bound Himself to save His elect people. (Heb. 6:17). A sacrament denotes an outward sensible sign of an inward, spiritual grace possessed by the recipient. An ordinance does not carry this connotation and is therefore not an altogether adequate expression for either Baptism or the Lord's Supper.

The Sacraments are important for the following reasons: 1. They are both instituted by Christ. 2. They are visible signs of the main truths of salvation. 3. They seal and confirm the blessings of the New Covenant. 4. They are a means of grace to those who rightly partake of them. It is important to note that both sacraments imply and presuppose repentance, faith and grace in those who partake of them. In other words, they are for believers only.

Baptism signifies union with Christ in His death, burial and resurrection. It is union with Christ by faith that secures our justification, our sanctification and ultimately our glorification. Immersion alone is adequate to symbolize union with Christ as His burial and resurrection, and is also fitting as a symbol of "the washing away of the corruptness of the old man beneath the water"[3] and the resurrection to newness of life by emerging from the water.

The Lord's Supper should be a service simple in form in which both bread and wine are distributed. It is helpful if a time is allowed for members to pray as they may be moved by the Spirit. The Lord's Table should not be so infrequent as to deprive believers of the strength which the sacrament is meant to impart and it is my view that it should not necessarily be confined to the Lord's Day, but I would not, as do some brethren, make a major issue of these details.

4. *Spiritual Life*

So far we have been considering the ideal church from the human, or subjective point of view. We may well ask what, in the eyes of God, forms an ideal church? The Lord's messages to the seven churches of Asia indicate that more than orthodoxy is required. It is possible for everything to be correct according to the letter, but dead in spirit. The believers at Ephesus had laboured patiently to add good works to their orthodox faith. Nevertheless, the church had left her first love and on this account, the candlestick was to be removed. For a church to be true, there must be genuine evidence of spiritual vitality. How do we define spiritual life?

Jonathan Edwards in *The Religious Affections* shows that more is to be looked for than moving testimonies, and appearances of love, zeal, fervour and assurance. For spirituality to be genuine there must be evangelical humility, the spirit and temper of Christ, tenderness of heart, and an all-round symmetry in the Christian life expressed not in word only, but also in practice. Bearing these factors in mind we will now examine four areas in which spiritual life should be in evidence.

(a) Worship

Those who say that they can be Christians without going to church show that they do not have the mind of Christ. In the 84th Psalm we see that the sanctuary of public worship is for the true believer. 1. The place of admiration for which he longs with the most intense longing (v. 1-4). 2. The source of his strength (v. 5-8). 3. The place of his supreme happiness, for there he meets with God Himself (v. 9-12). For His part the Lord declares that He loves the place of public worship more than all the private devotions of His people. (Ps. 87:2). This is not to disparage family worship but rather to show the pre-eminence of public worship.

The word used for worship in the New Testament could be translated "service". We gather to ascribe supreme worth to God and to give ourselves wholly to Him in love and obedience. The public worship of God should be reverent in that we have awe before a holy God. The angels cry, "holy, holy, holy, is the Lord of hosts, the whole earth is full of His glory." (Isa. 6:3, Rev. 4:8). We do not read that the angels crack jokes. Flippancy and lightness in God's house are out of place. Worship must be *humble* in that we realize that we are sinners, but *joyful* also, because we are redeemed from sin. This joy should be reflected in the melodious singing of psalms and hymns, suitably chosen in regard to their content. Worship ought to be *spiritual*. We should not have to rely on externalities such as special music items or ornate architecture. It should also be *prayerful* in that the worshippers should be led to entire dependence upon the sovereign grace of God for their every need.

The whole tenor of a worship service should be such that all ages are catered for, common sense allowing for the use of a creche for babies, and provision for young children to be instructed separately for part of the service if necessary.

A spirit of worship should be experienced at the prayer meetings where opportunity should be given for all believers to participate. Needless to say, an ideal church is one in which all concerns, activities and plans are laid before God in intercession. The times for prayer should be convenient so that all members have the opportunity of attending at least one prayer meeting a week.

(b) Holiness of Life

Holiness can be defined as separation from the world to the worship and service of God. It can also be understood as heartfelt conformity to the moral law or ten commandments. If we love God with all our hearts and minds we will fulfil the law, for love is the fulfilling of the law. (Rom. 13:10). The moral law will have a prominent place in the teaching and life of an ideal church. Holiness should be evident in the conversation of believers as Peter says, "so be ye holy in all manner of conversation". Sharing together of spiritual life and experience by way of fellowship is important. When those who profess the Gospel are reluctant to speak of anything else but worldly things it shows that they are in a poor spiritual condition.

(c) Brotherly Love

In the New Testament we see the wall of divison broken down between believing Jews and believing Gentiles. We also see those of many different nations and languages brought together into one united body. In any local church we ought to expect an exemplification of this unity. Professional men should sit side by side with those of humble occupation. Rich and poor, Chinese and Negro, Ceylonese and Argentinians should find spiritual fulfilment together in the same church in any locality. Happily this is the case in some of our churches, but in too many places assemblies tend to consist of one class only. We do not minimize differences of culture, background or temperament, but brotherly love should be of such power as to overcome these things. Pastors find that even when people are very much the same from the natural point of view, there can be terrible clashes of character or differences of opinion. Resentment, however, must be overcome. The emphasis on brotherly love throughout the New Testament is such that we must say that if this is not found in practice then a church is less than ideal.

(d) Evangelism and good works

Evangelism is not placed last because it is least in importance. In Israel there are two lakes, the one called Galilee and the other the Dead Sea. The Sea of Galilee is fresh. It takes in and gives out fresh water. The Dead Sea is deadly to life. It only takes in but does not give out. So any church which is solely taken up with the edification of its own members, without concern for outreach, is inadequate, and likely to be spiritually stagnant. The command to preach the Gospel to every creature, and to

29

teach all nations, is binding upon the churches until the end of the age. Every believer, if he has a true experience of salvation, has deep desires for the conversion of his relatives, his neighbours and workmates. He longs, too, for the conversion of the whole world, Jews and Gentiles, to Christ.

The local church should take practical steps to ensure that the Gospel is being made known throughout the locality at all times. It is here that good works are important. It does not help if people get the impression that the Gospel consists of words only, or even of special evangelistic meetings arranged for their benefit. If the lives of believers do not ring true; if they are guilty of shoddy work; if they are not zealous for good works; are not compassionate toward the needy, then evangelistic activity is likely to be fruitless. Without love the words of evangelism will be like a sounding brass. The hiring of special evangelists or the organization of special evangelistic campaigns will little avail when the churches are in a chronic spiritual state.

In a society in which people insulate themselves from others great stress ought to be laid on hospitality. It is possible to be very lonely in a great city for the simple reason that each family is living in a watertight compartment. This is particularly noticeable with flat-dwellers, many of whom watch events on the other side of the world on television but who rarely speak to their next door neighbours. The example of Cornelius (Acts Ch. 10) in the use of his home is noteworthy. Hospitality is essential for the office of eldership.

The local church should not only be involved in the task of evangelizing in its own annual crusade (that is evangelism from the 1st January-31st December) but should be concerned, too, with the establishment of other churches in the country. God's agent for evangelizing the world is the local church. Furthermore, if a church is ideal, prayer will ascend for churches in all nations, and practical support will be given for the establishment of true churches in other countries. The emphasis should be upon the establishment of churches rather than the establishment of missionary societies.

The mistake is sometimes made for a church to be enthusiastic about everything in general but support nothing well in particular. Resolution is needed to refuse to have too many interests. R. B. Kuiper in *God-Centred Evangelism* says, "The conveying of the evangel to the Antipodes is as deserving of the name *evangelism* as is the conveying of the evangel to one's next door neighbours." A church which is committed to evangelizing an area fifty miles away need not be less worthy than one involved in the establishment of a church in the jungles of New Guinea.

Application

It might be profitable, if each point outlined under the four main headings be considered in respect of the churches to which we belong. A warning is necessary.   The manner in which we contend for reformation is just as important as the changes we would like to see.   Brotherly love and patience are essential especially when we realize that reformation is the work of a life-time.

In conclusion we turn to two general points in which churches have degenerated from the Scriptural pattern, the first is practical, and the second, doctrinal.

1. *A weak ministry*

Neglect of the qualifications required by Scripture for elders has resulted in many entering the ministry who are not truly called or adequately equipped.   This has resulted in poor preaching, noticed particularly in the omission of the doctrines of grace.   These are vital as they concern our whole understanding of God and man.   A. W. Pink in *The Sovereignty of God* describes ten ways in which God's sovereignty is important, one of which is that the truth about God's sovereignty is the solid foundation of all true religion.   A weak ministry has not only led to a breakdown in discipline as to the doctrine taught, but also in the oversight and discipline of church membership or members.

Ways and means of recovering Biblical standards for the ministry is a large subject which would need separate treatment.

2. *The composition of a church*

The admission to church membership by baptism of the infant progeny of believers has been stoutly advocated by the Reformers and Puritans, and those who follow them in that conviction.[4]   John Owen[5] maintained that baptism is the symbol of regeneration and also that "nothing can be more unreasonable than that men should be taken into the privileges attending obedience unto the laws and commands of Christ, without avowing, or professing that obedience".   The profession required, according to Owen, consists of: "1. A competent knowledge of the doctrines and mystery of the Gospel.   2. A professed subjection of soul and conscience unto the authority of Christ in the church.   3. An instruction in and consent unto the doctrine of self-denial.   4. Conviction and confession of sin.   5. The constant performance of all known duties of religion.   6. A careful abstinence from all known sins."[6]

Now all infants of believers until they prove the contrary have, according to Owen, "a right to all the privileges of the church".[7]   This is a serious error which gives birth to more error as follows:—(i) The presumption that children are regenerate since they have a right to all the privileges of the church.   (ii) Reluctance to withdraw church membership from such children who are obviously only nominal in their attachment to the church.

The granting of baptism which Owen rightly terms "the seal of regeneration" to the infants of believers, thus leads in due course to a situation in which many, perhaps the majority, in a church are not regenerate. Once such people gain the ascendency a church becomes very far from ideal. This position not only pertains to those bodies which we call "sacral"— i.e. which embrace a whole society irrespective of the marks just outlined by Owen, but also to many churches which are Independent, but practise infant baptism. We maintain that it is fundamentally wrong automatically to include the children of believers in the formal membership of a church. We deny the charge made by Thomas Shepherd in his article *The Church Membership of Children*[8], that children must lack "the enjoyment of the special watch and care of the whole church", if they be not formal members of it. The composition of a church is vital. The place of children relative to a church is also vital. Children do not have to be baptized to enjoy the watch and care of a church. If a church consists of a truly regenerate membership and is blessed with a godly eldership it is unlikely that the children will be neglected. In striving for ideal churches we acknowledge the need for clear thinking as to the spiritual state of our children, their need for example, teaching and preaching.

Attention has been drawn to these general points which concern the Carey Conference in particular. The place of children in the church and their nurture is a subject requiring detailed attention. By printed papers and tape-recordings much can be done to further reformation. In the meantime it is the duty of all believers to pray and strive for local churches which will be a light to the community and a glory to God.

REFERENCES

[1] A preacher ought to analyse the current intellectual climate. By reference to matters and events which touch and concern the daily lives of his hearers he will be relevant, and more so, if he is able to bring the light of Scripture to bear upon daily problems.

[2] James Bannerman expounds under three heads: 1. Potestas dogmatike; 2. Potestas diataktike (power belonging to the church by way of administering ordinances); 3. Potestas diakritike (power concerning discipline, admission and exclusion) *The Church of Christ*, Vol. 1, p. 225 ff.

[3] *The Church of Christ*, James Bannerman, Vol. 2, p. 48.

[4] c.f. R. B. Kuiper, *The Glorious Body of Christ*, p. 208 ff. A. A. Hodge, *The Confession of Faith*, p. 344 ff. William Cunningham, *Historical Theology*, Vol. 2 p. 148 ff. Charles Hodge's Commentary on *I Corinthians*, p. 117 ff., and innumerable other references from books which we like most, and commend as best, but in which this serious error recurs again and again.   [5] Vol. 16, p. 12.

[6] Ibid., p. 15.   [7] Ibid., p. 22.

[8] *The Reformation of the Church*, edited by Iain Murray, p. 403.

3

The
Living
Church

by Erroll Hulse

A LIVING CHURCH SHOULD BE VIBRANT WITH THE LIFE OF CHRIST. EACH member contributes to the whole, a harmony of unity and worship being brought about which could never be seen by members on their own. Each individual believer is constantly deriving life from the head, even Christ, with whom he is in union. But it is when the body of believers meets together that the life of Christ is experienced in power. This is why the psalmist declares, "that one day spent in your Temple is better than a thousand anywhere else" (Ps. 84:10, TEV).[1] That is a strong statement. Many who live in difficult circumstances would dearly love to spend a few days in a peaceful, happy place for a few days. The text highlights the pleasure that is inherent in the worship of God. When properly experienced it has no rival.

So enthralled is the true worshipper with the life of heaven which he enjoys with others on earth in the sanctuary of Christ that he prizes that time as immeasurably superior to others. Confidently he can declare his love and preference for God's house and people as exceeding days of potential happiness elsewhere.

With Revelation chapter one in mind, I want to show how Christ is the life of a local church. He said that he was the resurrection and the life. In the vision given to John at Patmos we see him to be just that. In his victory over the grave he is the firstfruits of the resurrection and as the Church's glorified head he is her life.

Christ has been the source of the Church's life throughout history. He

33

has maintained her life through the centuries and it is most intriguing to observe the way in which he has sustained that life. Paul wrote to Timothy declaring that there is only "one mediator between God and man, the man Christ Jesus". It has always been so. Christ has always been the one to approach fallen men. He has always been the one bringing reconciliation, reconciling the Father to men, and men to the Father. Once reconciled it has always been the role of Christ to mediate on behalf of his people.

In enlarging upon the subject of the living church I wish to proceed as follows:

1. Christ the source of the Church's life-Revelation chapters 1-3.

2. How Christ has maintained the life of his Church through the centuries.

3. How the churches are to maintain their life today.

The last point particularly is relevant because Reformed practice is fundamentally different from Charismatic practice. A church living and practising on the basis of what has been established is different from a church inverted in an effort to re-live that which has been lived.

1. Christ the source of the Church's life—Revelation 1-3

Christ is the centre and life of the churches. This is portrayed in the vision seen by John at Patmos. The scene was one of surpassing splendour. Christ moves among the golden lampstandards which shine with a light derived from him who is all in all. The golden sash round his chest and the flowing robe remind us that it was the glory of his person that filled the temple when Isaiah was called. Isaiah saw him sitting on a throne, high and exalted. His robe filled the whole temple (Isa. 6:2). It is his temple and it is his sovereign right to call men like Isaiah into his service. The golden sash is a kingly rather than a priestly garment. It reminds us of his supreme sovereignty, that he is king of kings and lord of lords.

The source of life

Any doubts about the ability of Christ to sustain the churches of which he is the life and to which he is joined by spiritual union are dispelled by the facts portrayed in that appearance at Patmos. His hair "white like wool, as white as snow" reminds us that he is uncreated, without beginning, very God—the Father of eternity (Isa. 9:6). His eyes burn like fire portraying an omniscient intelligence, a gaze which penetrates all secrets and which perceives and understands all mysteries scientific or spiritual. He can put it into the mind of a Christian astronaut to remember a scientific detail, the omission of which would be fatal, at the same time sustaining the soul of that person in every way. His eyes see wicked thoughts and intentions and reflect holy wrath. Before those eyes every force or desire of evil will eventually be brought to total exposure.

The sight of brass when heated to a white heat is insufferable to human gaze. So is the glorious holiness of God's justice. It is upon the basis of justice indicated that Christ conducts his reign. It is upon the ground of justice satisfied by his atoning blood that his people are accepted. Those who remain in their abominations will in the end be trodden underfoot by the feet of Christ—burning like a furnace. The powers of darkness so feared by us for their sinister power will be trodden down by that king and universal judge.

His voice is as the sound of many waters altogether, awe-inspiring and majestic. His words are perfect, authoritative, magnificent, edifying and inspiring.

This is the man who imparts life and who sustains that life in the churches. With so glorious a living head we should expect believers to be alive. Especially should this life be evident in the churches of which they form a part. As we have seen in the previous chapter, it is helpful if a church is ideal and caters for the needs of whole families. It must be said, however, that while the marks of an ideal church may all be present and the organisation excellent, there may be deficiency in this essential matter of spiritual vitality.

Union with such a person is the guarantee of salvation and the assurance that all that we may stand in need of is found in him. But how is his life conveyed to those in union with him? The answer is to view his role as prophet, priest and king.

As high priest he represented us as the one who loved us and washed us from our sins in his own blood (v. 5). His kingly role is presented in detail. His eyes burn with an all-penetrating intelligence and his feet are like brass heated to whiteness in the fiery furnace, feet that will tread down and judge and consume all opposition.

The imparting of life

His prophetic role is the most prominent of all especially as it affects the churches. His voice is as the sound of many waters. All truth is mediated through him and from him must come the living message to all the churches. His encouragements, instructions and reproofs proceed through the messengers designated as seven stars in his right hand. It is helpful to observe these stars are symbols deriving their light from the one who is the uncreated eternal source of life. The symbol of a star reminds us of a light which is subordinate to and dependent on another. In him was life and the life was the light of men. "His countenance" says John "was as the sun shineth in his strength." He is like the sun at noon in full strength. All other lights are secondary, like planets revolving round the sun.

We are told quite plainly that the seven stars are Christ's messengers who deliver the message suitable in each case to the churches they represent.

The word in the Hebrew (*malak*) and in the Greek (*aggelos*) does not always refer to angelic beings but to those called from among men to serve. Malachi prophesied that God's messenger would be sent to prepare the way. The apostle John had to write to those messengers or servants. This is something we never do to angels in heaven. The fact that these messengers are held in his right hand indicates that they do enjoy a unique relationship to Christ—one in which they are directly responsible to him. This responsibility is very great but it is his right hand of omnipotence that holds and keeps them. Their commission, their understanding, their instruction, their message and their authority are derived from him who holds them. Since they bear authority as the ones sent and carry the message they are given, they approximate to the New Testament office of teaching elders who not only share the responsibility of overseeing the church but labour in the word and doctrine.

We have seen then from Revelation that Christ is the centre and source of the life of all his people and that this life is conveyed primarily through his work as prophet as he instructs the churches through the messengers whom he holds in his right hand. Suitable instruction, assurance, encouragement, reproof and correction for each church are sent by way of written message to the churches.

This is the basis or pattern for edification of the churches to the end of time. Christ does not appear to each messenger individually, nor to each assembled church individually, and certainly not to each individual believer. He appears to the apostles and through the apostleship the churches are edified. They are built upon the foundation of the apostles and prophets, Jesus Christ himself being the chief cornerstone (Eph. 2: 20).

Imagine the confusion if every individual believer claimed his own vision or his own direct leading! The Word is our only guide as it has come once and for all by the apostles.

How does the way in which spiritual life is mediated by Christ to the churches relate to the ministry and to the leadership role of the elders? Revelation chapters 1-3 is not the place to establish the fundamental principles of church government. We would begin rather with the pastoral epistles, passages such as 1 Timothy 3 and Titus 1. We should note, however, that the details of Revelation should be interpreted by the clear passages and that when this is done they are in harmony and confirm the New Testament pattern.

For instance, Christ viewed in the midst of the candlesticks confirms the New Testament order of churches. Each church is independent. Each is edified by Christ through those held in his hand. This confirms the concept that the authority to lead by way of teaching lies with the elders. The symbol of the Old Testament church was that of a single shaft from which sprang a row or single line of candlesticks: joined in one and all

"Guessens"—a forty-roomed house—is part of the Welwyn Evangelical Church. It has formed the temporary home of many young men, mostly students who have been introduced to vital Christianity in this way. Pastor Ian Tait has served as pastor at Welwyn for twenty-eight years. He is the author of chapter 10.

visibly connected.   Israel was a theocracy.   God ruled one nation which had different tribes but all were essentially bound as one.   Now the churches throughout the world are one in Spirit (Eph. 4:4-6) but separated geographically.   Each local church has its own government just as the seven churches of Asia were separate churches—receiving messages *not* through a single archbishop or pope set over all the rest of them, nor through a synod presiding over them all.   Each had a separate and distinct message borne by a distinct messenger—not one messenger over another but each one equal, and all subordinate to the one and only archbishop, the Chief Shepherd of our souls (1 Pet. 3:4).

2. How Christ has maintained the life of his Church through the centuries

In approaching this subject we are entering the realm of study which has come to be referred to as biblical theology which Geerhardus Vos defines as, "that branch of exegetical theology which deals with the process of the self-revelation of God deposited in the Bible".

The importance of biblical theology

There could hardly be a more relevant or important issue than this. Without it we cannot withstand nor refute the attacks that are made upon the Faith today.   For instance, when a miracle such as the swallowing of Jonah by a great fish is denied it is futile to get involved in technical details as to how a man could breathe inside a fish.   Rather we turn to the Bible as a book reporting the acts of God within the context of an overall, integrated and united revelation.   We accept the Godhood of God together with the way in which he has chosen to reveal himself.   When we say "the Godhood of God" we mean that God possesses all the atrributes of deity.   In particular we are reminded by that of the omnipotence of God—of his ability to create and to order, control and rule all that he has created.   His actions are supernatural.   Therefore we expect the revelation of himself in history to be characterised by the supernatural.

Biblical theology is the study of the acts of God in his self-revelation with particular interest in the unfolding of that revelation stage by stage and the lessons to be learned about God and his redemption of man at every stage.

It is like the erection of a building.   After the preparations section by section is added until the whole is complete.   If a good architect has designed the structure it will bear the marks of unity, proportion and beauty throughout.   While not being a building the Bible is perfect in unity, proportion and beauty.

Today we are confronted more strongly than ever with the challenge of those who are persuaded that we should be practising our Christianity with the same kind of signs, wonders and miracles as pertained in the time of the apostles.   Our answer to that challenge is biblical theology.

The signs, wonders and miracles of those times were the signs of God himself—his signature of attestation and approval written upon the testimony of the apostles as they gave witness to the Lord risen and ascended. God's acts are not the same but vary a great deal as history runs her course just as in the construction of a building the activity at the foundation stage is very different from that when the final touches are being made. When we read in Hebrews 2:4 of the signs, wonders and miracles and different gifts of the Holy Ghost the context demands that these were specific, unique and God-given confirmations to those who were eye-witnesses of Christ.

The subject of biblical theology can be approached by observing the progressive revelation of God's covenant. First we have a covenant of common grace made with Noah. Then there are the Abrahamic, Mosaic and Davidic developments in the unfolding of God's covenant of grace. Finally we have the new covenant. That is a major branch of part of the subject of biblical theology. Biblical theology can be built around the framework of the covenant progressively revealed, or it can simply follow the main great acts of God's grace as he builds up his people, intervening on their behalf and finally sending his son in fulfilment of his promises. I intend to follow the principle of biblical theology, in this case observing how Christ came to his people and how he sustained their life throughout their history.

Theophany

When we go back to the beginning we observe that he appeared by way of theophany (the temporary assumption of human form) at the important stages, namely, in the forming of a family and in the forming of a nation. In both cases he is the life-giver in the sense that he kept hope alive in Abraham (Gen. 18) and in Moses, and ultimately in the nation to whom Moses was sent (Exod. 3).

In the case of Abraham the promise of Christ was a promise of life— a promise to provide a son. It was a matter of creating life. We are reminded by Paul in Romans that Abraham believed Christ's promise to quicken the dead—he considered not his own body now dead, when he was about one hundred years old, nor yet the deadness of Sarah's womb, but was strong in faith.

Having kept the promise to multiply Abraham's seed we find that same progeny bound up in servitude in Egypt. The cry of the suffering people went up to God who heard their groaning.

We are concerned about life in our churches. How does it come? If a church is in bondage, or in the chains of tradition, or spiritually about to expire, how is that church revived? In the case of Israel in Egypt the revival began with the coming of Christ in the burning bush. The great "I AM" commissioned Moses with words. It was by the hearing of those words that Moses was renewed in his faith and by the conveying of the message received from the bush on fire yet not consumed, which is an apt picture of the Church in fiery tribulations yet not consumed. By this means the faith of the people was renewed. Life came from the life-giver through the hearing of words. A hearing church, that is a church eager and enthusiastic to hear and obey the Word of God, is likely to be a living church. The appearing of Christ to Moses in the burning bush may not have been a theophany in itself but subsequently theophany was the mode of communication as we read in Deuteronomy 34:10 "and there arose not a prophet since in Israel like unto Moses, whom the Lord knew face to face".

Subsequent to the Exodus in which the eating of the Passover lamb symbolised salvation and life, it is the One Mediator between God and man who counselled and instructed Moses. The same one who gave Moses the specification for the tabernacle and priesthood was the Rock smitten to give life-giving water to the people. "They drank from the spiritual rock that went with them and that rock was Christ himself" (1 Cor. 10:4, TEV).

Having come into the promised land "Israel served the Lord all the days of Joshua, and all the days of the elders that overlived Joshua" but there-after to that the nation fell on hard times. When it seemed as if the life of the nation was about to die there was given a unique and great fore-shadowing of how the spiritual life of God's people may be sustained through preaching. The angel of the Lord (which we understand by the way he spoke to be Christ himself) suddenly appeared at Bochim before the great assembly as the preacher for that day. Hearts were broken up. It was a day of life. That truly was the pattern of things to come. The way of revival is through preaching in which the Lord himself speaks relevantly to his people.

Theophany in the period of the judges

When the church is low and the people discouraged, and when the numbers are few and strength is feeble we should study those times when God's people were in similar circumstances. Such was the case in the days of Gideon. The land was invaded and overrun by Midianites. The cause was so weak that the remnant was compelled to eke out an existence in the hilltops and caves. Again it was through the hearing of encouraging words that actions of faith were inspired. Said Christ to Gideon, "The Lord is with thee, thou mighty man of valour". Gideon felt himself to have no strength at all. Yet these words imparted new life to him, and ultimately through his encouragement the people were revived in hope, courage and action.

Likewise in time of hardship the Lord appeared to Manoah's wife, and shortly after to Manoah and his wife together. He promised a son to the couple. He left them by way of going up in the fire from the altar (Judg. 30:20). With Gideon there had been a similar incident pointing to the fiery sacrifice that would one day be made by the Lord offering up himself (Judg. 6:21). Samson, while not being a lifegiver himself, sustained the hope of Israel by thwarting the Philistines. The low state of the people can be seen in their willingness to bind and hand over their own champion to their enemies. Surely this is a pointer to what was to come when Christ was handed over by his own people to Pilate for the sentence of crucifixion? Yet in his death he secured life for ever and achieved the greatest defeat of the enemy. Just as Samson slew more in his death than he had in his life (Judg. 17:30) so Christ triumphed over the greatest enemy in his death. Appearance by way of theophany was not the only way in which Christ encouraged and sustained the life of his people but we see it employed as a means during those early times.

Vision

A new age of prophecy was begun through the patient teaching ministry of Samuel (Acts 3:24). The example of Samuel is an inspiration to all who appreciate what we often refer to as the ordinary means of grace. Samuel was not a miracle-worker like Moses. Teaching and prayer (1 Sam. 12:23) were the means he employed in his systematic travels in circuit to establish sound faith and practice (1 Sam. 7:16,17). In the unfolding of further revelation following the times of Samuel we observe the employment of vision. This pertained particularly in the case of Isaiah (Isa. 6), Daniel (Dan. 7:9-13, 10:4-10) and Ezekiel (Ezek. 1:26-28). It is worth digressing for a few moments to note that in each case just mentioned there is what we might well call a "killing" work. Christ the great life-giver is also "a killer". He *kills* the love of sin. He exposes sinful propensities and their detestable nature and causes that his people should hate themselves for their own sins (Ezek. 36:31). Isaiah, Daniel, Ezekiel and John at Patmos all evidence feelings of appalling unworthiness to serve such a God. We recall Peter's reaction too when he had a glimpse of Christ's divinity. "Depart from me," he cried, "for I am a sinful man!" A ministry which does not expose sin so as to cause it to be hated and forsaken is a useless ministry. Those who are to minister to others in such exposure of the heart need to experience themselves a thorough and deep conviction of sin. Many who contend for the old values often have to bear the reproach of being out of touch and of being negative. Sometimes the reproach is deserved. On the other hand so much modern evangelicalism while being very "with it" can at the same time be entirely destitute of a really serious character. It is often light and flippant and worldly. You would never think that eternal life or eternal death were at stake. In a very few places is the sin-killing, the soul-convicting ministry of Christ in evidence. You will look in vain to find it in the popular evangelical glossies.

Incarnation

The incarnation was the next development in the life-giving process. This was no theophany. Now he was tangible among us. Simeon and Anna

41

held him in their arms in the Temple courts. The disciples looked upon him and could feel him (1 John 1:1). He had come to live among them. His body was the tabernacle of the eternal God. They beheld his glory, "the glory as the only begotten of the Father, full of grace and truth". When he rose from the dead there was a change in his body but it was essentially the same body. He was careful to impress this fact upon them. His body was the very first to be glorified, yet in all characteristic features (including in his case the retention of his wound marks) it was absolutely and essentially the same body. It may be that he will be the only one in glory with a scarred body. All the redeemed will have unscarred bodies only because his was wounded.

What is the difference between his body then as he moved among his disciples and walked with the two on the road to Emmaus and now that he is in heaven? The difference surely is that now he is in glory. There is no veiling of his Godhead. That which was always there during his earthly life and which shone out briefly on the mount of transfiguration is now open and unveiled.

We are now in a position to stand back and view Christ's mediatorial work in perspective particularly as it relates to his office as prophet. First he appeared by theophany to Abraham, to Moses, to several in the period of the Judges. He also appeared to a large assembly on the one occasion during that time. Second he appeared by way of open vision to Isaiah, to Ezekiel and to Daniel. Third he came by way of the incarnation. Finally he appeared in his glory to John at Patmos and in doing so showed us the way in which we are now to live by him—not by immediate prophecy, or by vision, or by a present incarnation, but by his Word now completed, explained, expounded and applied by those appointed, whom he holds in his right hand.

Completion of the apostolic work

Our position today is one of greater certainty and clarity as far as the foundations of the faith are concerned. Some regard it ridiculous to think that our position is superior to that of Paul.[2] But it is not absurd when we reflect more deeply about it. Are not the Scriptures described as "a more sure word of prophecy"? We can rely much more on an established and proven word than we can on the oral recital of visions or inspirations that are not proven. Having no final form of Scripture to appeal to, Paul had a constant battle to get the believers of his time to reject the false apostles in favour of himself whom they sometimes despised (2 Cor. 10:10). The Christians of the apostolic era were dependent on revelation which had to be tested. There seemed to be no shortage of false apostles (2 Cor. 11:13). The believers had to face the problem of sorting out the false from the true. The Ephesians were commended by Christ for their detection and rejection of false apostles (Rev. 2:2). The situation in those times was one of uncertainty. Theirs was a period of construction and formulation. Ours is one in which we rely on a revelation that has passed the test and which is infallible. Our task is easier and our position better because we possess the more certain word of prophecy which according to Peter is more dependable and reliable than dependence on an oral testimony which could easily be distorted or soon lost to posterity. The written Word cannot be altered.

A major difficulty with the Charismatic movement is that we are presented with further prophecies and direct revelations. All these have to be examined. In each case we are confronted with uncertainty. Is it true or false? With the Scripture we have certainty. Through the indwelling of the Holy Spirit we have direction and power to interpret. Our mandate is to conquer the world: to occupy and win all nations for Christ. That is our commission and we have all we need for the task. We need not go back to the apostolic age. As much as our Lord's present glory transcends his earthly role as humble servant to death, by so much does our age transcend that. Did he not give us the unqualified assurance that it was better for him to leave and send the Spirit. Whatever the joys may have been, the handicap or disadvantage of having to depend on his earthly whereabouts was very great. Now he rules from heaven and the Holy Spirit is at work everywhere in the most intimate way possible, namely, by indwelling our hearts.

The Holy Spirit came for the first time in great power from the glorified Lord on the basis of his completed work on the day of Pentecost. In that sense it was a day of birth. The apostles in particular were empowered. As far as Scripture is concerned the apostolic age terminated with the revelation given by the Lord to John. The concluding words seem to endorse that (Rev. 22:17-21).

The final revelation given at Patmos is an appropriate conclusion to all the process of self-revelation that had gone on before—a revelation revealing the Son and the Father. The Church through history has been sustained in her life by that process and the Church on earth today lives by a knowledge of the whole from Genesis to Revelation.

3. How the Churches maintain their life today

How then are we to live? The answer is by "every word that proceedeth out of the mouth of God" (Matt. 4:4). The emphasis of the New Testament is consistent. The Word is to be preached in all seasons (2 Tim. 4:2). The flock is to be fed (Acts 20:28, 1 Pet. 5:2). The doctrine is designed to save preachers and hearers alike (1 Tim. 4:16). The purpose of the ministry is to ground and establish all believers in the truth so that they will be built up and not be blown about by every wind of doctrine (Eph. 4:7-16, Col 1:28).

The principle of the truth being written down is stressed (Rev. 1:11,19, 2:1,8 etc.). The written word is to be expounded and applied. All other means of life are secondary to this and supplementary. Nothing must be allowed to supplant the primacy of preaching. Some hanker after signs, others long for eloquence, and some exalt human wisdom, but God's way of saving men is by preaching (1 Cor. 3:21-23). We cannot return to an age of theophany or of vision. We do not anticipate having Christ back in the flesh by way of incarnation. Nor can we expect to repeat again the special and extraordinary witness of the apostolic age.

It is not by going back to any constituent part of the revelation that we are to live, but by understanding the relation of the constituent parts to each other, and the relevance of the whole as it applies to us in our experience today.

It does not help to try to supplement our way of life or worship by looking for direct inspirations, or prophecies, or interpretation of tongues. All kinds of problems arise if we are in doubt as to the motive, origin and substance of a new prophecy. It may be argued that the material in a prophecy is of a personal nature only without reference to any doctrine. If that is the case, then we are still left in doubt about the motives behind the direct message and also whether it is truly of divine origin or whether merely human. In any case it is the work of the person of the Holy Spirit to make personal application and give direction and guidance through Scripture. Now that he has come to indwell believers and give them understanding of what he has written in Scripture his work is capacious in a way which it never was before.

The conclusion is reached that we should resist the temptation to think that because we live by Scripture alone without any attempt to return to former times of inspiration that our life, worship or service is dull and boring. If it becomes boring the error lies not with the fulness of our provision but in the defects and shortcomings of human nature. This is the era of the Word which is our treasure and the fulness of the Holy Spirit who is our guide. We do not rely upon or require theophany or special vision, nor should we crave signs. Spurgeon speaks well to the point in a sermon on Thomas (John 20:27).

"Crave not wonders because *it is dishonouring to the sacred Word to ask for them.* Will you cast suspicion upon the Holy Ghost, who, by his word, bears witness to Christ?

Crave no signs, because *it is unreasonable that we should desire more than we have already.*

Crave no signs, because *it may be you will be presumptuous in so doing.* Who are you to set God a sign?

Again, crave no signs, for *this craving is highly perilous.* If Thomas' faith had grown to be so little that, if he continued insisting upon this and that, as a sign or evidence, that faith of his would get down to the very lowest; yea, he would have no faith left!"

How is the church to live? How is she to practice? By hearing and by heeding! The churches are to live by hearing the Word and keeping it. The sentimentally inclined think in terms of people and events that have made them important or interesting, like the woman who cried, "Blessed is the womb that bare thee". The emotionally inclined think in terms of hugs and kisses and bodily expressions of ecstasy. The hyper-Calvinists think in terms of hearing and debating without sacrifice, and without the involvement of going in to all the world. The intellectually inclined think in terms of head knowledge and learning. But Christ tells us who are the truly happy ones, the ones who have his approbation, "Yea rather blessed are they that hear the word of God, and keep it!" (Luke 11:28). A living church is a church which loves the preaching of the Word, loves the God of that Word, loves the people born of that Word, loves the fellowship of the people who base their lives on that Word and love the good works commanded by that Word.

Thus a living church is a church which is applying and practising the Word that has come and which has been expounded and confirmed by the Lord of the Patmos vision. A living church is a church in union with that Lord who has given the revelation. The issue of life is hindered, not helped, when believers try to repeat or complete that which is already complete. New visions, extra biblical revelations and presumptuous claims of messianic leadership are marks of the cults. Acceptance of and submission to the Word, conviction of sin, repentance toward God and faith in Christ are the overwhelmingly central issues and emphases of the church living. May such spread round the globe and when the nations cry, "O how I love thy law", it will be the day when that Scripture will be fulfilled "that the kingdoms of the world are become the kingdoms of our Lord, and of his Christ".

[1] Unless otherwise stated Scripture quotations are from the King James Version.
[2] In a review of *The Baptism of the Spirit and Charismatic Gifts* published by the BEC which appeared in the *Evangelical Times* Basil Howlett derides the idea that we are in a better position than Paul.

4

The *Implications* of *Baptism*

by Erroll Hulse

BAPTISM MAY BE DEFINED AS THE FIRST OF TWO SACRAMENTS COMMANDED and instituted by the Lord Jesus Christ for his Church, to the effect that every person who becomes a visible member of that Church does so by being submerged in water in the name of the Father, Son and Holy Spirit. Several further explanations and definitions will be helpful before we proceed with our subject proper.

You will observe that I have used the word "submerge" for "baptism" because to immerse, to baptise and to submerge are synonomous. I have in my library a treatise published in 1865 by T. J. Conant, an exhaustive study of the word *baptizō* in which he cites 236 cases of the use of the word in the Greek language. The context is cited in each case. This study shows that for about 800 years, in the centre of which the New Testament was written, the word *baptizō* possessed the definite, stable and universal meaning of "I immerse" or "I submerge". Herbert Carson in his paper on the mode of baptism, describes some of the straits to which the advocates of sprinkling are reduced in order to sustain their theory that there is ambiguity about the meaning of the word *baptizō*. They say that it could mean to sprinkle (*rantizō*), but since the latter word was ready to hand and *unambiguously* denoted sprinkling, the apostles would doubtless have used it had they intended sprinkling to be the mode. To Greek speaking people *baptizō* is synonomous with immerse and if I use the word interchangeably it is because there is every warrant on linguistic grounds for doing so. Because they know the meaning of their own language[1] the Greek Church use the mode immersion exclusively for baptism.

Then you will see that I prefer the word "sacrament" to "ordinance". There are several practices, such as preaching or the assembling of ourselves together, which God has ordained, *ordained* being the word from which ordinance is derived, but there are only two ordinances to which our Lord binds himself by oath. The Latin word *sacramentum* means oath and it is suitable that we use the word sacrament for both baptism and the Lord's Supper since our Lord binds himself to be present where these are faithfully practised and to bless them to the participants.[2] Moreover he binds himself to fulfil without fail the salvation symbolised in baptism. From the second century the term "seal" was used as a synonym for baptism (2 Cor. 1:22; Eph. 1:30, 4:30). Hermas put it this way: "Before a man has borne the name of (the Son of) God he is dead; but when he has received the seal he layeth aside his deadness and resumeth life. The seal then is in the water; so they go down into the water dead and come up alive. Thus to them also this seal was preached. . . ." A seal is like an oath. God, who cannot lie, will perform what he has promised. The abuse of the idea of sacrament by sacramentalist teachers of all kinds who attach power to the actual elements of water, bread and wine ought not to deter us. The want of a better word than "*sacrament*" disposes some to use, not to the exclusion of the word "ordinance" but in preference to it.

In the Gospels we find that our Lord includes baptism in the great commission (Mark 16:15, 16; Matt. 28:19, 20). Believing and being baptised are so fundamental that they are put together. "He that believeth and is immersed shall be saved; but he that believeth not shall be damned." Immersion is a necessity, not for salvation—the dying thief had no opportunity to be baptised—but for obedience. Any true believer or disciple not immersed remains in a state of disobedience to an express command of the King. Immersion then is a necessity for obedience.

Accordingly, we read in the book of Acts that all who were brought to faith were baptised with little delay. This was so at Jerusalem, Samaria, Caesarea, Philippi and Ephesus. Though previously immersed with the baptism of John, the disciples at Ephesus were immersed again. This was essential to signify properly their union with Christ. If I am asked whether valid baptism is possessed by people who have been sprinkled as believers my reply is in the negative. We should proceed as did Paul at Ephesus to do what was commanded by our Lord and properly signify union with Christ. This is not possible with sprinkling or pouring. Let us grasp this well: it is not the faith of the candidate alone that is important; it is the Lord's person and the believer's union with the Lord that also require declaration and portrayal.

Obedience to Christ's command about baptism is illustrated by way of practice in the book of Acts whereas its meaning is explained in the epistles. The sense of immersion is admirably portrayed than in the very heart of Paul's treatise on salvation, given to the Romans. Union with

47

Christ is as total and all-embracing as immersion itself. The entire person is brought into symbolic union with Christ in his death, burial and resurrection. This complete identification with Christ is central both to justification and to sanctification. Union with Christ by faith is the spring both of justification (Rom. chaps 1-5) and of progressive sanctification (chaps 6-8). It is fitting, therefore, that two central principles of Christianity, justification the foundation, and progressive sanctification the superstructure, be symbolised by the initiation rite of burial and resurrection with Christ.

In writing to the Colossians Paul repudiates any further need for the rite of physical circumcision on the grounds that believers have experienced spiritual circumcision. By virtue of union with Christ a whole transformation of character has taken place. The old, unregenerate nature has been stripped off and cast away. A radical and complete change has taken place. Believers have been raised with Christ to walk in newness of life. The Colossian believers had portrayed all this in their immersion, symbolising their union with Christ (Col. 2:11, 12). There was therefore no need whatever for circumcision. From this passage the observation should be made that only those who have been born again of the Spirit are fit candidates for baptism. Excellently does baptism signify our completeness in Christ. If we are complete in Christ then there is nothing extra that can be provided by Jewish rites. Further, Paul shows that baptism is confined to those who have faith in the operation of God who raises the dead.

While believers' baptism also symbolises the washing away of sin (Acts 22:16) and the remission of sins, the preponderant idea throughout the epistles is that of union with Christ. The fact of having died in union with Christ is always expressed in the aorist and it is a pity that this is not always translated in the past tense in the King James Version. The walking in union with Christ and hence in newness of life is, of course, in the present tense. Not only Paul but Peter too stresses this union. Noah and his family, secure in the ark, were tided over into a new world by the flood which destroyed the ungodly. Those joined to Christ and in his death by faith are tided over to the resurrection world (1 Pet. 3:18-22).

During the last few years we have seen an upsurge of interest in the subject of the baptism of the Spirit. The connection between Spirit baptism and water baptism is close. Water immersion follows Spirit baptism and portrays it. Baptism by the Spirit into union with Christ and his body, the Church, is declared in 1 Corinthians 12:13 and Galatians 3:27.

The four instances of the Holy Spirit having been given, reported in Acts (Pentecost, Samaria, Caesarea and Ephesus) are diverse in character and not intended to provide a formula for an experience. Rather these are narrated to demonstrate beyond all disputation that the Holy Spirit had been given to believing Jews and Gentiles alike. That is precisely the way in which the apostles understood the issue and the way they applied it (Acts 15:8, 9).

We consider now the implications of baptism for the local church in respect of the following:

1. Evangelism
2. Preparation of disciples for baptism and church membership
3. The Lord's Table and transient communion
4. A powerful witness
5. The purity of the church
6. The unity of the local church
7. Infants and children in the church

1. Evangelism

"Therefore go and make disciples of all nations," commanded our Lord, "baptising them in the name of the Father and of the Son and of the Holy Ghost, and teaching them to obey everything I have commanded you. And surely I will be with you always, to the very end of the age" (Matt. 28:19, 20 NIV). The implications of baptism for the local church as it respects the great commission are clear. It forms part of that commission. We cannot fulfil the command without immersion. The words *make disciples* express an imperative. Since all power is at the command of Jesus we have all that we require in the work of making disciples. That he is with us to the end of the age, employing his power on our behalf, shows that the command is binding on all churches of all generations.

The very idea of immersion into union with Christ tells us what a Christian is and what we are aiming at. The two clauses beginning *baptizontes* and *didaskontes* are co-ordinate, both indicating *how* the nations are to be discipled, that is, by baptism and teaching. Therefore baptism is an essential and integral part of evangelism.

Baptism into the triune God reminds us that reconciliation to the Father by the atonement of the Son, and consequent indwelling of the Holy Spirit must be a reality before the act of baptism. The baptism of disciples that have been won could hardly bring into clearer focus all that is involved in evangelism.

2. Preparation of disciples for baptism and church membership

The solemnity of baptism should be emphasised to those who request it and the possibility of apostasy should be faced before the sacrament is undertaken. Baptism is a once and for all sacrament symbolising a once and for all death in Christ and a once and for all resurrection in Christ. For one who has publicly identified with Christ to repudiate union with him is unspeakably solemn. The epistle to the Hebrews, in particular, deals with the question of backsliding and apostasy, the one leading to the other. The two climactic passages of the letter (Heb. 6:4-6, 10:26-29) intimate plainly that there can be no recovery from apostasy. These passages can be used to warn backsliders of the fearful implications of denying their vision with Christ as voluntarily expressed in their immersion.

The first context (Heb. 5:11-6:9) is particularly meaningful with respect to our subject because the writer declares baptism to be within the scope of the basic fundamentals of the faith. In the context he is speaking of "the first principles" of God's word (5:12), and "the foundation" of the faith (6:1).

What did the Christians of the apostolic era esteem as the fundamentals of the faith? What constituted the basic principles of the profession of faith made by them (Heb. 10:23)? What was regarded as "elementary"? Six matters are suggested in Hebrews 6:1, 2 and these stretch from the genesis of Christian experience, that is repentance and faith, to the consummation, namely, the resurrection and judgment to follow. Between the first two and the last two we have washings (baptismōv) and laying on of hands. The early Christians understood plainly the difference between Christian immersion and other washings exemplified by the baptism of proselytes and that of John the Baptist. The laying on of hands was a long-established practice in Israel and was carried over with a number of different meanings attached to it into the practice of the early Church. It accompanied the giving of blessing (Mark 10:16), of healing (Mark 6:5ff) and of ordination (Acts 6:6, 1 Tim. 4:14).

So great was the expectation of the blessing of the Holy Spirit in confirmation of the fact that he was Christ's gift to believers that we find the laying on of hands accompanying baptism; in the conversion of Paul (Acts 9:17), at Samaria (Acts 8:17) and at Ephesus—"and when Paul had laid his hands upon them, the Holy Ghost came on them".

Hebrews 6:4-6 declares the tragedy of apostasy. Partaking of the Holy Spirit, participation in the good word of God and the powers of the world to come, and enlightenment are experienced leading to open confession of faith. This is followed by a turning away and putting Christ to open shame. Baptism expresses repentance, faith and an open confession of union with Christ. Therefore to repudiate one's baptism is to repudiate Christ and his Gospel. The experience involved, participation of the Holy Spirit, enlightenment in the truth and confession of Christ does not belong to infants. Therefore it is inappropriate to goad young people about forsaking a baptism to which they were subject as infants whether they liked it or not. It is also out of place to apply Hebrews 6:4-6 to those, who while they have heard the Gospel many times, have never professed experience of its powers and have never made a public profession of faith.

Once it is clear that a person understands the implications of baptism and has repentance toward God and faith in the Lord Jesus Christ, how long should be the interval before baptism? That there was no delay seems to have been the case in the New Testament. The Jerusalem converts were baptised on the day of their conversion. As soon as Peter saw that the members of the household of Cornelius had received remission of their sins through Christ and that they possessed the gift of the Holy Spirit he asked, "Can any man forbid water, that these should not be baptised, which have received the Holy Ghost as well as we?" (Acts 10:47). How can we justify the sometimes considerable delay before we baptise converts? The answer to this may be that a clarity and certainty existed in the period of the apostles which made immediate immersion acceptable. That there was such clarity and certainty in the days of Pentecost is demonstrated inasmuch as those who were immersed at that time continued stedfastly in the apostles' doctrine and fellowship, and in breaking of bread and in prayers (Acts 2:42). Even with our long delay and careful preparation we rarely achieve such a standard with our converts. Three further factors which do not apply in the situations in which we find ourselves now should be remembered. The first is that the Holy Spirit had drawn and prepared these people and made them willing and zealous enough to travel long distances to Jerusalem from all parts of the then known world. The second is that their zeal seems to indicate that they were well taught in the Old Testament Scriptures. The third is that to profess openly identity and union with the very person who was hated and rejected by the Jewish hierarchy was a costly business. It was dangerous and therefore decisive. One had to be truly sincere and sure to take so momentous a step.

The Philippian jailor was baptised without any delay. His faith, though born suddenly, was decisive and it is helpful for us to remember that this is the principal issue to discern. Were the apostles wrong to act so promptly? For instance, could it not be charged that the baptism of Simon the Sorcerer (Acts 8:13) was precipitous? We claim infallibility for the apostles in the writing of Scripture but not in all their actions or decisions. Furthermore, we must not base the norms for the treatment of baptismal candidates on the exceptional and anomalous instances of apostasy. Caution and testing must be balanced with charity and the remembrance that faith newly born does not have the same proportion and stature as faith matured. The young in faith often have a very imperfect knowledge. It is helpful if the credibility of a Christian profession is tested by the officers and by those members of the church who are acquainted with the candidate. Although no human assessment can be infallible, yet once reasonable assurance exists there need be no delay whatsoever.

According to the Lord, life eternal consists of a personal, loving knowledge of the Father and the Son by the Spirit (John 17:3). It is imperative, therefore, that such knowledge should exist in a person before baptism.

It is the responsibility of the elders to show that such knowledge must be experimental and not intellectual only. Inevitably this involves counselling from the elders and an oral testimony by the candidate to the elders. I am sure we would all reject the notion that we must accept people as Christians on the slender basis that they give intellectual assent to the doctrines of the Faith and that they are not guilty of scandalous living. There are millions of nominal Christians in the world who give assent to a creed, commit no outward crimes, but who are dead to God and dead in sin. Philip required not an assent from the eunuch only but also that he believe with *all his heart!* (Acts 8:37).

The very nature of baptism reminds us of the necessity of regeneration. Union with Christ spells regeneration. To be baptised by the Spirit into Christ is the same as regeneration. We must insist, therefore, on evidence that a man is God's workmanship, created in Christ Jesus unto good works. We must insist on evidence that a man is a new creature and that all things have become new for him (2 Cor. 5:17).

Every candidate should pass the three basic tests which John repeats over and over again in his first epistle. He must pass *the moral test*, that is holiness of life (1 John 3:9). The candidate must pass the *social test*, giving evidence of genuine love for the Christian family (1 John 3:14, 15). Furthermore, he must pass the *doctrinal test* (1 John 4:2), in that he possesses a personal, living and clear perception that Jesus Christ is the Son of God. Otherwise how will he overcome the world? (1 John 5:45). It is to be noted that Jehovah's Witnesses and Mormons do not have this personal knowledge of Christ. Even though they may give lip service to it when pressed, they never confess him as Lord. It is not a comprehensive knowledge of the 1689 Confession of Faith that is required, or an understanding of the doctrines of grace and the five points propounded by the Synod of Dort, but saving faith. That the elders know and believe the Confession and be conversant with all doctrine and teaching is paramount. Candidates for baptism and church membership should not be in conflict with the doctrines of grace or with the Confession as a whole. Not to understand doctrine is one thing, to be at loggerheads with it is another.

In Puritan times churches adopted covenants outlining all the responsibilities of and expectations from members. Some churches retain these. We retain the use of our covenants and articles even though they date back to 1887. But we also use contemporary literature to help clarify responsibilities involved in church membership: all new members are acquainted with these before being accepted. The next question is whether the judgment of the elders should be regarded as adequate for the introduction of candidates or whether such should be required to give an oral testimony before the gathered church. Many prefer a public testimony and there is much to be said for it. It should never become mandatory. We should remember the mistake of the Church from the second century onwards of introducing rites and ceremonies not required in Scripture. Nevertheless, having said that, we must lay equal stress on the liberty we have been given in Christ to decide on whole areas of practical detail, judging and discerning what is most edifying and helpful in different areas of culture and background. According to the local situation we are free to encourage oral testimony if it accords with the church and is of benefit.

It is of great importance to remember that baptism must never be separated from church membership. Disciples are baptised into Christ Jesus the head and at the same time immersed into his body the Church. Abiding in Christ includes abiding in the church (Jn. 15:1-6). No person should be baptised unless it is baptism into a specific body of believers. Even those living a peripatetic existence such as pilots and air stewards must have some ultimate place of refuge, fellowship and responsibility. They, even more than others, need all the spiritual support that a church can provide.

The Ethiopian eunuch might be cited as an exception since he was not baptised into a church. Somehow he missed the revival on at Jerusalem. We do not know what believers already existed in his home country of Ethiopia or whether he was the first convert. At any rate the sphere of his union and of his responsibilities was in his native country and to that he returned with the seal of baptism. Paul too was baptised on his own but integration with the Church followed as soon as the fears of the Christians about him were overcome.

When church members have heard the testimony of the applicant for baptism he should withdraw for opportunity to be given for discussion. If the elders have done their work well there is very little likelihood of objections being made to the entrance into the church of the candidate. If some scandal or substantiated evidence of hypocrisy is revealed, then the elders can defer the application until it is sorted out discreetly. The opportunity for discussion and reflection is ideal as it helps to integrate the membership. The appearance before the church of one who is shortly to be immersed into the life and body of the church provides opportunity for all members to be reminded of their responsibilities, not to mention the encouragement derived through hearing an account of what the Lord has done in drawing souls to himself. Before leaving this question of oral testimony the question should be asked whether any Scriptures can be offered in its support. As already intimated it is not expressly commanded. It is interesting to note that it did take place under John the Baptist's ministry. Confessing their sins they were immersed (John 3:6). Timothy made "a good profession before many witnesses" (1 Tim. 6:12). G. R. Beasley Murray argues cogently that this profession was made by Timothy at the commencement of his Christian life, that is at his baptism, and not at his ordination.[3] Other references which seem to encourage oral testimony in the way suggested are Matt. 10:32; Mark 8:38; Romans

10:9, 10; Psalm 66:16; Psalm 119:74. Of these Psalm 66:16 is particularly eloquent: "Come and hear all ye that fear God, and I will declare what the Lord hath done for my soul." Provided that abuses are avoided, particularly that of superficiality by way of copying others or saying things simply because they are expected, and that the other cautions that have been mentioned are observed, testimony surely has a place in the local church.

3. The Lord's Table and transient communion

The baptism of the believer involves him in all the life of the local church. Having been baptised the disciples continued stedfastly in the apostles' doctrine, and fellowship and breaking of bread and prayers (Acts 2:42). Baptism represents the birth, the Lord's Supper the festive manifestation of Christianity. Baptism is initiation into the body; the Supper is part of the sustenance and nourishment of that body. It follows, therefore, that the birth and the initiation precede the feast. The Supper prefigures the great Wedding Feast to come. *First* let the wedding garment of imputed righteousness be procured, then the sitting down at the table; *first* the seal of baptism signifying inclusion in the New Covenant, then the right to enjoy the benefits of the New Covenant; *first* the seal of water and then the seals of bread and wine; *first* the sign of union, then the blessing of c﹐mmunion; *first* the washing away of sin, then fellowship with those who have likewise been washed.

The communion supper expresses the following truth: grateful remembrance of the Lord's death as the only way of salvation; participation in the blessing of the New Testament; fellowship in Christ, and the sharing in the hope of his return to glory. It is inappropriate for those who have not entered into the reality of these verities to participate. By its very content the Lord's table is proclaiming that it belongs to those alone who have been baptised into Christ's body the church. If it be objected that the issue is a private one and that it is written, "but let a man examine himself" (1 Cor. 11:28) it can be pointed out that Paul was addressing the baptised members of the church at Corinth many of whom were under judgment, being weak and sickly, because of their abuse of the Supper. He was not addressing all and sundry but brothers whom he exhorted to tarry one for another.

Everything should be done decently and in order. It is disorder and confusion if nominal Christians, known hypocrites, and those who have no consistent Christian testimony are able to sail past those new disciples and genuine converts who are submitting to baptism and church membership before participating in the Lord's Table.

The first communion after baptism is an appropriate time to give formal or public welcome to newly baptised members. Expression in prayer of joy and gratitude from a member of the church, as well as words of encouragement, exhortation and edification from one of the elders is most fitting (Heb. 10: 22-25).

One of the most important implications of believers' baptism is the consideration of visitors who have not been immersed as believers. Do such qualify for the Lord's Table and should they be invited? If they are invited, what effect will this have on those disciples who are in the process of being made but who have not yet themselves been baptised and are therefore not yet ready for the Lord's Table? It is at this point that we must take into account the fragmented and divided church situation of today. Allowance must be made for multitudes of genuine believers who have only known denominations in which the tradition of infant sprinkling has prevailed for centuries. It would be wrong to unchurch such by denying the essential bond of faith in Christ that unites us.

The tension is between the need to maintain a consistent discipline in the local church on the one hand, and on the other the need for a recognition of the visible church of our Lord in its multifarious forms all over the world. Some have thought they have solved the problem by claiming that the Lord's Supper belongs to the local church only and should therefore be confined to the members of the local church. But that will not do, because visiting Christians do come to stay for varying lengths of time and it is hardly consistent to assert that we will have fellowship with them in all the means of grace but not the Table.

The answer, surely, is to focus on the central issue, namely, consistent church membership. Is it not fair to say therefore that we welcome fellow believers providing they hold a consistent church membership with an evangelical church? If they decide to stay in the area, then it is reasonable that they should submit to the order of the church if they wish to join it.

4. A powerful witness

Is baptism just an outward symbol, intended only as a simple act of obedience or is it a sacrament attended by the presence of God? Are we to expect the powerful work of the Holy Spirit in the hearts of those who are present and especially in those who are the subjects of the sacrament? The answer is in the affirmative. As the Father attended the immersion of his Son with words of highest approbation and as the Holy Spirit came down upon Jesus in the form of a dove, so we by faith should anticipate (and in most instances do experience) the manifest blessing of God. Sunday is the market day for our souls but when baptisms are included then it is a time of festive joy *par excellence*.

We should not wonder at the fact that the Holy Spirit should be active in an unusual way on these occasions. Baptism portrays the greatest truths we possess: the forgiveness of sin through union with Christ in his death, and the possession of newness of life. Celebrated is deliverance from all the powers of evil which formerly imprisoned us. To the Corinthians, some of whom had been the most evil characters, Paul (probably referring to their baptism) said, "but you were washed, but you were sanctified" (1 Cor. 6:11 NIV).

From the human side we see baptism as the confession of the believer's faith in Christ as his whole salvation. We see him submit his body to be buried and to be raised again as a token of his glad appropriation of God's gracious provision. This act is "the indispensable external expression and crowning moment of the act of faith".[4]

God's part is to confirm mightily the reality of all that is visibly expressed. We are confirmed and emboldened in our faith to know that as surely as Jesus died effectually to save us, so surely our sins, too, have been washed away. As surely as our eyes behold the rising again of the one buried, so surely have we been raised up to have union with Christ in his present reign. As the candidate comes out of his grave so will he be raised on the last day. Preaching should accompany baptism. The relevance and significance of the sacrament should be highlighted, this being a means by which the Holy Spirit vivifies the event and makes it an effectual and a lasting blessing to those present. This does not mean that a separate or special sermon specifically on the subject of baptism needs to be preached for each enaction. If it suits the theme or subject, part of the sermon may be used to expound upon and apply the subject to the hearers. If not, then prior to the baptism a brief exposition on a passage relevant to the subject is appropriate.

It is helpful if baptism takes place in a natural setting. The baptism of our Lord was a public event. It can be, and often is, a most powerful witness to those present who have not yet trusted in Christ for salvation. Think of the stir created when Jesus openly identified himself with sinners before John and all the people. When a man emerges from the world and identifies himself boldly and completely with Christ's death and resurrection it sometimes has an awakening effect on his worldly associates. Likewise, when a member of an unbelieving family believes with all his heart and determines to be baptised into Christ and his Church, the public portrayal of all that is involved in leaving one domain and entering another is striking and convicting to other members of the family who are yet unconverted. For the candidate, for the local church and for all who from the outside may witness the symbolic act, baptism is fraught with the presence and mighty blessings of the same triune God into whom the believer is baptised.

5. The purity of the local church

The main New Testament analogies describe the Church as a body made up of living members. The analogy of the human body predominates (2 Cor. 12:12-17, Rom. 12:4-8). Of necessity all parts of the human body must be alive. The Church is depicted as a temple of living stones (1 Pet. 2:5), and as a vine with living branches (John 15:1-8). Believers' baptism is God's way of providing a safeguard for the purity of the church. As has been seen baptism brings the meaning of what it is to be a Christian into clear focus. Only those joined to Christ and justified and sanctified thereby, qualify for membership of Christ's living body, the Church.

Inasmuch as multitudes of unregenerate people have become members of Christian churches by means of infant baptism there could not be a more practical implication of believers' baptism than this. When practised according to New Testament principles there is no greater or better safeguard for the purity of the church.

In the churches where it is practised, infant sprinkling nullifies and destroys true baptism for the simple reason that when the time of regeneration does come the outward, visible, conscious experience of union with Christ in the sacrament has been removed. It no longer exists.

The gradual increase of those within a church who *possess church membership* by natural birth, but who are strangers to the new birth and who have not God's laws written in their hearts will, if it does not destroy that church, causes it to lose its New Testament character. It is thereby turned into a body in which the true believers meet within the framework of a dead carcase—that is, *ecclesiolo in ecclesia—a little church within the church*, or more descriptively a little living church within a big dead one. This is true of all the great Sacral Churches such as those in Scandinavia, England, Scotland, Holland and South Africa. The Greek Orthodox and Russian Orthodox Churches are further examples. Evangelicals have testified that the latter have been guilty of cruel persecution of evangelical believers. From the time of Abel to Peter's imprisonment up to the present day the "unspiritually religious" have always persecuted the true seed of those who are spiritual through the second birth.

The mischief that is caused through neglect of believers' baptism can also be seen in the half-way covenant expedients which plagued the New England churches from about 1645. The subtle destruction caused by the admission of those who were nominally Christians but who showed no credible evidence of regeneration is illustrated in the case of the church at Northampton, Massachusetts where the famous Jonathan Edwards was the minister. This church experienced one of the most extraordinary revivals of history and yet this same church expelled Jonathan Edwards in 1750. He had been the minister since 1727. He was voted out by 230 votes to 23. The central issues concerned Edwards' refusal to baptise some children and the standards to be maintained for participation at the communion table.[5]

6. The unity of the local church

If the body is pure in its composition by virtue of the fact that all members have been baptised into it by the Spirit, then there is no excuse for disunity. We are all one in Christ Jesus and this spiritual unity transcends all other considerations whether of race, nationality, status, cultural or political background.

Believers' baptism safeguards at one and the same time the purity and the unity of the local church. We should not be surprised, therefore, to observe the dignity and importance accorded to baptism when we find it included in what must surely be the most powerful and comprehensive, and yet most brief statement on unity to be found in Scripture, namely, Ephesians 4:4-6.

Having described the amazing grace of God and the wonder of Salvation Paul in Ephesians 4:1-6 appeals to believers that they should walk in a way which accords with such divine magnanimity. *The* foremost expression of such a gracious and generous calling is earnest effort to maintain the spiritual unity in the church that has been created by the same effectual calling. The grandeur of that unity is outlined because the privileges commonly enjoyed should act as a powerful incentive to maintain unity.

To start off with, there is only one body Ephesians 4:4. This Paul has illustrated in the long preceding passage beginning at chapter two and verse eleven. Ephesians 4:1-6 is the climax, conclusion and application of that context which forms the most detailed statement in the Bible on this subject of unity. There is only one body which includes both Jewish and Gentile believers. Every one in the body possesses the Holy Spirit. Every one has experienced the same calling by which every one is given the same hope of expectation of eternal life. Every one is joined to the same head, even Christ, and all have the one faith. Some regard that faith as inward faith that savingly joins the believer to Christ while others take the faith as the truth of the Gospel. Some believe both for both are true. In any case objective faith (and verse 13 in the same context may well point to that as the primary meaning) is not meaningful unless appropriated by inward faith. All believers are made children by adoption and all have the one Father who is the Sovereign God.

These factors (all prefixed with the word ONE) and baptism are the possession of all believers without exception. No mortal outside the body of Christ possesses so much as one of these blessings. To have one is to have all. How are we to understand baptism in the light of the context which concerns unity and especially in connection with the great stress on *oneness*?—*one* Spirit, *one* Faith, *one* calling? Paul is reasoning thus: You have one Spirit indwelling you; division into two is therefore incompatible. You have one Father; division into two is therefore unthinkable. You have one calling to one eternal home; division into two or more parts is totally inconsistent.

In answer to the question as to the place of baptism in the context we note that Paul is saying that every one in the body of Christ has the *one* baptism, therefore division is incompatible. But does everyone in the body of Christ have baptism? Yes Indeed! One cannot be in the body without baptism, that is without the baptism of the Spirit (1 Cor. 2:12, 13, Gal. 3:27, Rom. 6:3, 4).

The last cited Scripture will serve to illustrate the point. The union described by Paul in Romans 6:3, 4 is experimental in character. That cannot be denied when we consider the force of his appeal in Romans six as a whole. Paul is reasoning with the believers concerning something which they have experienced. The outward sacrament of immersion perfectly symbolises that experience. It is an experience of inclusion into the body of Christ by the Holy Spirit. The foremost objective realities of the Gospel are declared in the ordinance, realities which are now expressed experimentally.

Those who have believed and been immersed as believers well understand the force of these passages from personal experience.

The disciples at Ephesus had been immersed as believers (Acts 19:5) to signify their union with Christ and with the trinity (Matt. 28:19). Thereby the inward had been sealed and signified by the outward.

The implication of baptism for—local church unity is obvious. The sacrament symbolises baptism in the trinity and into the body of Christ the Church. Incorporation into the local church is something shared by all the members. The privileges and responsibilities of the Gospel in which a church is united are rehearsed every time a believer comes forward to be baptised.

Baptism is effectively destroyed by granting it to infants who may never believe. Certainly not one of the momentous realities pointed to by the seven great ONES of the passage (Eph. 4:4-6) is expressed by an infant. None of the aforegoing can be said to exist in an infant who may not come to faith in the future. Should that infant later experience these momentous realities by the one effectual calling, then both he and the church are deprived of the means ordained by God to celebrate that union. A few drops of water sprinkled many years ago in an unremembered and unconscious past is the most miserable and wretched substitute for a person who comes into union with Christ. That person now desires that union with Christ be expressed. It is a union realised existentially in an experimental present and enjoyed now by the candidate, and by the whole visible local church of which he has become a part. The baptism of a believer is a festive occasion of joy and delight redolent of all the meaning expressed by Paul in Ephesians 4:4-6. Baptism expresses initiation into God triune and culminates in the realisation of the glorious hope of which the calling was the invitation. A Church constituted of believers all of whom have experienced these realities and expressed them in the obedience to Christ's command, "he that believeth and is baptised shall be saved," should be a church strong in grace and unity.

Before taking up the next point I would suggest that the one baptism of Ephesians 4:5 is the baptism of the Spirit into the body of Christ symbolised in water immersion. The water immersion is not essential to salvation but it is desirable in the interest of clarity, experience and unity. The paedobaptist error has been the source of endless confusion and division in the history of paedobaptist churches. Our brethren in some of the paedobaptist denominations confess that the great splits in their churches have often been caused by the vexation and anomalies of infant baptism. Certainly this vexation is highlighted in the history of the half-way covenant debate in America already referred to.

7. Infants and children in the local church

The charge made against us as Reformed Baptists is that we fail to see the corporate nature of the covenant and the very crux of paedobaptists' objection to our practice is that in denying baptism to our infants we are doing less for them than was done for the children of the Jews, the Covenant people, in the Old Testament administration. They feel this to be scandalous in the highest degree.

In response we aver that we appreciate most heartily the corporate nature of the covenant and the continuity of its nature but we appreciate no less its diversity and the contrast and difference between the Old and New Covenants upon which the Scripture itself insists (Heb. 8:7ff.).

Since this matter is of the utmost importance it warrants careful attention by way of explanation.

First as to the corporate nature and the continuity of the covenant, we would stress that the covenant is God's sovereign administration of grace, divine in its origin, disclosure, confirmation and fulfilment. God contracts monergistically to redeem; that is, from and by himself.[6] To Noah he revealed that he would preserve the material world, in order to achieve his purpose; to Abraham he revealed that out of him he would make a nation and that he would give them a land. The Mosaic covenant was made with that people promised to Abraham, even with the whole nation, that God would be their God. For their part they had to be faithful to the laws given to them. A further revelation of God's covenant purpose is called the Davidic covenant in which it was revealed that all the blessings and provisions of the covenant would come through a Messiah who would in himself embody all the covenant blessings (Ps. 89:1-4).

The New Covenant is the climax and complete revelation of all that God has prepared for his people in redemption. The sum total of all the details revealed in the progressive stages of the covenant are fully and finally disclosed in the New. David's greater Son reigns over a new nation in which every member from the least even to the greatest has a spiritual nature. To have the laws of God inscribed on the heart in new birth is essential and fundamental for membership in the New Covenant community.

That there is corporateness we can see, since spiritual people who were born again were found within the Old Covenant nation of Israel. Continuity is evident because God progressively revealed different aspects of his sovereign mercy. But the Scriptures insist that equal justice must be given to the differences between the old and the new. Now what is the difference between the New Covenant and the Old? Hebrews 8:6-13 is decisive in answering this question. There was certainly fault to be found with the old which demanded that it be removed to make place for the new (Heb. 8:7, 8).

The first and most obvious difference is that the new covenant is *new* in contrast to the old. The word used in Hebrews 8:13 *gēraskon* is a strong Greek word denoting "ageing into decay". Another strong term is used, namely *aphanismov* which is a word used for wiping out a city or obliterating an inscription. The old was so old as to be near vanishing away! Let us make no mistake about it, the old covenant way of salvation is now totally and irrevocably obliterated. As a way for us to follow for salvation it is wiped out, annihilated. Any tendencies whatever to return to it as a basis of salvation is denounced by Paul in the most vehement terms (Gal. 1).

The second difference to be noted is that the new covenant is internal, that is, it is written on men's hearts and minds. All members of the new covenant nation under king Emmanuel obey God out of love. They have all been born again. They are all children of the spiritual circumcision. The old, unregenerate nature has been replaced by a new spirit and a new heart. By contrast, the Old Covenant (and it is specifically the Mosaic covenant that is referred to in Hebrews 8, Galatians 3 and 2 Corinthians 3) was external inasmuch as every single person born into the nation of Israel was obliged to be obedient. Whether they felt like it or not they were all in the absolute sense required to obey. Serious rebellion was subject to the death penalty. Does this mean that it was all legalistic and that there was nothing spiritual about the Old Covenant? Such a conclusion would be false indeed. The spiritual was contained within the external. Now in the new covenant the spiritual and inward aspects are brought into focus. This is the stress of Hebrews 8:10, 11. "I will put my laws into their mind, and write them in their hearts—for all shall know me, from the least to the greatest."

A third contrast is the stress on forgiveness in the New Covenant. Of course there was forgiveness in the old: the priesthood and the sacrifices all pointed to the provision that would be made by the Lamb to come. But for clarity about forgiveness and justification by faith on the grounds of accomplished redemption the new is like the meridian sun for clearness compared with the old which may be likened to the long wintry shadows of a Scandinavian winter's sun. Hence the stress, "for I will be merciful to their unrighteousness and their iniquities will I remember no more" (Heb. 8:12).

With these factors in mind we remember that circumcision was mandatory for all born into the Old Testament community. Circumcision was the sign and seal of the covenant. Obedience to all the laws, national and ceremonial, was obligatory and circumcision acted as a reminder of that. Now it is contested that baptism has taken the place of circumcision and all the infant progeny born of Christian parents should be baptised.

But this idea is based wholly upon the Old Covenant and no amount of special pleading about corporateness and continuity can make up for the fact that the differences between old and new covenants stressed in Hebrews 8:6-12 are ignored. Neither by command nor example can we find infant baptism in the New Testament. That rite is based on the old covenant as B. B. Warfield says: "The warrant for infant baptism is not to be sought in the New Testament but in the Old Testament."[7]

Observing the differences between the Old and the New Covenant we must insist that baptism be given only to those who have the credentials of new covenant status, namely, that they have renewed hearts and know the Lord. Not to observe the difference, but to act on the basis of the Old Covenant leads to the terrible confusion of sacral societies, whole populations or whole denominations being regarded as Christian through the sprinkling of water.

The New Testament knows of two categories, namely, baptised communicant members of the body of Christ and, unbaptised non-communicant members. The baptism of infants creates a third category: baptised non-communicant members.

In conclusion we must face the charge that we have less for our children that the Hebrew nation had for theirs? The answer to that is simple. To be born into the orbit of Christian teaching, love and nurture is a privilege immeasurably greater than that of circumcising male infants on the eighth day. John the Baptist, in seeing the Messiah, saw more than all the prophets before him including Moses and in respect of his office was accounted by Christ greater than them all. Yet the least in the kingdom of heaven is greater than John. The least in the kingdom can now appreciate all the work of Christ completed, something which John could not see. Children born into Christian homes enjoy privileges immeasurably superior to those of the Old Testament times. Christ is set before them as the triumphant all-powerful redeemer. Even John the Baptist did not see that!

---

[1] Calvin said that it was evident that the term *Baptism* means to immerse entirely, and it is certain that the custom of entire immersion was anciently observed in the Church. Nevertheless he felt that the mode should be left free to the diversity of countries (he is probably referring to climate). To Calvin the sign was represented either by immersion or sprinkling.

[2] It is the early use of *sacramentum* that is valuable. In everyday usage it was employed to describe a pledge or security deposited in public keeping and also as an oath taken by a Roman soldier, to the emperor. Later the word was taken to mean 'mystery' and the Vulgate renders the Greek *mysterion* (Eph. 5:32; Col 1:27; Rev. 1:20) as sacramentum.

[3] *Baptism in the New Testament.* p. 203ff.

[4] N. P. Williams. *The Fall and Original Sin*, p. 31. Quoted from G. R. Beasley Murray. ibid. p. 274.

[5] This history of The Halfway Covenant is described by David Boorman in *The Puritan Experiment*, the report of the Westminster Conference 1976.

[6] The Greek word for covenant is *diathēkē*. For all normal uses the Greek word for an agreement is *sunthēkē* as between two countries or as in marriage between two people. *Sunthēkē* describes an agreement entered into on equal terms. *Diathēkē* in contrast to that denotes not an agreement but *a will*. The covenant God makes is not argued or bargained over. As in a will the testator decides what he will do with his estate so in God's covenant God's mercy is divinely Ordained.

[7] *Studies in Theology*, p. 399.

5

The Mode of Baptism

by Herbert Carson

LET ME BEGIN ON A PERSONAL NOTE. WHEN I WAS STRUGGLING WITH THE issue of Baptism some years ago the question of mode was a secondary question. The matter of supreme concern to me was the subject. As an Anglican I was familiar with the rubric in the Baptismal Service which directed the minister to dip the child in the water discreetly and warily. Provision was made for sickly children on whom water was to be poured. Later on, of course, I became aware of Spurgeon's caustic comment on the large number of sickly babes at Anglican fonts! However the exception, even if it was only observed in theory, did indicate that from the prayer book standpoint immersion was the obvious mode. Indeed you may recall John Wesley's early troubled days in Georgia when his literal enforcement of the rubric landed him in difficulties. It has not, therefore, been my sojourn among Baptists which has led me to see immersion as the biblical mode. It has simply meant that I have appreciated its significance by actual practice rather than by a nod of theoretical assent. Furthermore it has confirmed my scepticism at the special pleading to which the advocates of sprinkling seem to be reduced. In other words my basic position is that the plain, simple and obvious meaning of the term "Baptise" in the New Testament is to dip and it is only what we may term translators' indecision or cowardice which has landed us with an unnatural word which does not represent anything but a failure to translate!

I do not propose to spend time on the etymology of the word βαπτίζω. All I need to establish is that the primary meaning of the word is "dip" and this I can discover by consulting a lexicon. That a skilled etymologist may discover in some linguistic bypath far from the highway of normal usage a Greek author who uses it in a sense which may be induced to yield the rendering "pour"—this does not trouble me or upset my position at all. When the obvious and generally used meaning of a word is established then in order to interpret it in the unusual sense in any context we would need a very clear indication that the latter was in view. For an author to use a word whose normal connotation is clear to all but which may on a rare occasion be used in another sense, and not to indicate that his usage is out of the ordinary is simply to promote ambiguity. In the case of the word we are discussing (βαπτίζω) the ambiguity would be more inexcusable since he had a word readily to hand which would have conveyed the idea of sprinkling, *i.e.* ραντίζω.

To ignore that word and to employ a word which without very precise qualification would suggest another mode is the kind of writing we might expect from a man who is very limited in his vocabulary, but certainly not from a man whose precise usage of language is seen in the nuances of Romans or Galatians. If Paul was a stumbling foreigner we might excuse him as we excuse the Englishman whose French leaves a lot to be desired but Paul was far removed from such a gauche position. There is, of course, the further factor and an even more vital fact that to say he used βαπτίζω but meant ραντίζω is not merely to accuse him of slipshod linguistic usage but to indict the Spirit of God of culpable ambiguity.

The question then to be discussed in this paper is this—do the theology of Baptism and the descriptions of Baptismal practice in the New Testament confirm the general linguistic usage? Even more important we shall ask the supplementary question—Is the mode in the New Testament a matter of primary significance as far as the ordinance is concerned or only of minor concern? Is it in fact an important element in the ordinance or is it a secondary detail to be settled largely by personal taste? In endeavouring to answer these questions we shall begin with the theology of the ordinance and make our primary appeal there. The descriptions of baptismal practice will come in the second place as a confirmatory testimony. We shall begin, in other words, by probing the theological significance of baptism. Having done that we shall then examine the way in which people were baptised and we shall, I trust, be in a position to say why they were baptised in the particular mode which was employed.

We begin with Rom. 6: and at once must deal with the objection that the reference to baptism in v. 4 does not refer to water baptism at all but to the baptism with the Spirit. Certainly this would get small support among the commentators and it emerges from a failure to appreciate

65

the prominence which baptism clearly had in the thinking of the New Testament churches. It was such a vivid experience for them that in referring to it they easily passed from the sign to the thing signified. Indeed Peter so naturally speaks of the sign accomplishing something (baptism does now save us) I Pet. 3:21, that he at once has to qualify his statement lest someone twists it to produce a magical view of the ordinance. So he adds "not as a removal of dirt from the body but as an appeal to God for a clear conscience". Paul is surely using the term in a similar way in Rom. 6. The spiritual reality is of course in view. But it is the ordinance which sets forth that spiritual reality. After all it must be remembered that the primary purpose of Rom. 6 is not to work out and expound a doctrine of baptism. It is to reject any antinomian teaching which would pervert the doctrine of justification by faith into a licence for sinful living. Paul's concern is with holiness of life. His argument is that the Christian has died to sin. It is no longer his habitat. Hence it should be intolerable for him even to contemplate any trifling with sin. You died to sin, he says; You have risen to newness of life in Christ; you must therefore walk accordingly.

It is in this context that he makes appeal to their baptism. You have been baptised—this is his argument—well you must realise what your baptism signified. It declared your death to sin and your rising with Christ. It set forth the radical change involved in the new birth. The man you were in Adam has died, the man you are in Christ has risen to newness of life.

Behind this argument is his basic contention that a believer is one who is united to Christ. United with Him by eternal choice (Eph. 1:4) we were united with Him at Calvary when He died for His people and in the experience of the new birth we were experimentally united to Him. So we are involved by union with Christ in all that He has done and all that He is. We have been crucified with Him, we have been raised with Him, we live with Him, we shall reign with Him.

Now it is all this which is represented and set forth on baptism. Indeed so vividly is it declared that Paul uses of the sign, language which really belongs to the spiritual reality—we were buried therefore with Him by baptism into death. The reality is the work of the Spirit who baptised us into the body of Christ. But it is the plunge in water which vividly sets forth this spiritual baptism.

It is at this point that we must notice in v. 4 the introduction of the thought of "burial". By baptism we were buried with Him with a view to our resurrection with Him. Now John Murray argues (and Hendriksen follows him in his commentary on Colossians) that this says nothing about the mode of baptism. He contends that to argue that the burial and resurrection theme imply a particular mode of baptism would lead us to say that being planted with Him and being crucified with Him must also refer to mode and it would be hard, so he maintains, to find immersion in these pictures.

But this objection, I believe, fails to observe the basic fact that the whole passage is not about baptism at all but about holiness. Baptism is introduced by way of illustration. But a preacher might well be indignant if his illustration is forced to conform to the whole subsequent development of his sermon. You introduce an illustration to make a point clear but you move on in your argument and you may very quickly employ another illustration or you may move from illustration to metaphor. This surely is what Paul does here. He illustrates one aspect of his basic theme by his reference to baptism in v. 4, and he goes on to employ other pictures in vv. 6 and 7. If he had been expounding baptism he might well have been charged as Professor Murray charges us with confusing the issue. In fact it is simply that Paul is using his liberty to expound the truth and Murray would put him in a homiletical strait-jacket.

There is a further vitally important point. It is the reference to burial. He has already in v. 3 spoken of our union with Christ in His death. Now in v. 4 he reinforces this by the conclusion which he draws from our baptism that we are buried with Him. So baptism does not simply represent identification with Christ in His death, it declares our burial with Him and at this point the significance of the mode becomes very obvious. Baptism is not simply a bath—it is this of course, with the significance of cleansing—but it is also a burying, and the total immersion of the baptised is a vivid representation of burial.

We must look further at the stress on burial in the apostolic gospel. In I Cor. 15 Paul gives the essential elements in his gospel. They were three —Christ died; He was buried; He rose again. We might well ask why Paul mentions burial as a distinct element and the $\kappa\alpha\iota\ \acute{o}\tau\iota$ which introduces it makes it as distinct an element as the death and the resurrection.

The answer would seem to be twofold. His burial represented the final point in His identification with His people. So John describes His burial as being in accordance with the burial custom of the Jews (John 19:40). Then again it was an essential confirmation of the fact that He had truly died and so it becomes an attestation to the supreme miracle of the resurrection. The burial of Christ is therefore no incidental fact but a significant element in the total pattern.

The believer in Rom. 6 is united with Christ. He has died with Christ. His death has not been a make-believe. Paul is not arguing for some psychological trick of self-persuasion. He is saying that our death has actually taken place. We have been identified with Christ in His death. But just as His burial confirmed the reality of His death so our burial has born witness to our union with him in his dying and to our own death. Baptism is the instrument here—the preposition used is διά. It is by means of baptism that this has been effected. Again the sign and the thing signified converge. But it is the very vivid character of the sign which enables sign and thing signified thus to converge. It is the symbolic immersion, a ceremonial drowning if you like, which sets forth the identification of the believer with Christ at the final point of His burial in the sepulchre. It is hard to see how a few drops of water could convey such a lesson.

It is surely clear how specious is John Murray's objection that our interpretation of v. 4 requires us to be consistent and apply vv. 5 and 6 similarly. The point is that Paul does not say that "we have been crucified with Him by baptism" but he does say "we have been buried with Him by baptism". It is not the manner of dying which is in view but the reality and the finality of it, and it is this which baptism sets forth by embodying the thought of burial and by illustrating it so forcefully.

When we turn to Col. 2:11-12 we find the same kind of argument. Again it is in the context of practical exhortation. At Colossae there was false teaching. There were Judaistic elements but also traces of what later came to be developed into various forms of Gnosticism. Paul's answer is similar to the one he gave in the Galatian situation. It is to point to the fulness of Christ and to the consequent completeness of the salvation which He has worked out and which by the Spirit's working has been applied to the believer. To import the restrictions or the demands of the false teachers is not only to adulterate the gospel but is to deny the all sufficiency of Christ and His work. In Christ dwells all the fulness of the godhead bodily and we have come to fulness of life in Him.

The emphasis is thus on the completeness and radical character of the new birth. It is no mere ceremonial change but a deep inner transformation. So he introduces the idea of a spiritual circumcision which we have received. It is clearly in contrast with the literal circumcision which was so constant a theme of Judaising teachers. Ours is a circumcision "made without hands". But equally important is its far reaching character. It has involved the "putting off the body of flesh in the circumcision of Christ". Hendriksen points out that the verb ἀπεκδύσει has a double prefix ἀπο and ἐκ. Thus the thought is of "the putting off and casting away" of the body of flesh. The latter phrase is also significant. It is not merely the removal of a piece of flesh as in circumcision. It is the whole body of flesh which has been removed. Now circumcision as Geerhardus Vos so well expounded[1] had a spiritual significance. The fact that it dealt with the organ of procreation indicated that it was the very life of a man which needed radical divine surgery. Now this inner significance of circumcision has found its fulfilment in the circumcision of Christ. It is thus the "entire evil nature" to quote Hendriksen again which is put off and cast away.

Now it is this radical change which is declared in baptism. The use of the participle "buried with him" indicates that this is not a further statement but is by way of explanation and illustration of the point he has been making. The reality is the new birth which has involved a death and a resurrection, the death of the old man and the birth of the new. We are again in the same realm of thought as Rom. 6. Baptism declares death and burial and resurrection and it is the burial in the water which so vividly sets this forth. A few drops of water which hardly moisten a man's brow do not inconvenience him and do not alter his condition very much. But to plunge him in water and to immerse him in the water is a vivid interference with his ordinary condition. It is an extraordinary action, almost a violent action, and indeed symbolically a killing action. But it is only such an action which can adequately declare a death, a casting away, and a rising again to newness of life.

Turning from this brief summary of some of the elements in the theology of baptism we must look at the actual practice as recorded in the Gospels and in Acts. The question we ask is whether the plain and obvious meaning of the narrative confirms the deduction we have drawn from our theological premises. We begin with the baptism of John, for while there was a significant difference in the implication of John's baptism and the gospel ordinance, as we see in Acts 19, yet the employment of the same word without any qualification would lead to the conclusion that in action and procedure there is a continuity from John's baptism to that administered by the apostles.

Both Matthew and Mark record that Jesus was baptised "in" the river (Matt. 3:5; Mark 1:5). The preposition used is ἐν. It can be argued that he went down and stood in the river in order to be sprinkled but common sense surely rules out such an absurdity. As an Anglican I baptised adults by effusion but I never needed to get them to stand in a bath for the purpose! All I needed was a very small amount of water. But Mark goes further in 1:9 and uses the preposition εἰς. He was baptised "into" the river. The plain implication is that in some way he actually entered into the water and the most obvious conclusion when the primary meaning of the word is to dip is that he was immersed. To speak of dipping someone in the water is expressive enough but to speak of dipping them into it is even more so. Incidentally, one can see the absurdity of translating βαπτιζω here as sprinkle or pour. You can dip someone in the water but you cannot sprinkle them into the water unless you have used a mincer beforehand!

This conclusion is confirmed by the description of Jesus' subsequent emergence. He went up out of the water (Matt. 3:16) ἀνέβη ἀπο τον ὑδατος. Note that He did not simply come up from the river but from the water. He was not standing on the verge and then climbed to the bank. He came from the water. In Mark's account in 1:10 he uses the preposition ἐκ to describe the emergence. (ἀναβαινων ἐκ του ὑδατος).

Let us look at the verb and the prepositions employed here. The verb ἀναβαίνειν means to ascend. It can be used literally of an ascent from lower ground up to a hill. In this case the starting point was the water.

Further, the idea of ascent presupposes that of descent. Paul develops this in his great statement of the ascension in Eph. 4:9. The ascent of Jesus presupposes His previous descent, ἀναβαινω presupposes καταβαινω and this was into the depths τα κατωτερα μερη. To apply this to the baptismal accounts we may say that the coming up of Jesus implied a previous going down. The whole picture speaks of immersion.

But look further at the prepositions. Ἐκ introduces the place from which the separation takes place. Hence it is used especially with verbs of motion. Ascent from the water points to disengagement from an element where one was previously. Take for example Rev. 13:1 where the combination of ἀναβαινω ἐκ is used of the beast rising from the sea and in Rev. 17:8 of the angel from the abyss. One could hardly argue that in either case they were at the edge or on the surface. In fact they come to the surface. It is precisely this kind of usage which we see in the gospel account of Jesus rising from the water.

The preposition ἀπο has, says Arndt and Gingrich, trespassed in the New Testament in the domain of ἐκ. It has basically the meaning of separation, with the same link with verbs of motion. Hence we are led to the same conclusion.

I must confess that I feel almost the futility of having to labour what seems so obvious. It is like the eucharistic controversy in the past when one had to strive to demonstrate that "do this" really only means "do this" and not "sacrifice this". Well, it is only the existence of the extraordinary insistence on sprinkling or pouring that drives us to the necessity of demonstrating that dip in the water means dip and that come up out of the water means just that!

By way of postscript we should note the comment in John's gospel about the location of the Baptist's ministry. It was at Bethabara because there was much water there (ὑδατα πολλα). Such an explanation would be utterly pointless if in fact sprinkling had sufficed. A gallon of water would go a very long way with that particular mode. There would certainly be no need whatsoever for the kind of facility which was available at Bethabara.

Turning to the practice in the Acts of the Apostles the most explicit description of the mode is in the account of the baptism of the Ethiopian eunuch in Acts 8:36-39. Here we have the two contrasting verbs καταβαινειν to go down and ἀναβαινει to come up. Earlier I noted how these two were linked together in Eph. 4:9 and I suggested that the idea was implicit in Matthew and Mark. Here however it is not merely implicit but quite explicit.

It is I suggest a quibble to argue that because they are both said to go down into the water therefore it is invalid to infer that such a descent involves immersion since Philip also was there. This is to demand a precision of language beyond the limits of normal usage. To say that a doctor and patient went into the surgery together certainly implies that part of their action was common, but the ultimate action was distinct. So too an immersion presupposes both the baptiser and the baptised going down into the water, but the intention in view is obviously that the recipient of the ordinance might be immersed. I say "obviously" for if pouring or sprinkling was sufficient it baffles me why they should both have to go down into the pool together. Was one of them incapable of taking some water in a basin? Indeed on the assumption of sprinkling or pouring the mention of the pool becomes even more inexplicable. A man would not have been travelling down a desert road without a water bottle. He would have had some to spare surely for the perfunctory sprinkling which goes by the name of baptism. But in fact apart from special pleading the simple and obvious meaning of the passage seems quite clear. The pool of water suggested the possibility of baptism. It was clearly of sufficient depth for them both to go down into the water. He was dipped in the water and he came up after his immersion to go on his way rejoicing in the assurance of his new birth and the assurance brought through the administering of the ordinance which had come to him through the preaching of the Word and through the administering of the ordinance.

We turn to the narrative of the giving of the Spirit on the day of Pentecost. This is presented as the baptism of the Spirit. Jesus refers back to John's baptism and forward to the baptism of the Spirit—you shall be baptised with the Holy Spirit not many days hence (1:5). Now the recurring phrase to describe the gift of the Spirit is "pouring out". This is true of the original language of Joel which Peter saw fulfilled on the day of Pentecost—"It will come to pass in the last days saith God that I will pour out of my Spirit upon all flesh". The phrase recurs in v. 18. So in v. 33 he speaks of the Spirit being "shed forth". The same language is used in the account of the conversion of Cornelius in 10:45 "on the Gentiles also was poured out the gift of the Holy Spirit". So Peter described the incident in similar terms saying that the Holy Spirit fell on them.

The argument then is that as the mode of the coming of the Spirit is described as pouring and since it is also represented as baptism then pouring is a legitimate mode for the administration of baptism. Indeed they would go further and say that the baptism of the Spirit cannot be interpreted in terms of immersion. They were not dipped in the Spirit but the Spirit was poured out upon them.

We begin to see the flaws in the argument when we find that various images are used to speak of the coming of the Spirit and if we use them to establish the mode of baptism we end in absurdity. While the gift of the Spirit is presented as pouring the result of His coming is filling. He fills the house, enveloping the disciples. They are filled with the Holy Spirit. In other words no one word adequately describes the gift and so different terms are employed. But we cannot allow the conclusion that therefore a variety of modes is admissible for one would be forced to ask what mode is indicated by being filled! In other words unless we are to become quite ridiculous we are forced to conclude that the issue of mode simply does not enter here.

To return to Rom. 6, the mode of baptism is prominently in view because it is precisely the truth presented by the mode, namely burial with Christ and resurrection, which is being set forth. But here in Acts 2 this is not the kind of truth which is being declared and so there is no special emphasis on the mode of the coming of the Spirit. What is in view is the inauguration of the new age which begins with the gift of the Spirit. The visitations in Samaria, in the case of Cornelius, and at Ephesus, are similarly inaugurations of the new age for particular special groups—for Samaritans, for Gentiles, for the disciples of John the Baptist. Because it is this element which is in view the precise mode of the coming of the Spirit is not in the forefront. The main points are, first, the plenteousness of His coming hence the copious pouring out; secondly, the completeness of it hence the filling of the house; thirdly, the purifying effect hence the tongues of fire; finally the wonderful consequences hence their being filled. The only valid conclusion is that it is the initiatory aspect of baptism which is in view not the precise way in which it is administered, and to try and produce a theory as to the mode of water baptism on such a basis is to miss the point and to end in absurdity.

REFERENCES

[1] *Biblical Theology,* p. 104.

6

The Implications of the Lord's Table

by Dic Eccles

THE SUBJECT OF THE LORD'S SUPPER IS A LARGE ONE AND IT WOULD BE impossible to do justice to it in a short paper like this. Besides, it has been ably treated elsewhere (see particularly the following books which are thoroughly recommended: Kevan—*The Lord's Supper*, Owen—*Sacramental Discourses* (Works vol. 9), Bruce—*The Mystery of the Lord's Supper*). We concentrate here on those aspects of the Lord's Supper which touch upon the local church.

1. The Church and the Lord's Supper

The Lord's Supper is usually treated in works of dogmatic theology under the general heading of ecclesiology (the doctrine of the Church). Sometimes the impression is given that this is quite arbitrary, a mere matter of convenience: more out of a lack of anywhere else to put it than out of a conviction that this is where it rightly belongs.

Here is the question: Is there a connection between the Lord's Supper and the Church? Or is the Lord's Supper a separate and isolated subject without any relation to the doctrine of the Church? To my mind this is a vitally important question to ask and one that has been overlooked too often by Baptists. I have found very few books on Baptist principles or the Baptist doctrine of the Church which deal with it.

I have two propositions:

(a) The Lord's Supper is a Church Ordinance

The Lord's Supper was instituted by our Lord for the Church, rather than primarily for individual believers who partake. The Lord's Supper is rightly administered only when it is in the Church.

The Scriptural evidence for this is as follows:

(i) References to the observance of the Lord's Supper in the church. Paul describes the Lord's Supper in Corinth as "When you come together as a church . . . for the Lord's Supper" (1 Cor. 11:18,20 and see also vv. 22,33,34). In Acts the same pattern can be observed: "We gathered together for the breaking of bread" (Acts 20:7); "They continued stead-fastly in the apostles' . . . fellowship, in breaking bread" (Acts 2:42).

There is not a single reference in the New Testament which gives any instance or which can be construed in any way as giving an instance of the Lord's Supper being observed by an isolated, lone individual.

(ii) The Supper is a showing forth (1 Cor. 11:26). There can be no showing forth except in company. In the New Testament teaching there is no place for the Lord's Supper being observed in private.

(iii) In all the passages which give the institution of the Lord's Supper the verbs of command are plural (Matt. 26:26-29; Mark 14:22-25; Luke 22:17-19; 1 Cor. 11:23-26). This is often brought out in the Authorised Version by the use of the old-fashioned "ye". In Matthew 26:27 Jesus is reported as saying "All of you, drink of it". The Lord's Supper is clearly intended to be a corporate thing.

(iv) 1 Corinthians 10:17—"Since there is one bread, we who are many are one body." Paul brings out teaching about the Church in this verse bas-ing his instruction on aspects of the Lord's Supper. He was able to do this because there is a vital and essential connection between the two. It is not just a matter of theological classification, typical of the academic quibbles some theologians delight in, but a matter of vital spiritual dependence. If there is no Church, there can be no Lord's Supper.

(v) 1 Corinthians 11:22—"Do you despise the church of God?" There were appalling abuses of the Lord's Supper in the Church at Corinth, and in bringing teaching and correction to them Paul uses this remarkable expression. He says that their behaviour, their disorderliness, their dis-unity was a "despising of the Church of God". It was not, mark you, a despising of the Supper, not even a despising of the Lord who instituted it, but a despising of the Church. The abuses were of the Supper, but their actions were a despising of the Church. How could Paul say that? The only answer is that we cannot comprehend the Supper apart from the Church. There is a vital and essential relation between the two. The Lord's Supper presupposes the Church of Christ.

Now we must ask exactly what this means. What is the Church? The New Testament uses the word in two ways: (1) to describe the universal

74

Church (e.g. Eph. 5:25, "Christ loved the Church and gave himself for it") and (2) with reference to the local church (e.g. 1 Cor. 1:2, "To the church of God which is at Corinth"). For which of the two, the universal Church or the local church, did Christ institute the Lord's Supper? What I want to show in the second proposition is that the Lord's Supper was instituted for the local church.

(b) The Lord's Supper is an Ordinance of the Local Church

It follows from the very nature of the universal Church that this is so. The universal Church is the body of the elect from every place throughout all ages. It has no earthly organization, no earthly discipline, no earthly ministry. It has no ordinances. There is no sense in which we join in the Lord's Supper with the church in heaven. The Lord's Supper, then, as an ordinance of the church, is an ordinance of *the local church*.

The second argument we can present for this proposition is the emphasis in the Scriptures given above on the meeting of the church. "When you come together as a church" (1 Cor. 11:18; see also Acts 20:7). The universal church does not have meetings. It does not "come together". Therefore the Lord's Supper is instituted for the local church.

We fail to understand the Lord's Supper fully until we see it in this light. It is true that the individual believer is benefited by the Lord's Supper. It is true that he remembers the Lord in his death and this is the primary thing in the Supper. But there is also this element in it: that it is rooted ·in the context of the local church. As such it has several far-reaching implications for the local church, namely in its fellowship and its discipline. Before turning in more detail to these questions, four matters warrant a briefer comment:

1. The New Testament knows nothing of denominations. The word "church" in the singular is never used to describe a provincial organization with a number of local churches or congregations under its jurisdiction or incorporated in its fellowship. In view of this, the Lord's Supper must not be regarded as being instituted for groups of churches or what we would call denominations. There is no such thing in terms of Scripture as denominational communion.

2. Occasionally, reports are heard of the Lord's Supper being held at conferences, Assemblies and association meetings. I simply want to ask: what possible justification can there be for such practices? The Lord's Supper is an ordinance of the local church, and it is an expression of the fellowship of the local church. If it is observed outside the context of the local church, it ceases to be the Lord's Supper.

3. Baptism is also an ordinance of the local church, and cannot be understood aright apart from the local church. Baptism and the Lord's Supper are closely connected for this reason. By baptism a believer

enters the fellowship of the local church, and by the Lord's Supper that fellowship continues to be expressed.

4. The connection between the church and the Lord's Supper must not be viewed as the Church being the custodian of the Lord's Supper for the purpose of dispensing grace to the public. This idea arises from an erroneous doctrine of the Church which goes back to the time of Constantine, the Roman Emperor.

Constantine made Christianity the official religion of the Roman Empire. His reasons for doing this were basically political, arising from his conviction that the function of religion was to provide stability and unity in society, to weld society together through every citizen's following the one religion and observing its ceremonies. These ideas are known as "sacralism". Constantine had problems in making the establishment of Christianity effective in this way because there were many characteristics of the Church which did not fit into the sacralistic pattern.

Sacralistic religion is characterised by three things. First, there is ease of initiation. If every citizen is to embrace one official religion, it is necessary to make it easy for him to join. Second, there is a lack of emphasis on standards. If great demands are made on the adherents, there is a possibility of losing them and that is a risk that cannot be taken. Third, there is an emphasis on ceremonies. If high standards are rejected, there is nothing left but ritual. The devotees must feel that they derive something from their religion and the ceremonies provide this. Sacralistic religions commonly regard their ceremonies as actually imparting some benefit (such as the essence of the divinity) to those who partake. However, the church had been characterised by its distinctiveness and its separation from unbelievers and by its preaching which made a division between men. The Lord's Supper was observed as a remembrance of Christ in his death by those who believed. But sacralistic ideas gradually took over in the Church. Universal and indiscriminate baptism became widespread; there was a drop in moral standards; the emphasis on preaching declined and the Lord's Supper came to be regarded as a ceremony which conveyed grace to the partakers. The Lord's Supper came to be called a "sacrament"—the word used to describe the ceremonies of the sacralistic cults of the Roman Empire which imparted benefit to the adherents.

The significance of this for our subject are obvious. The doctrine of the Church was materially altered at this time and, with it, the understanding of the Lord's Supper. The Church became a dispenser of grace to the public through the sacrament of the Lord's Supper. The Lord's Supper became a ceremony which imparted grace and it became the right of every citizen.

One of the difficult areas in the administration of the Lord's Supper is that there are many today who regard the Church as the dispenser of grace to the public through the Supper. Refusal to allow an unbeliever to partake can cause him great distress because of this error in that he comes to regard the church as acting in an unChristian way in barring him from the grace he needs. An explanation of the sacralistic concepts that lie behind his ideas and our reasons for rejecting them can go much of the way towards resolving such difficulties.

Some today advocate that the Lord's Supper should be termed a sacrament. I must confess that I am not happy with that. The pedigree of the term is dubious, to say the least. Its etymological origins are innocent enough, but by the time it came to be applied to the Lord's Supper it plainly had a meaning that was far removed from the biblical teaching. Also, the word means things to some people today which we would not intend to convey and our use of it would only lead to confusion. It must also be said that the usual alternative that is put forward (i.e. "ordinance") is not satisfactory either. There are other ordinances in the Church, for example preaching and the disciplinary censures, which are different in kind from baptism and the Lord's Supper. Perhaps terms such as "symbolic ordinance" or "covenant ordinance" could serve to make the necessary distinction.

It has been possible only to touch on this question of sacralism and its effect on the doctrine of the Lord's Supper. Those who wish to look further into the matter are recommended to these books: Verduin—*The Reformers and their Stepchildren*, Bender—*The Recovery of the Anabaptist Vision*, Verduin—*The Anatomy of a Hybrid*.

2. The Local Church and the Fellowship of the Lord's Supper

In 1 Corinthians 10:16 Paul describes the Lord's Supper as communion: "The cup of blessing which we bless, is it not the communion of the blood of Christ?" The word he uses is *koinonia:* fellowship, sharing. Now the question is, fellowship with whom? Is it fellowship with Christ, or is it fellowship among those who partake? It seems quite clear that Paul has in mind that the Lord's Supper is an expression of fellowship among those who observe it.

He begins the chapter by describing the people of Israel in the wilderness as being all under the cloud, all passing through the sea, all baptized unto Moses in the cloud, all eating the same spiritual food and so on. They shared these experiences together. They were united in them. The context of verse 16, then, is the fellowship among men. In verse 17 he goes on to speak of the unity of the body: "We who are many are one body." Quite clearly this verse is stressing what the different members of the Church share in common, and what brought them together in fellowship.

The fellowship Paul is speaking about in verse 16, then, is not fellowship with Christ but fellowship among believers. That is not to say, of course, that the Lord's Supper is not fellowship with Christ, just that Paul is not talking about that fellowship in this verse. Our understanding of the Lord's Supper must therefore include this: that it is an expression of the fellowship of the local church. Indeed, it is the greatest and highest expression of that fellowship. There are several specific matters which are implied in this:

(a) *Mutual acceptance*

Each individual participant comes to receive the Lord's Supper because he has faith in Christ and in his work on the cross. He knows the grace of God shed abroad in his heart. In eating the bread and drinking the wine he remembers the Lord and gives thanks for the grace of God given to him.

But there are others present who make the same profession. The believer hands the plate and the cup to the person sitting next to him. This action expresses the conviction the believer has that the others present with him know the grace of God as he does. It is a confession that the others are his brothers in Christ.

The church, in allowing this situation, is also acknowledging that those present are, as far as it it is able to judge, true believers in the Lord Jesus Christ. The church, when it admits someone to the Lord's Supper, is saying that it accepts him as a believer.

The same thing is true of baptism, of course. When a person is baptized, not only is he making a personal profession of his faith in Christ, but the church also, in baptizing him, is saying that it accepts that he is a believer.

This aspect of fellowship, the acceptance of each other as believers, is important. It is a great encouragement to all, and particularly to those who have a tender conscience.

(b) *Equality*

The Lord's Supper is an expression of the sameness of each person who partakes. All are present on the same basis: that they are sinners saved by grace through faith in Christ. It matters not whether they be Jew or Gentile, bond or free, male or female, university professor or dustbin man, Duke or commoner, black or white—they are equal in coming to the Lord's Supper. The Lord's Supper is a leveller of men.

The Lord's Supper, then, is an expression of what ought to pertain in the fellowship of the church as a whole. No-one, because of what he is in daily life, should have any eminence in the church of Christ (Jas. 2:1-4). Each person, in taking the Supper, is saying that he accepts this equality and that he pledges himself to observe it in every aspect of the church's life.

(c) *Unity*

Paul's treatment of the Lord's Supper in 1 Corinthians is to teach the unity of Christians and the unity of the local church which is implicit in the Communion.

The local church is one body (1 Cor. 10:17), and when it comes together for the Lord's Supper it is giving expression to that. In the Corinthian church, however, there was disunity. There was party spirit, and the whole church was split deeply into factions. But this was not the only aspect of their divisions. It would appear that they met together for fellowship meals and that their disunity was manifesting itself there: some had plenty and some had little; some over-ate and were drunk whilst others went hungry. Paul argues from the Lord's Supper that this situation was wrong. The disunity that was manifesting itself in all sorts of different ways was inconsistent with their taking the Lord's Supper (11:18-20). Their actions were disorderly—so much so that the Lord's Supper that they thought they were holding had become so distorted that it was not the Lord's Supper at all. "When you come together as a church, it is not to eat the Lord's Supper" (v. 20). It was their purpose in coming together to eat the Lord's Supper, but because there was disunity amongst them, when they ate the bread and drank the wine which expressed unity, it made a mockery of the Lord's Supper.

This is why in verse 22 he describes the abuses of the Lord's Supper that prevailed in Corinth as a "despising of the church". It is because the Lord's Supper expresses the fellowship and unity of the church. Where this unity does not exist, and the Lord's Supper is observed, a strange mockery is perpetrated, a gross inconsistency is indulged.

If there is disunity in a church, the Lord's Supper cannot be the Lord's Supper. The bread may be eaten, the wine may be drunk, the words of institution may be used, but it is not the Lord's Supper. That is the measure of the seriousness of this expression of unity implicit in the Supper. When there is disorderliness or division in the church, these problems should be resolved before the Lord's Supper. If such things are countenanced and tolerated, the Lord's Supper will be a sham and a hypocrisy, and it will be stripped of its significance.

(d) *Commitment to one another and together to the Lord*

Fellowship means not only that the believers possess the same things together in Christ, but also that they give themselves to one another in the Lord. The Lord's Supper is an expression of this general Christian principle. In eating the Lord's Supper, we are giving ourselves to one another and expressing our acceptance of our obligations to one another in fellowship. What is entailed in such obligations is taught in 2 Corinthians 8:5; Ephesians 5:21; Philippians 2:4; 1 Thessalonians 5:11 and 1 John 3:16-18.

The participants not only commit themselves one to another in the Lord, but also in fellowship together they commit themselves to the Lord. Paul, commending the believers of Macedonia, says of them, "They gave themselves first to the Lord and then to us" (2 Cor. 8:5). In taking the Lord's Supper the believers acknowledge that "they are not their own, they are bought with a price" (1 Cor. 6:19,20). They acknowledge that they are under obligation to live according to the rules of Christ and that certain acts of behaviour are inconsistent with their profession. They are, in the act of eating, pledging themselves to desist from these and live to Christ. Paul (1 Cor. 10:21) puts it like this: "You cannot drink the cup of the Lord and the cup of devils; you cannot be partakers of the Lord's table and of the table of devils." He is applying this, in the context, to the question of meat offered to idols, but his argument indicates that there is a general principle involved, and that this is not the only application. His statement clearly indicates that when the believers take the Lord's Supper they are acknowledging in the act that there are moral obligations resting on them, and they are expressing that they accept their responsibilities. In this sense the Lord's table is a holy table.

Now, before leaving this aspect of the subject, a number of general comments must be made:

1. It is a matter of regret that this expression of fellowship, intrinsic to the Lord's Supper, is not emphasised more among us. We tend to be characterised more by the attitude that the participants come to the Lord's Supper for what they can get out of it. The Lord's Supper, in its very nature, is completely opposed to such self-centredness.

The expression of fellowship in the Lord's Supper is very precious and we must do what we can to recover it and preserve it. It is important that Christian people be taught these things, so that they know what is involved in their taking the Lord's Supper, and can play their part in the fellowship. Eating the Lord's Supper is a stimulus to Christian living as a whole.

2. The church must not be indifferent to the casual attitude displayed by some towards the Lord's Supper. There are those who feel that they can attend if they want, or they can absent themselves if they want. Attendance at the Lord's Supper is an obligation—it is an expression of fellowship. Not only do those who stay away rob themselves of the benefit of remembering the Lord and of fellowship with the other believers, but they are also robbing the church of what it is entitled to expect of them: their fellowship. Indeed, the question should be asked whether they are in fact in fellowship with Christ, since it is so inconceivable that they should not desire to have fellowship with him and with his people at the table.

3. I want to make comment on the mode of the Lord's Supper. I have never been able to understand why we baptists as a whole are so insistent

on the mode of baptism whilst at the same time we are not particular about the mode of the Lord's Supper. Yet there are clear biblical grounds for insisting on the use of a single loaf of bread and a single cup. Paul in 1 Corinthians 10:16,17 argues from the fact that they used a single loaf and a single cup to show that the Corinthian church was one body in Christ and that their divisions were a denial of fellowship. The word translated "bread" may also be translated "loaf", and the adjective "one" would indicate that this would be preferable here: "the one loaf that we break". From his argument there can be no doubt the bread and the wine are intended to symbolise not only the body and blood of Christ given for his people, but also the unity and fellowship of the local church. There is a need for these things to be taught and applied so that those who partake are aware of them.

The point I am making is this: are we not losing this aspect of the symbolism, and thereby losing the symbolic expression of fellowship, if we do not use the single loaf and the single cup?

3. The Local Church and the Discipline of the Lord's Supper

As a church ordinance, the Lord's Supper is a matter for the jurisdiction of the local church. The church is to provide for the Lord's Supper, and it also has the responsibility of ensuring that it is properly observed. This means that the church, through the elders, is to exercise discipline over the conduct of the service itself to ensure that there is no malpractice. Since so much depends on who partakes of the Supper, the church is also to exercise discipline over who is admitted. In establishing all this, let me demonstrate first of all that:

(a) *Discipline is to be exercised over the Lord's Supper*

(i) To preserve the fellowship of the local church

Discipline must be exercised to ensure that the precious fellowship of the Lord's Supper is preserved. Where, through malpractice or the disunity of the members, this fellowship has been lost, steps must be taken to recover it.

Paul tells us that we are to "endeavour to keep the unity of the Spirit in the bond of peace" (Eph. 4:3). The word "endeavour" used here is a strong and intensive word indicating the use of great effort. It is not synonymous with our weaker expression "try" or "make an attempt". He reminds us by this that the preservation of unity and fellowship has to be worked at. Fellowship does not happen by magic, by sitting back, but is only achieved by specific endeavour. Having achieved such fellowship, it can only be maintained by continuing effort.

Fellowship in the Lord's Supper does not just happen. Endeavour must be given to this also. A great responsibility rests upon the individual members to play their part in this, but also the church as a whole through the ministry of its elders has a responsibility in it. The church must ensure that the Lord's Supper does express fellowship. That is to say, the church must exercise discipline over who is admitted to the table to ensure that each one who participates can and does express that fellowship *i.e.* that they are believers and are living a consistent Christian life. Unless this is done, those who come to the table have no assurance that all who gather are in fellowship, and consequently there can be no expression of fellowship through the Supper.

(ii) Because the Scriptures indicate that this is so

Two passages of Scripture are of particular relevance. In 1 Corinthians 5:3-5 Paul gives instructions on how the church at Corinth was to act over the man guilty of incest; he tells them that they were to invoke the censure of excommunication. He then, in verse 11, enlarges the subject from the particular instance to the general principle. The church was to withdraw from anyone who professed to be a believer but who was openly practising gross sin. The church was instructed not to eat with such persons. Taking meals with other people was considered at this time to be an expression of approval, of acceptance, in fact of fellowship. The eating referred to here is an ordinary meal. However, it is inconceivable that Paul would intend the church to refuse an ordinary meal to such a person and yet receive him at the Lord's Supper, which is a far greater expression of fellowship. We must therefore see the injunction not to eat as including the Lord's Supper.

Therefore, let us take note of this fact: it is possible for the church to refuse the Lord's Supper to certain people. More than that—it is its responsibility to do so. Discipline is to be exercised over the Lord's Supper and control is to be exercised over who may be permitted to partake.

Again, in 2 Thessalonians 3:6,14,15 we have the same command, that the church is to avoid those who are unruly; the church is to withdraw from them, it is not to associate with them. I call attention to this Scripture because in verse 16 there is an additional element that is important. Those who are the subjects of this disciplinary action of the church are not enemies, and the bringing of this censure does not involve the church in regarding them as such. They are not to be treated as outsiders, as unbelievers, but as brothers. This means that this censure is not excommunication. It is a suspension of the privileges of fellowship which, though very serious in itself, falls short of actually putting the offender out of membership. It may be objected that treating someone as a brother involves the expression of fellowship and that there is a contradiction here. That is so, of course, but the extraordinary situation has arisen from the brother's unruly conduct which is itself a violation of fellowship. This means of withdrawing fellowship from him (i.e., the more obvious and open expressions of fellowship like eating with him) is designed to indicate to him that his actions are contrary to fellowship, so that he may be restored to full fellowship. The admonishing or warning of him as a brother (v. 15) is along these lines.

The censure of suspension from fellowship will be expressed in many ways, and included in it will be suspension from the Lord's Supper. It can be seen from this that the church through its elders has the responsibility of exercising discipline over those who partake, and of determining who is eligible to come.

(b) *The Responsibility for Discipline over the Lord's Supper rests upon the Local Church*

In what has been said above it ought to be clear that the responsibility for the discipline to be exercised over the Lord's Supper belongs to the church. The censure of withdrawal or suspension of fellowship is the institution of Christ for the church, and is given specifically for the maintenance of its fellowship. The claim is made, however, that the responsibility for deciding who may partake of the Lord's Supper rests with each individual. If that is so, however, then the censure of suspension from fellowship is rendered impossible to apply.

The practice of giving an open invitation to people to join in the Lord's Supper cannot meet the requirements of the need to preserve fellowship. It is putting the onus on the individual member of the congregation in such a way as to make it impossible to exercise proper discipline. It opens the door to the possibility of abuse and disorderliness. The expression of fellowship in the Lord's Supper is entirely lost.

This point has nothing to do with the relationship between baptism and the Lord's Supper. That is a separate issue. There are churches who restrict the Lord's Supper to those who are baptized as believers and who give an open invitation to "all who follow Christ and are baptized as believers by immersion". This also is putting the responsibility for participation on the individual. The decision whether to participate is left to him in such a way that it is impossible to apply a proper discipline. Now someone will say, "What about 1 Corinthians 11:28 which says 'Let a man examine himself and so let him eat?' " However, this Scripture is not talking about the same thing. The question in 1 Corinthians 11 is not whether a person may partake of the Supper, but that, when they do partake, they should do it in the right way. What the Corinthians were to examine was not their warrant to partake (that is assumed), but their manner of partaking. Verse 27 speaks of "drinking the cup of the Lord unworthily". That does not mean that they were unworthy to take the Lord's Supper, because none is worthy. Albert Barnes, who has no axe to grind on this question, says in his commentary on this verse: "Most persons interpret it as if it were *unworthy* and not *unworthily:* and seem to suppose that it refers to their personal qualifications, to their unfitness to partake of it, rather than to the manner in which it was done. It is to be remembered, therefore, that the word here used is an adverb and not an adjective, and has reference to the manner of observing the ordinance." What Paul says earlier in the chapter backs up the point being made that it is the church's prerogative to exercise discipline in the Lord's Supper. In verse 2 he says, "Now I praise you that you remember me in all things and hold fast the traditions even as I delivered them to you." Verse 23 makes it clear that among these traditions was the Lord's Supper- "For I received of the Lord that which also I delivered unto you, that the Lord Jesus, the same night in which he was betrayed, took bread." The church at Corinth (as a church) is commended by the apostle for its acceptance of its responsibilities for the administration of those ordinances that he had passed on to it, and included in these responsibilities is the oversight and disciple of the Lord's Supper.

We must get away from the idea that the church is the dispenser of the Lord's Supper, and that all who wish to partake should be allowed to do so. That is an idea that is rooted in sacralism. It is not a biblical concept.

(c) *Those whom the Local Church should admit to the Lord's Supper*

Having established that it is the local church that is to determine who shall be admitted to the fellowship of the Lord's Supper, we must now consider to whom these privileges should be granted.

(i) THE FELLOWSHIP OF CHURCH MEMBERS

It is quite plain that, because the Lord's Supper is an expression of the fellowship and of unity of the one body, the local church, the only ones who can properly express that fellowship are those who are in it, that is, the members of the church. If we adopt any other position, this fellowship that is expressed in the Lord's Supper is lost to us.

It was stated earlier that the Lord's Supper is a church ordinance. It is so in this sense also, that the church gathers in fellowship in the Lord's Supper.

(ii) THE PLACE OF VISITORS

Does this mean that the possibility is ruled out of visitors joining with the church in taking the Lord's Supper? There are some who would say "yes" to that. But such a response is not scriptural. In Acts 20:7 we are told that Paul gathered with the church at Troas in breaking bread. As a visitor to the church he was welcomed to the fellowship of the Lord's Supper. Those who maintain a rigid "members only" rule try to make out that Paul as an apostle had a right to take the Lord's Supper with a church he was visiting. This, however, does not meet the case. The verb is in the first person plural: "we gathered together". Evidently Luke was present also. Verse 5 tells us that there were seven other people from various churches in Paul's party. The "we" must include them also.

Visitors do not have any right to partake of the Lord's Supper in the church they are visiting, since they are not members there and are not therefore part of the fellowship. It is only the members that have such a right. But the church may invite visitors to join in the fellowship of the Supper if it so desires. In such a case the visitors will be specifically and personally invited. The situation is analogous to that of meals enjoyed by a family. Each member of the family has the right to sit down at the table for the meal, and it would be unthinkable to expect the head of the family to invite them to do so. The members of the family are in a special position. But a visitor who was present with them would not dream of sitting down unless he was invited to do so. It would be presumptuous and offensive if he did so, because he was a visitor. But, insistence on the rights of the members of the family does not preclude the possibility that they may extend such an invitation to a visitor if they so desire.

Whom may the church invite as visitors to the Lord's Table? As we begin to answer this question, let us note the point that the church is the one to decide what visitors are to be invited. It is not to be left to the visitor himself to decide. It would be totally incongruous if the church could exercise discipline over its members and could withdraw the fellowship of the Lord's Supper from a member but could exercise no control over who is welcomed as a visitor to the Lord's Table. Prerequisites for visitors to partake of the Lord's Supper are:

a. The visitor must be a believer. In taking the bread and the wine, a man is symbolising that he has taken Christ by faith and is resting on Christ's sacrifice as the ground of his redemption. If he takes the Supper, but does not have that faith in Christ, the symbolism becomes hollow. The church cannot tolerate the enactment of such a lie.

b. The visitor must be a member of another church. He must be in fellowship with another church and under its discipline in order to be able to express true fellowship with the church he is visiting. Spiritual nomads or tramps or those of a sermon tasting disposition who wander here and there and who will not accept their responsibilities anywhere to any church will not be able to fellowship properly in the Lord's Supper in a church they are visiting. It would do despite to the fellowship of the church, and seriously undermine its discipline, if they were allowed to do so.

c. The visitor must be in good standing with his church. He must not be under discipline in his church. He must not be out of fellowship with his church. He must be an active member. Sometimes what happens is that someone has a disagreement with his church, and he runs to a neighbouring church and tries to take the Lord's Supper there. Such lack of respect for the fellowship and discipline of his own church needs to be corrected by the church where he is a member. It is unruly for another church to extend fellowship to one in such a position, and it will be found to be disruptive to the fellowship and discipline of both churches and injurious to the individual involved. Of course, the individual caught in such a situation may not always be in the wrong, but at least the whole question must be carefully examined.

There are also cases of individuals who maintain membership with a church so far away that it is impossible for them to be involved in true fellowship in it. Such people attend other churches and often expect to have the privilege of partaking of the Lord's Supper. Although they are members of a church, they cannot be regarded as being in good standing. It ought to be made clear that these comments do not apply to those who have recently moved to a new area, but to those for whom this situation has been true for years.

(iii) BAPTISM AND THE LORD'S SUPPER

There is an essential and vital relationship between baptism and the Lord's Supper, although it is an indirect one.

By baptism a believer comes into membership with the local church. As a member of the local church he comes in fellowship to the Lord's Supper. Baptism is the initiation into fellowship, and the Lord's Supper is a continuing expression of that fellowship. The connection between baptism and the Lord's Supper, therefore, involves a middle term, the fellowship of church membership, a middle term that must not be forgotten.

The argument that baptism is a prerequisite to partaking of the Lord's Supper involves this middle term. It is really based on the arguments presented in Erroll Hulse's paper on baptism. In the New Testament, a believer is a baptized believer; a church member is a baptized member. In the New Testament there is no infant baptism; baptism is the immersion of believers.

What about visitors: are they in a different position? Is it possible for a baptist church to welcome to the Lord's Table as visitors those who have not been baptized as believers? To answer this question the point needs to be made first that both ordinances are instituted by Christ. Both are therefore equal. Whatever practice we adopt, we must not allow ourselves to give more importance to the one than to the other. We are under Christ, and we are not at liberty to say that we can disregard one in favour of some supposedly higher concept of the other. For this reason, ordinarily, visitors should only be received to the fellowship of the Lord's Supper if they have been baptized as believers.

The question of the godly person who is a convinced paedobaptist and who is in membership of a sound paedobaptist church is a difficult one. Some distinction ought to be recognized between various people who have not been baptized. There are those who admit that they ought to be baptized and who have not been; there are those who will not properly face up to the issues. These, surely, are in a different category from those who are convinced of the paedobaptist position. The former are disobedient and unruly; the latter are not, for they are seeking to follow the Word of God as they understand it and are faithful members of their churches. For the latter group, some case can be made out for their inclusion as visitors in the Lord's Supper, largely on the grounds of the extraordinary situation of genuine difference of opinion between Christians on these questions. Certainly, where a church makes use of paedobaptists in preaching it does seem very inconsistent to then exclude them from the Supper.

A word of caution must also be given in this: there can be no such thing as a permanent visitor. There are those who attempt to be such, people who do not join the church and yet who meet regularly with it. They will not accept the responsibilities of membership (often for perfectly good reasons, such as being convinced paedobaptists), and in this situation it is not right that they should be able to enjoy the privileges of membership. Therefore, when there are those who live in the area who are not one with the church, whilst they can be welcomed as visitors to the Supper when they first attend (assuming that the prerequisites are fulfilled), this cannot be allowed to go on indefinitely.

(d) *The Practice of Discipline in the Lord's Supper*

Many churches have encountered problems in seeking to apply these principles. Most of these problems arise from the practical arrangements they have adopted in the conduct of the Lord's Supper. Two things seem to be essential for the discipline of the Lord's Supper to be orderly and honouring to God:

(i) There should be an opportunity for the elders to ascertain the standing of visitors so as to ensure that the prerequisites for visitors to take the Supper are properly regarded. This really means that adequate time should be allowed.

(ii) There should be an opportunity for the elders to give a specific and personal invitation to those visitors whom they wish to meet with the church in the fellowship of the Table.

A solution which meets these requirements may be suggested. The problems of administering the Lord's Supper with respect to visitors mostly centre around the difficulty of speaking to them when the Lord's Supper is held at the end of a public worship service. The solution consists in challenging this practice and suggesting that the Lord's Supper be held separately. There is no need, even, for the time of the Lord's Supper to be announced.   This will be known to the members.   When visitors are present at a public service, the elders will have an opportunity to speak to them and, if they are believers, enjoy their fellowship.   In this situation, they can give an invitation to them to join the church in the Lord's Supper and can tell them at the same time when it is to be held.   At the table the elders can inform the members who the visitors are.   In this way the precious element of fellowship in the Lord's Supper will be preserved, and the church in gathering for the Supper can have confidence that all who are present, including the visitors, are one in Christ.   Another advantage that commends this arrangement is that the inevitable rush that attends the Lord's Supper when it is tacked on at the end of a service can be avoided.

4. The Local Church and Joy in the Lord's Supper

We have attempted to look at the significance of the Lord's Supper for the local church, and in so doing we have had to consider a number of problems and touch on some aspects that are controversial.   There are thorns on this rose.   But he is a pathetic man who goes into the garden only to look at thorns.   So, in conclusion, let us look at the joy of the Lord's Supper.

There is joy in true Christian fellowship.   There is joy in remembering the Lord in his death; in recalling his great love towards us; in remembering his sacrifice on the cross.   There is joy in realising that our sins are forgiven, in acknowledging all the blessings we have received through the cross.   There is joy in renewing our pledge of devotion to him to whom we owe so much.   There is joy in imparting ourselves to our brethren. Above all, there is joy in acknowledging the glory of God.

Paul describes the cup of the Lord's Supper as "the cup of blessing" (1 Cor. 10:16).   The word he uses is "eulogia", which can be translated either as "blessing" or "thanksgiving", and which is transliterated into English as "eulogy".   The same word comes in Ephesians 1:3, "Blessed be the God and Father of our Lord Jesus Christ", and he goes on to describe all that God has done for his people in his grace, and every privilege that they have in Christ.   There is joy in that "blessed".   There is joy in the thanksgiving.

Now, I ask, why is it that so often we have long faces when we come to the Lord's Table?   Why do we feel we have to look grey?   Why is it that our communion hymns are set to such morbid tunes, to dirges? There is a particular outward appearance of piety which is characterised by a bleak and sombre solemnity and we seem to be beset by it particularly at the Lord's Supper.

Let me make it clear that I do not mean that we should be irreverent. The privileges of the Lord's Supper are tremendous—awesome.   But true joy is not incompatible with reverence.   Nor does true reverence mean that we cannot be joyful.

Sometimes, in our church, at the Lord's Supper we sing the hymn "Come, let us join our cheerful songs", and we like to sing it to a good, extrovert tune (Lyngham)—a joyful tune.

Come, let us join our cheerful songs
With angels round the throne.
Ten thousand thousand are their tongues,
But all their joys are one.

"Worthy the Lamb that died," they cry,
"To be exalted thus!"
"Worthy the Lamb!" our lips reply,
"For he was slain for us."

7

ℱellowship in the ℒocal Church

by Colin Richards

THE WORD FELLOWSHIP COMES FROM THE GREEK WORD *KOINONIA*
Koinonia is derived from *koinos* meaning common and can be defined as
"a relation between individuals which involves a common interest and a
mutual, active participation in that interest and in each other". (*Word
Studies in the New Testament*. M. R. Vincent. Vol. 1. P. 228.) The
word *koinonia* is often, although not always, rendered in the Authorized
Version by the English words communion or fellowship. Now fellowship
is an exceedingly broad subject so I want to confine myself to one aspect,
namely, the fellowship of believers within the local church. That fellowship is dependent on two things:

1. Fellowship with God and with his Son Jesus Christ

The Biblical basis for this statement is found in 1 John 1:3 and 7: "That
which we have seen and heard declare we unto you, that ye also may have
fellowship with us: and truly our fellowship is with the Father, and with
his Son Jesus Christ. But if we walk in the light, as he is in the light, we
have fellowship one with another, and the blood of Jesus Christ his Son
cleanseth us from all sin." The fellowship of believers in the local church
is dependent on the fellowship that believers have with God and with his
Son, Jesus Christ. As to its origin, it must be stated that there can be no
fellowship between believers unless there is fellowship with God. As to
its quality it must be stated that the kind of fellowship we enjoy with one
another is dependent on the kind of fellowship we enjoy with God. If
this is so, then any study of the fellowship of believers in a local church

should concern itself with the personal disciplines of reading the Scriptures, prayer, self-examination, fasting, and all kindred matters.

2. Fellowship with members of our family

It is clear that this point is not applicable in all cases, since a Christian could be the only Christian in a family. Yet the principle that fellowship within the local church is related to fellowship within the family is vital to those it does concern. The biblical basis for this statement is to be found in 1 Timothy 3:4 and 5 where an elder is described as "One that ruleth well his own house, having his children in subjection with all gravity; (For if a man know not how to rule his own house, how shall he take care of the church of God?)" Paul's argument here is that spiritual life in the church never rises above the spiritual life in the home. In this passage of scripture which deals with the qualifications for the office of elder, Paul is insisting that if you want to know what a man is or will be in the life of the church, you must examine the spiritual qualities of his home life. So it is proper to argue that the fellowship of believers in a local church is dependent upon fellowship in a family. If this is so, then any study of the fellowship of believers in a local church should concern itself with the spiritual responsibilities of family life: the responsibilities of husband and wife separately, toward each other, and to their children.

Now it must be emphasized at this point that if we are concerned for fellowship in the local church (and particularly to raise the quality of that fellowship), then those called to preach the Word of God must deal regularly in their preaching with these practical areas of reading the Scriptures, prayer, self-examination, fasting, and the varied responsibilities of family life. For the Word of God to be brought to bear upon the consciences of church members with light and life in these vital realms will bring incalculable blessing.

The fellowship of believers in a local church comes to visible expression in three ways:

1. In corporate, public worship

The content of corporate public worship should include such things as reading the Scriptures, preaching, singing, collection, baptism and The Lord's Supper. It cannot be said too strongly in a day of emphasis on activity that we Christians should be worshippers of God before anything else. The chief end of man is to glorify God and if we fail to glorify God in our worship we will fail in every other area of life. Heaven is a place of perfect fellowship, and public, corporate worship should be the nearest thing to heaven on earth.

Now I am sure that we are all concerned to see the standard of the worship in our local church raised. For some the answer rests in changing the order of the content of our meeting—so much so that "no-order" becomes an order *par-excellence*. Such matters are not irrelevant, but our chief fault does not lie in that direction. It lies principally, I believe, in two other directions, preparation for public worship and public worship itself.

It lies firstly in the need to prepare ourselves for corporate public worship. There is today great emphasis laid upon participation in worship, but our first concern should be with preparation for worship. We may find little difficulty in preparing ourselves outwardly. We wash our faces and our hands and dress ourselves presentably. But how much more important it is to prepare our souls. "Who shall ascend into the hill of the Lord?" asks the Psalmist, "or who shall stand in his holy place? He that hath clean hands"—if this can be taken in the non-metaphorical sense we could say that the outward preparation is not irrelevant, yet clearly not the most important part of our preparation, for the Psalmist continues—"and a pure heart; who hath not lifted up his soul unto vanity, nor sworn deceitfully' (Ps. 24:3, 4). Preparation for Sunday worship should not be too difficult for most of us, since Sunday is a day free from the usual cares of our business—although an ill-spent Saturday coupled with a late night to bed can rob us of much good when we meet with God's people on the Lord's Day.

The mid-week meeting is much more difficult. We come to the meeting physically tired because of a day of business, or, in the case of a mother, because of a day of toil in the home. We may in coming to the meeting have left our work in fact, but not in thought. Even if work is behind us in thought, yet we can still be adversely affected by the cares of the day. But the task of preparation is not impossible. The Lord knows and understands our weaknesses (Ps. 103:13, 14) and has promised to supply our every need (Phil. 4:19). A brief prayer on entering the building where God's people have met to worship is not enough. Neither must we expect that the content of the earlier part of the worship meeting will bring us to a right state of heart in time for the sermon. The fact that this is sometimes our experience is not a rule to be followed, but an occasion of gratitude for God's mercy to us.

We must be deliberate in this matter. We must give ourselves time, however short, to prepare ourselves for the momentous privilege of meeting with God. The great need as we come to worship with the Lord's people is that our hearts should be cleansed of all known sin. We should endeavour to come into the congregation of God's people with repentance, with joy, with a sensitivity to the Scriptures, whether read or preached, and above all with a sense of expectancy that is indicative of worshipping a gracious and omnipotent Saviour.

It lies secondly in the need to participate in corporate public worship, To be present at the times of worship is not enough. There must be participation as well. Participation involves attention of such an order that we are not disturbed by any noise, avoidable or unavoidable. If you have a company of children in your congregation it is easy to be distracted by their noise—even by the noise which is quite legitimate. Now, if we have no children or if our children can sit still without causing any distraction, one way to help our concentration is to sit in front of those children that may cause a disturbance. It shows lack of thought to sit at the back of a congregation and be affected by noise and movement that hinders thorough concentration, when there is no necessity to be sitting in such a position, particularly if there are empty seats at the front just waiting to be filled!

Our participation in public, corporate worship demands the use of our minds. We must

> *Shake off dull sloth, and joyful rise,*
> *To pay our morning sacrifice.*

There is the need, too, for audible participation by the congregation. Let the "Amen" be hearty at the end of the prayers (1 Cor. 14:16). There ought to be opportunities somewhere within the life of the fellowship for prayer and general ministry for all members of the local church. Although this is an area that bristles with problems we cannot ignore it or else we are guilty of failing to take seriously the words of Paul in 1 Corinthians 14:26; "When ye come together, every one of you hath a psalm, hath a doctrine, hath a tongue, hath a revelation, hath an interpretation." We

Colin Richards expounding The Word

93

must seek to enter into every detail of our worship—the Scripture reading, prayer, singing, sermon, even the notices! Our Lord spoke of the Pharisees as a people who "draweth nigh unto me with their mouth, and honoureth me with their lips; but their heart is far from me" (Matt. 15:8). Who of us can claim never to have been guilty of that condemnation?

The Lord's Supper seems to epitomise all that I have said thus far. The Lord's Supper is a fellowship meal (1 Cor. 10:16). It is a meal which expresses fellowship with God and with other believers. There is an obvious emphasis on preparation in the solemn warning given in Paul's description of this special ordinance: "Let a man examine himself . . ." (1 Cor. 11:28). The eating of the bread and drinking of the wine is a visible reminder of the need to feed on Christ by faith.

That is why I am sure there is great value in the Lord's Supper holding a more prominent place in our worship. It is never to be considered more important than preaching. It is not a means of special grace. A means of grace—yes; but all we can derive spiritually from the Supper we can derive from preaching, but the Lord's Supper is a special means of grace. Calvin in his "Articles concerning the organization of the Church and of worship at Geneva in 1537" writes: "It would be well to require that the communion of the Holy Supper of Jesus Christ be held every Sunday, at least as a rule." It is not the weekly observance of the Lord's Supper that would *ex opere operato* resolve our problems in preparing ourselves for and in participating in public worship, but it is a pointed reminder of those principles which govern all our corporate worship.

2. In informal, private fellowship

I am a little uncomfortable with the term "informal" fellowship, but it does convey the concept I am trying to describe; namely, fellowship other than corporate public worship of the gathered company of believers. Because we are building-orientated in our corporate public worship, fellowship seems to be too much confined to a building. How can we break through this established pattern? There are two things that can be done:

(a) We must encourage one another to see that talking on spiritual topics is an integral part of our meeting together. One may feel like locking the door after the "Amen" of the benediction to prevent folk disappearing rapidly without engaging in spiritual conversation. Needless to say that is not the answer. Christians must be instructed to realize that, having been engaged in corporate worship, having been affected profitably by the content of such a meeting, there is no better occasion for our speech to be possessed of grace (Col. 4:6) so that we may minister grace to our hearers (Eph. 4:28). If improvement can be seen in this area, it will naturally lead to the second thing that can be done to encourage informal, private fellowship.

(b) The Lord's people must be encouraged to visit one another regularly.

In an old church covenant drawn up for a Particular Baptist Church in Cambridgeshire in 1843, point 15 reads: "That we will make conscience, as we have opportunity, to visit one another; and in our visit to make it our business to inquire into each other's spiritual state; and spend that little time we may be together in communicating some spiritual thing to each other, and not in idle talk and foolish jesting or in exposing the sins and infirmities of our neighbours, or other professors; (as is the shameful practice of the present day) but in endeavouring to promote each other's edification and comfort in the Lord." There is good scriptural precedent for this conduct. There was a man in the early Church named Onesiphorus of whom Paul says he "oft refreshed me and was not ashamed of my chain. But when he was in Rome, he sought me out very diligently, and found me . . . and in how many things he ministered unto me at Ephesus, thou knowest very well" (2 Tim. 1:16-18).

3. In personal, practical care

This is a vast subject in itself and only the bare outline can be given. Such care involves what we say and what we do. There is a limitation to this kind of division, but I think it will suffice.

(a) *What we say.* The Scriptures exhort and give examples of how we should encourage one another (2 Tim. 1:16-18), instruct one another (Acts 18:24-28), reprove one another (Gal. 2:11f.), pray for one another (Phil. 1:4), share our experiences with one another (Rom. 12:13). So much could be said on each one of these areas raised but I will briefly comment on just one: the need to pray for one another. In Philippians chapter one, verse four, Paul writes: "Always in every prayer of mine for you all making request with joy." Paul's care for these Philippians evidenced itself in a truly comprehensive prayer. The words to underline are *always, every, all.* Paul prays for all. In every prayer Paul prays for them all. Always in every prayer Paul prays for them all. What a difference this would make to our fellowship if this aspect of practical care were conscientiously observed.

(b) *What we do.* We are to show personal, practical care in the realm of our possessions. There is not space to demonstrate from Acts 2:44,45 and 4:32-37 that there was no common fund, compulsory or voluntary. I believe that these two passages teach that as need arose in the early church so Christians sold their possessions in order to meet that need. There are two principles that govern our conduct in the use of our possessions to help those in need. Firstly, whilst retaining "ownership" of what we possess, none of us are to say that what we possess is our own (Acts 4:32). Secondly, when need arises every man, according to ability, is to give to every man according to need (Acts 4:34,35). These two principles help to highlight the radical difference between Marxist Communism and Christian communism. The former says, all thine is mine: the latter, all mine is thine. These two principles concern not just our goods, but our money, our time, and our skills.

Having dealt with the three ways in which the fellowship of believers comes to visible expression in the local church, I now want to cover the same ground again but to approach it in an even more practical way. I want to arrange the material under the following headings:

1. The building in which we meet.
2. The meetings that we hold.
3. The size of the fellowship.
4. Hospitality.
5. The role of the elders.
6. Cultural enjoyments.
7. Revival.

1. *The building in which we meet.* A building hired or owned could easily be described as a convenient inconvenience or an inconvenient convenience. Little things affect great issues. The doctrine of God's providence is an illustration of that. It is important that in our public worship we sit together. To see a congregation (often small) scattered around a building (often large) is detrimental to worship. The singing is affected. It affects the preacher, or at least should do. It is important that he sees every one of the congregation and particularly their reaction to his preaching. Furthermore, it is important to consider what the outsider thinks of such a spectacle. Fellowship spells togetherness and yet what is seen is a visual exemplification of "you in your small corner and I in mine".

Talking to one another in our buildings must be encouraged to a greater extent. We have already commented on this. Such an activity must not be seen as a "bit tagged on to the end of our meeting" even if in practical terms it often is that. It is not to be seen as some exercise for the young, or the enthusiastic or for those who "like that sort of thing". The event of worship ought to lead naturally to spiritual conversations. If it does not, something is radically wrong.

Such conversations ought not just to be with other Christians but also those in our congregation who are not Christians. Indeed, the events of worship can provide great opportunity to speak to these people. A sermon may have been preached on the law of God, or there may have been an exposition on the freeness of the Gospel—and there are those in our congregation who need such a ministry. We have been praying for these people and now there is opportunity to speak to them at the close of the meeting. Who knows what good can be done? Clearly care and discretion are needed so as not to do spiritual harm to anyone, but the fear of a mishap should not paralyse us. The great commission demands that we implement its commands "beginning at Jerusalem" (Luke 24:47), and our place of worship admirably fits that description. If we show enthusiasm in knocking on the doors of the unconverted but do not speak to the unconverted sitting in the congregation, we open ourselves to the charge of hypocrisy. These conversations should be concerned with ministering grace to our hearers (Eph. 4:28). The scope is unlimited. In a day when the people who come to our meetings often do not live close to each other, and in a day when the pace of life is exceedingly fast, to exploit such conversational opportunities is an application of that far-reaching principle of "redeeming the time" (Eph. 5:16). I cannot forbear saying at this point that pews do seem to add to the already formidable obstacles in the way of implementing these ideas. Chairs do make the task easier. You can control the number of seats and instead of having to move physically out of the place of worship to an adjoining hall or even further afield to a home—you turn your chair around and begin.

2. *The meetings that we hold.* It is imperative that we keep our public meetings as few as possible since there are other things to do in life than just meet together, even if it is for fellowship. There are family, business and social responsibilities that need to be fulfilled. It is good, too, that all members should attend every meeting. Such a practice is an encouragement to all who attend. Anxiety and grief caused because certain faces are missing at the meeting can distract us from the holy exercise in which we are engaged. But such a standard can only be expected if we keep our meetings to a minimum. To have meetings every night of the week encourages disintegration of fellowship in a local church. It is good, too, for the church to meet without the presence of non-members, whether they be Christians or not. The church is a family and as in the natural family so in the spiritual, it is not easy to share everything and be open in a mixed gathering. In a living situation there should always be things to share and discuss together—matters which are personal as well as those affecting the church as a whole, or matters concerned with society in general. At such meetings, which ought to be held regularly (say once a month), there should be specific prayer for people or things that could not easily be mentioned without some difficulty or embarrassment in a normal congregation gathered at the usual midweek prayer meeting. This meeting might be a good starting point for the ordinary members of the church to participate audibly in the public gatherings of God's people. On these occasions one does not have the problems normally associated with a mixed congregation: not knowing who may attend, or having people present who are not subject to the discipline of the church. These meetings can encourage audible participation naturally and easily since their prime purpose is not for the preaching of the Word of God, but for mutual fellowship.

You may object at this point and remind me that such meetings could easily lead to argument and discord and thereby reveal the low spirituality of the church, and do more harm than good. Our Presbyterian friends speak of the Independent congregational church meeting as the terror of the church. Church meetings can engender terror! It has been suggested that a simple test of the spirituality of a church would be to call a church meeting to discuss a controversial topic and then let all who were present be given an opportunity to speak. No one would deny that such meetings are beset with dangers. The answer to the objections levelled against meetings of this kind is simple: the abuse of what is right is never a reason for its discontinuance but rather for a wise control of such meetings. If these meetings provide a kind of thermometer to test the spiritual temperature of a church (and I would insist that they do) then that is for the good. There is no virtue in convincing ourselves that all is well when it is not, or in covering up what is wrong and should be dealt with. The Christian faith calls for realism of the highest order. Since the church is a family, I cannot really see a place for segregated meetings—women's meetings, men's meetings, young wives, and endless variations of young people's meetings. The church consists of all those who are one in Christ. We are marring this unity and thereby the growth and development of God's people by making the church look like some departmental store. The only exception to this might be the "Sunday School" so called. But even here we must be clear about the issues at stake. Children of Christian parents are to receive their instruction at home and then in the worship service, in attendance with their parents. Some would insist (and I believe with biblical justification) that at such services there should be no children's address and that children should stay (noise permitting!) for the whole length of the meeting and not retire to some Sunday School or "Junior Church" (a most mischievous expression).[1]

Clearly we have a duty, because of the demands of the great commission, to reach and teach all children, including those children from non-Christian homes. We are to preach the Gospel to every creature. I would have thought that "children" in their teens and above could and should be treated as adults and, therefore, could quite easily be cared for spiritually by the kind of meetings arranged for adults. Even when reaching the children from a non-Christian home and below teenage, again certain particulars must not be overlooked: (i) Is Sunday the best day for such an activity, particularly if Christian parents are taking their own family responsibilities seriously and instructing their children? Sunday can easily become a day of continuous meetings and so parents cannot give proper attention to that all-important task of teaching their children. (ii) Is a "church" building the best base for such a work? Why not the home? Is this not the place where real people are seen living in real situations? Does not a godly home expose the shallow and dissatisfying life of the world? It ought to do so. Does not this give real incentive for Christians to be more evangelistically involved in the life of the church? It is so easy for us to have such a conception of "the church" as the agent for evangelism that we think of "the church" as some phantom body stalking the land and we forget that the church is made up of people like us. To use our homes in order to reach children from unconverted homes would not merely involve Christians with children but affect all those who live in the homes of those children—so much so that our evangelism at this point would be "house" evangelism. Therefore, all other things being equal, the home as a base for operation is less artificial and more attractive than the church building. Obviously, each local church must decide for itself in this matter.

In addition, we must not forget that our thrust in evangelism must be to reach the head of the home and not his children. Remember only one in fifty children reached by the Sunday School (a conservative estimate) remains intellectually convinced of the Christian faith and becomes a church member. I say "church members": some are not necessarily even Christians.

Lastly, under this heading, we must remember not to be afraid to be adventurous and willing to experiment in church life. We shall not be reluctant to do this or rash in our actions if we engage in a constant revision of all our activities. We should do this not just in the light of Scripture but in the light of the particular circumstances of our own fellowship. The principles that govern church life are unalterable because they are rooted in God's infallible and inerrant Word, but the application of those principles will vary from age to age. Much thought needs to be

This picture taken at the church of which Colin Richards is the pastor illustrates the form of fellowship following the services. The photos for this chapter are by Sylvester Jacobs.

given regarding the distinction between our worship meetings for the church and our evangelistic meetings for the unconverted. The gap between us (believers) and them (unconverted) is widening in terms of church relations, so that the welding together of these two things: the worship meeting and the evangelistic meeting, is getting more difficult. I am not suggesting that we should not be evangelistic in our worship meetings—we should, we must. Unconverted people will be present, unconverted professing Christians will be too and they need to be un-masked. The truly converted need to hear the Gospel regularly since their reaction to it is a test of their spiritual state. If our evangelistic meetings are building-based, and they ought not to be exclusively so, then it is necessary sometimes, depending on the particular thrust of the meeting, that we dispense with hymns, prayer, and even a Bible reading. There may be occasions when it is right to depart from the traditional sermon format and engage in a public conversation with a congregation by means of questions and answers. This is not to minimise the place of preaching in our evangelism, it is simply to recognise that there are other ways of publicly presenting the Gospel to men and women. (One Greek word "dialegomai" which the Authorized Version rendered "preached", "reasoned", "dispute" (Acts 17:2, 17; 18:4, 19; 19:8, 9; 20:7, 9) can carry the meaning of dialogue).

3. *The size of the fellowship.* The church is a family. Paul describes it as the "household of faith" (Gal. 6:10). Now, if a fellowship is too large the family spirit can wane and disappear, and cliques and groups can all too soon develop underneath one umbrella. If a fellowship is too large all the gifts will not be exploited to the full. Of course, it may be possible for a group within a church, who come from a particular geographical location, to be separated (with two elders as a minimum) in order to form another gospel church. Such a procedure adds quality to the life of a fellowship as new needs arise, as new experiences emerge, and, above all, as a new sense of expectancy pervades the church's life.

When does a fellowship become too large? The answer to that question would depend on how many children of believers there were in a given congregation to the number of church members and how many unconver-ted and Christians yet non-members there were in a given congregation in proportion to the number of church members. Other factors would include the age and maturity of the fellowship or the number and/or ability of elders in the church to facilitate the separation of a group of members into a new gospel church. I would have thought that as a general rule, when a fellowship has reached a membership of 70-100, it has reached a point where a mutual separation of some of its members into a new gospel church is more than desirable.

In stating that a fellowship can become too large, it must not be overlooked that a fellowship can be too small. Stating the problem differently and more pointedly, a fellowship of Christians without God-appointed officers

100

can hardly be regarded as ideal or complete—and some would say, and I think with justification, that such a fellowship could hardly be considered a church. In Titus 1:5 the absence of elders in Crete merits the comment of Paul that "things . . . are wanting . . ." and so elders must be appointed. To appeal to Matthew 18:19 "where two or three are gathered together in my name . . ." is an unfair warrant to claim the name church. Christ's presence among Christians constitutes Christian fellowship but more is required if such fellowship is to be denominated church fellowship. Not every heap of bricks is a wall, not every regiment of soldiers is an army. Surely we who believe in the independency of the local church and, therefore, of its self-government ought to insist that a church so called possesses the instruments of government or else we are issuing an open ticket to anarchy.

Now, it is easy to describe the malaise; it is not so easy to find a cure, and it is much more difficult, having found this cure, to implement it. But here is a suggestion: an elderless fellowship ought to place itself under the care of a church with elders and seek for those elders to govern its affairs until it has elders of its own. Such a proposition has problems but then the issue we are trying to resolve has problems too, and of a more serious kind.

4. *Hospitality*.   If we accept the conversion of Lydia as being in principle typical of all true conversions, it is fair to say that when the Lord opens our hearts one result of that is that we open our homes (Acts 16:14, 15). This is further confirmed by the example of the Philippian jailor.   This man having been saved, we read that he washed the stripes of Paul and Silas and "when he had brought them into his house, he set meat before them, and rejoiced" (Acts 16:33, 34).

The Scriptures not only exhort Christians to be "given to hospitality" (Rom. 12:13) but to "use hospitality one to another without grudging" (grumbling, murmuring) (1 Pet. 4:9). Now although the scope of these two exhortations goes beyond the opening of our homes to one another as Christians, it does include that. The most common objections in people's minds concerning the exercise of hospitality are, Have I space? Can I afford it? To these I would answer: we can all do something and we need not be extravagant. A woman concerned to give as good a meal as she and her family received or indeed better can involve herself in great expense, but often this is unnecessary.

A Christian home is perhaps one of the chief weapons in our armoury in tackling the various needs of our complex world. Francis Schaeffer in his book *The Church at the end of the twentieth century* states: ". . . there is no place in God's world where there are no people who will come and share a home as long as it is a real home . . ." (P. 131). Schaeffer goes on to contend that if we Christians are going to use our homes meaningfully to reach the unconverted of the twentieth century, we must be prepared to take what he calls an "unantiseptic risk", e.g. a girl with sexual disease sleeping between our sheets, or entertaining a drunk who may vomit on our carpet! To meet the challenge of the world at this point is not easy—but then it is not at this level that we begin. We begin by opening our homes to fellow Christians. Indeed, if we cannot do this it is foolish to think that our homes will ever be open meaningfully to those outside of Christ. The Scriptures exhort us to entertain strangers (Heb. 13:2) but that is not too easy a place to begin—we begin by opening our homes to fellow Christians and more particularly to fellow members of our local church. What is the value of such hospitality being extended to other church members? In each other's homes we can share our joys and sorrows. In each other's homes we can learn how ordinary other people are. In each other's homes we can learn to pray with one another (the public prayer meeting is not the easiest place for some Christians to start to pray). In each other's homes we can learn from one another—how to care for our children, how to conduct family worship. The possibilities are endless.

5. *The role of elders.* It is the Lord's intention that each local church should have elders (Acts 14:23; 20:17, 28; Phil. 1:1; 1 Thess. 5:12; Titus 1:5; Heb. 13:7, 17, 24.). Their duties are described in the New Testament in the following way: they are to be examples to the flock (1 Pet. 5:3); they are to feed the church of God (Acts 20:28); they are to rule (1 Tim. 5:17); they are to teach (1 Tim. 3:2); they are to labour in the word and doctrine (1 Tim. 5:17); they are to take heed to and watch for the souls of men (Acts 20:28; Heb. 13:17). Their duties can be reduced to two heads: the public preaching of the Word of God and the personal, private care of individual believers.

In a day when there is a renewed interest in the Reformed Faith, it is easy to stress the primacy of preaching in the local church so as to forget the need for the personal care of individual men and women and young people. A prayerful reading of "The Reformed Pastor" by Richard Baxter would do much to maintain a right balance in this realm of the elder's duties. The personal care of believers by the elders should be exercised not only in the formal meeting of the church when believers are gathered together, but in their homes too. Indeed, to maintain a regular visitation of all members with the intent of inquiring into their spiritual state and so ministering suitably to their needs would do much to raise the spiritual level of the fellowship.

Sometimes the general application of the Word of God in the pulpit needs to be more particularly applied to the individual believer in his or her home. We must at times create a situation in which a Nathan says to a David "Thou art the man". Reproof is not the only thing that needs to be applied in this way—although, sad to say, it is by far the most common —so does instruction and comfort and these, of course, should be applied when required. This care should not be exercised so as to deal with present and immediate problems only, but should be exercised so as to prevent the occurrence of problems.   Roots of bitterness soon spring up and defile (Heb. 12:13) and so mar the work of God.   The God-appointed shepherds need constantly to care for the sheep and guard them against such perils, for their own sake and for the sake of others.   God has appointed elders to "prepare God's people for works of service that the body may be built up" (Eph. 4:12 N.I.V.) and such activity inevitably enriches the fellowship of all.

6. *Cultural enjoyments.*   "The earth is the Lord's and the fulness thereof: the world and they that dwell therein" (Ps. 24:1).   In the face of such a verse of Scripture, the Christian should not hold a secular-sacred distinction in his or her thinking.   The Christian can legitimately have an interest in all spheres of life provided they are subject to Christ's Lordship—art, literature, music, physical recreation.   Indeed, the Christian ought to have an interest in one or more of these realms else his or her "spirituality" will be stunted and ugly.   This contracted and distorted Christianity invites that just criticism from the world that Christianity makes us less than human.   We do well to remember the words of Gresham Machen delivered in an address on "The scientific preparation of the minister" in which he alludes to Christianity and culture.   He says: "Instead of destroying the arts and science or being indifferent to them, let us cultivate them with all the enthusiasm of the veriest humanist, but at the same time consecrate them to the service of our God.   Instead of stifling the pleasures afforded by the acquisition of knowledge, or by the appreciation of what is beautiful, let us accept these pleasures as the gifts of a heavenly Father."[2]

It is not the church as such that should involve itself in these realms except, of course, where the church's work inevitably touches these realms. The task of the church is to preach the gospel, but the individual Christian can and should be involved in these cultural enjoyments.   It is good, for example, that our children meet regularly for games, or modelling, or some nature trail, or just for a long muddy walk.   In the area of cultural enjoyments, there is a justification for that deep longing among so many— the segregation of our people into groups according to age or sex.   What children and young people (who come from a Christian home) do need today is the company of their own age and/or sex (although not exclusively) in the ordinary things of life—and that in an atmosphere that does not create undue tension with the Christian principles that have already shaped and moulded their lives.   At the cultural level, segregation is imperative.   One can hardly imagine an aged couple wanting to negotiate a long and hazardous ramble, or teenage boys wanting to learn the art of dress making.   These pleasures are engaged in not as an evangelistic outreach that is a perversion of evangelism.   They are not to be formally concluded with that indefinable thing called an "epilogue" that is a perversion of worship.   We engage in these pleasures for their own sakes, to the glory of God.   Such activities are tremendously beneficial to the spiritual life of the church.

7. *Revival.* This matter is not least in importance, although it is the last matter I want to deal with. To experience times of refreshing from the Lord's presence (Acts 3:19) is of paramount importance. Surely it cannot be disputed that the need to know "the years of the right hand of the most High" (Ps. 77:10) is our greatest need at this moment of time.

The Bible speaks of the *koinonia* of the Holy Spirit (2 Cor. 13:13) because any Christian fellowship emanates from the activity of the Holy Spirit in terms of its origin, its continuance, and its perfection. If this is so, then we need to remind ourselves constantly that the particular, detailed concerns of this subject do not of themselves achieve anything worthwhile —we need God the Holy Spirit to take hold of these things and prosper them in our hands.

[1] The most excellent article entitled "Children and the Sermon" by Iain Murray in *The Banner of Truth*, issue 108, September 1972, gives a more detailed treatment of this matter.
[2] *The Banner of Truth* Magazine, issue 69, page 18.

8

Discipline in the Local Church

by Dic Eccles

THERE HAS BEEN, OVER THE LAST HUNDRED YEARS OR SO, AN INCREASINGLY haphazard and lackadaisical approach to the matter of fellowship within the local church. The local church as the body of Christ, a living organism, has been forgotten, and we have seen an atomistic concept take its place. Church members have little idea that they are a part of a whole; they regard themselves as answerable to no-one but themselves; they are, in their own opinion, simply Christians who happen to go to a particular church with a number of other Christians. It is possible that they find opportunities of service within their church but, again, their conception of this is that their work is their own affair.

There are historical reasons for the development of these attitudes, chief among which is the departure of churches from the biblical faith in the middle of the last century. This led evangelicals to opt out of involvement in the churches and, instead, to involve themselves with interdenominational societies. Inevitably, the standing of the church declined and over the years it has been forgotten that the church is the instrument of God for evangelism and mission and for the growth and encouragement of believers.

The outcome of these developments is manifestly unscriptural and there is a crying need for a return to the scriptural pattern. Reformation is receiving a good deal of attention at the present time and this is to be welcomed wholeheartedly. If there is to be any misgiving, it is that this movement is not yet universal. Scripture teaching must be rediscovered and applied in the churches.

One area sorely in need of reformation is the sphere of *discipline*. Perhaps this is an unfortunate word to use nowadays, since to some it conveys overtones of harshness, rigidity, lovelessness and cold vindictiveness. What is meant by the term is that God has provided a certain order for churches and this order is revealed in Scripture. This order concerns the organisation, government and fellowship of the church. When a believer joins a church he is putting himself into the hands of a body which, through the elders, will minister to his needs, and in everything he will be in subjection to the church. He will be expected to play his part to the full as an organ in the body, so that the body as a whole does not suffer. What happens when there is a disruption of this order, when the peace and fellowship of the church are violated ? The church, according to Scripture, is empowered to act to maintain its order.

Scripture is the authority for belief and practice of the church, no less than for other matters. It declares how the church should be organised and governed and what should be practised. No attempt is made here to prove these statements. They are assumed in this article and what follows is based upon them.

Contrary to popular opinion, a great deal is said on the subject of church discipline in Scripture. An orderly presentation of this teaching is attempted in what follows.

A. The Need for Maintaining Church Order

The need for the local church to control its life and maintain its order follows from the conception of the "gathered church", the "ordered church" and the "voluntary principle".

1. *The Gathered Church.* The church is a fellowship of regenerate people, and the church must receive into membership only those who are believers. The value of this is lost if it is not maintained, and those who turn back on their profession, or who give the elders reason to believe that they are not truly converted, must be removed from the membership. The "gathered church" means a church made up, not of those who once credibly professed to be called out of the world to Christ, but of those who still hold to that profession. (1 Cor 1:2.)

2. *The Ordered Church.* The church stands for the truth of the Gospel and for Christian morality. It exists to bear witness to both in the world and, in order to further this, it has an ordered structure and fellowship. If its standards are violated by a member, action must be taken to restore its order, both for its own purity and for the sake of its witness. (Tit. 2:1-5.)

3. *The Voluntary Principle.*[1] When a person joins a church he does so because he desires to, and not because he is forced against his will. In so doing, he is taking upon himself privileges and responsibilities. These responsibilities include making a full contribution to the life of the church, and living a consistent Christian life at the personal level. Since he has willingly agreed to these, the church is right to act when they are violated. (2 Cor. 8:5; Acts 2:41.)

4. *Scriptural Warrant.* Examples of the churches in the New Testament maintaining their order in this way are abundant. They cover many different situations, including offences against the peace and fellowship of the church, heresy, sin in the personal life of a member, disputes between members and disputes between churches. (Matt. 18:15-20;

Acts 15:1-33; Rom. 16:17; 1 Cor. 5:1-2; 2 Cor. 13:1-2; Gal. 6:1; 2 Thess. 3:6, 11, 12; 1 Tim. 1:20, 5:20; Tit. 1:13, 3:8-11.)

B. The Purpose in Maintaining Church Order

1. *The Preservation of the Spiritual Life of the Church.* The church, in maintaining its order, is acting in self preservation. Its life is spiritual and sin can destroy it. If sin is tolerated in its midst, the whole life of the church suffers and the fellowship is marred. (1 Cor. 5:6; Rev. 2:14-16, 20.)

2. *The Preservation of the Church's Witness.* Sin and error, if they are overlooked, deny the message preached by the church. A telling witness demands consistency. The church acts against sin within itself in order to continue an effective witness. (Tit. 2:1-5.)

3. *The Discouragement of Sin among the Members.* When the members know that the church will take action to maintain its order, they are discouraged from sin. This is heightened if they see discipline being maintained. (1 Tim. 5:20.)

4. *The Restoration of the Offending Member.* The church is acting for the good of the one who has sinned. It is giving proof that it takes a serious view of sin in the Christian. It goes a lot further than this however. The real aim is that the guilty person should be restored to full fellowship in the church. Discipline should not be exercised with a vindictive or arrogant spirit but with Christian love and humility. (2 Tim. 2:24-26; 1 Cor. 5:5; Gal. 6:1; 2 Cor. 2:6-8; Rev. 3:19.)

C. The Means of Maintaining Church Order

1. *Maintaining a Regenerate Membership.* It is vitally necessary for the spiritual life of the church that only converted people are admitted into membership. But the church's concern must not end there. That is only the first line of control. The membership is maintained of converted people. Those who show that they are not converted ought to be removed. Mistakes can be made in deciding that a person is converted. The first acceptance should not be final, though in practice it so often is. The important principle that should be accepted is that the church should be made up of those who are converted, and that is not the same thing as those who once satisfied the church that they were converted. This is not to say that the faith and experience of all the members should always be on trial, but rather that those who give positive cause for doubt should be reconsidered. Those who give evidence that they are not converted should be removed from membership, and no others.

Lapsed members would fall into this category, and those who make an open denial of the Faith and of their profession. Except in extremely exceptional circumstances, this should also include those who have moved away from the district, although time should be given for such to find another church and seek membership there.

Removing a person from membership should never be done without ministering to the person concerned. Unless it is impossible to trace him, it should never be done without his knowledge.

2. *Instruction and Exhortation.* The teaching of the church should include detailed instructions on Christian living and standards of behaviour, on the personal level and within the corporate life of the fellowship. It is not merely the public preaching of the Word that is in view here, but the particular application to the individual in private, through pastoral care.

The private and pastoral side of teaching is also important in cases of departure from the church's standards. When a member is guilty of a fault he should be visited by the elders, reminded of the truth and encouraged to follow it. (Gal. 6:1.)

3. *Censures.* The church also has open to it certain censures which (except in grave cases) should be used only when private exhortation and pastoral care have failed. The censures are made before the whole church met together, and are by the church as a whole.

It needs to be emphasised, that the spirit in which they are given must never be vicious or vindictive. They must be exercised with love and compassion. In all its actions the church must be merciful. (2 Cor. 2:6-8.)

It is essential that the members are aware of the church's position in its control over them. They should be reminded of this from time to time. More important still, it should be made certain that new members, when they join, fully understand this. It will avoid misunderstanding and ill-based indignation, if the two fields not commonly observed today (pastoral exhortation and censure) are specifically explained to prospective members, before they make their final decision to join the church. They cannot take offence at the church's controls and censures, if they knew that this was how the church would respond to unruliness. Besides this, the purpose of the church's control will be defeated if censure is applied with no forewarning.

For the same reasons, this activity of the church must be constant and consistent. It must not be the spasmodic launching of a sudden purge. (1 Tim. 5:20-22.)

The church must be scrupulously fair in the exercise of control. There must be no favourites whose offences are overlooked, and those who are disciplined must not feel they have been singled out. (1 Tim. 5:21.)

D. The Censures of the Church

There are three censures open to the church.

1. *Rebuke and Warning.* A person who is guilty of a fault should be visited by the elders and rebuked privately. (Tit. 1:13.) He should be encouraged to repent and mend his ways.

If, however, he refuses this rebuke, he should be called to a special meeting of the church and rebuked and warned before them all. (1 Tim. 5:20.) The warning consists in pointing out that if he repeats his behaviour he will be brought under the second censure. No other action is taken by the church, but he will be ministered to by the elders.

Situations which would warrant rebuke and warning would include: grumbling; anger; quarrelsomeness; rumour-mongering; heartlessness toward a brother in exposing his weakness or criticising him harshly; indulging in unprofitable matters which disrupt the peace of the church; neglect of church meetings (including business meetings) and neglect of responsibilities to the church.

2. *Suspension.* This censure consists of the withdrawal of the privileges of membership, including partaking of the Lord's Supper, participation in prayer meetings and business meetings. The most important New Testament reference in this connection is 2 Thess. 3:6, 14, 15. In the operation of this censure the offender is not to be treated as an outsider, but "as a brother". Its purpose is that he may be "ashamed". This censure is maintained until the offender has confessed his sin, righted the wrong and given a credible assurance that he will not continue in the sin. It cannot continue indefinitely, however, and if after encouragement and warning the offender persists in refusing to respond, it may be necessary to bring him under the third censure. (Tit. 3:10.)

Suspension must be accompanied by the ministry of the elders, with a view to restoring him to the full privileges of membership (Gal. 6:1). In certain cases, where an offence is public knowledge (whether this is because the state brings a prosecution, or because of some other reason), it may be necessary for the church to make the fact of its censure public knowledge. Ordinarily, such matters are confidential business and should not be made public, neither should members pass on such information to outsiders. Where such knowledge already exists, however, it will harm the church's witness and, in order to minimise the effects of this, the church's expression of disapproval of the member may be made public knowledge. In cases of serious sin, a token period of suspension may be advisable, even though repentance may have been manifest from the outset.

Situations warranting suspension include: refusal to receive and acknowledge the first censure (2 Cor. 12:21; 13:2); continuing in sin after a public rebuke; deliberate and calculated disruption of the peace of the church; slander against another member; leaking of confidential church business; false doctrine; grave sin and guilt in state criminal proceedings.

3. *Excommunication.* Excommunication, or putting someone out of church membership, is a very grave action. It should be done only when no doubt of guilt exists and when there is no repentance. It must be preceded by suspension, so that an opportunity for repentance is given.

The Corinthian church was commanded to excommunicate a member (1 Cor. 5:1-5). He was guilty of a particularly offensive, immoral relationship, but it is important to note that this was not the reason for his excommunication. The reasons were that he was open and blatant in it, even to the point of boasting, and that he did not repent. (2 Cor. 12:21; 13:2.) The action the church was to take is described as "delivering to Satan" (cf. 1 Tim. 1:20), which should be understood as delivering to the sphere of Satan's kingdom, *i.e.* outside the church (1 Cor. 5:2, 13; Matt. 18:17). This censure is designed for the guilty man's spiritual welfare and salvation (1 Cor. 5:5; 1 Tim. 1:20).

This censure does not preclude the possibility of further action by the church, either in making information available to the authorities that may lead to a state prosecution, or in bringing a private prosecution in the state courts. These kinds of actions will be extremely rare, but circumstances may warrant it, *e.g.* in cases of misappropriation of funds.

Excommunication is not irreversible. A person who has been put out of the church can be received back into membership, provided he or she has repented. The case of Corinth can be cited here. Although there is no absolute proof that the Corinthians followed Paul's command, it seems certain that the incestuous man was excommunicated. I take 2 Cor. 2:6 and 9 to refer to the action taken against him. Note the concern that overwhelming sorrow might destroy the offender (v. 7). Paul mentions forgiveness (v. 10). This clearly opens up the possibility of reinstatement.

Excommunication involves the treating of an offender as an ordinary outsider (Matt. 18:17). If it is right to buy a loaf of bread from an unbeliever, or say "hello" to him when you see him, so it is with an excommunicated member. Love is still to be shown (2 Cor. 2:8). Excommunication does not involve the severing of social contact or banning from public services. This has not always been recognised and actions similar to those of the Taylorite brethren have been practised, down to cutting the dining room table in half. The more extreme group of Mennonites, Flemish Mennonites, practised "shunning" as well as "banning". This applied to husband and wife, parent and child. The Flemish Mennonites insisted it included "bed and board".

E. The Special Place of Officers

The ministry of the church is through the elders. They are responsible for the teaching and encouragement of the members, for the execution of church censures and the pastoral care of the subjects of censures. (Heb. 13:17; Acts 20:17, 28; 1 Pet. 5:1, 2; 1 Thess. 5:12; Gal. 6:1.)

The manner of dealing with sin in an elder or a deacon differs from the manner of dealing with other members of the church.

1. *Receiving an Accusation Against an Elder.* An accusation against an elder is more serious than against other members. Elders are more vulnerable than others to accusations. For these reasons, an accusation should be heard in the presence of several witnesses so that every word may be established. (1 Tim. 5:19.)

2. *Sins of Office.* Officers take on themselves responsibilities and if they fail to live up to these they will render themselves liable to the church's censure. Sins of office include: failure to fulfil the duties of office; using privileges for personal gain or selfish prestige and instigating party spirit. (1 Pet. 5:2, 3.)

3. *The Censure of Removal from Office.* An elder or deacon who receives a church censure cannot continue a spiritual ministry, since this depends so much on the confidence the other members have in him. He should automatically become subject to a special additional censure, removal from office. It is likely to be a long time before the church will feel able to reappoint him to a ministry over them.

It may be advisable, while an accusation against an officer is being heard, to suspend him from office until the matter is settled. For this reason such proceedings should not be prolonged, but should be dealt with as speedily as possible.

F. Association Between Churches and the Maintaining of Church Order

1. *The Need for Association.* As in other matters, there is a need in regard to church order for churches to be in fellowship. This needs to extend to agreement on a common practice. Unless this is achieved, churches will be susceptible to troublemakers who move from one to another, leaving behind them a trail of devastation which may take years to repair.

Those who are censured in one church should not be accepted into membership by another. All too frequently what happens is that a member takes offence at being censured, resigns from his church and then applies to another for membership, where he is accepted without any questions being asked. This militates against the spiritual good of the person concerned, leaves the receiving church open to the same trouble as the first, and may cause strained relationships between the two churches.

2. *Transfer of Membership.* A system of recognised procedure of transfer of membership is needed in this situation. A church approached by someone asking for membership and who is resigning his membership from elsewhere, should write to that church and ask for its fellowship in transferring the member. That church should not agree to transfer a member who is under censure, however strong the temptation to be rid of a troublemaker. Details of the person's baptism should be given, and it is of help to the receiving church to be told what service has been rendered by the one transferring membership. In some cases it may also be helpful for the receiving church to be told details of past censures on the transferring member so that the elders in his new church can minister most helpfully to his needs. All this information should be confidential between the elders.

3. *Letters of Introduction.* 2 Cor. 3:1; Rom. 16:1, 2. Letters of introduction and commendation can be given to members who move away, or who go to live in another area for a period of time. Those who do move to a new area should be encouraged to join a church in that area by transfer. It is pointless and unscriptural for them to maintain membership in their original church, since they are playing no part in it, nor enjoying its privileges. Sentimentalism and nostalgia probably play a large part in the desire to keep up old ties, but it is not necessary to maintain a meaningless membership to preserve prayerful interest and fellowship.

G. Church Courts

1. *The Need for Church Courts.* Christians are forbidden to go to law against their brethren (1 Cor. 6:1, 7). There are two alternatives put forward. One is to receive and suffer the wrong done patiently and mercifully and not seek any reprisal (v. 7). This is by far the more preferable. The other is to have the matter decided by a wise man in the church (v. 5). From the style of argument used by Paul, it is to be concluded that this is a minimum, and does not preclude the possibility of several wise men, or elders, making judgment.

2. *The Calling of Church Courts.* Members who find themselves in a situation with a brother which cannot be resolved privately can ask the elders of the church to pass judgment (Matt. 18:15-17). If the injury claimed is proved it may involve the wrongdoer in a censure (v. 17).

In cases where a quarrel between members is disrupting the fellowship of the church, the elders should call for the dispute to be heard before them. It may be necessary to rebuke both parties.

3. *Courts of Churches in Association.* Occasionally disputes may arise between members of different churches. The only way these can be

properly settled is by the churches concerned meeting together, through their appointed representatives (elders), and deciding, in fellowship, what action is needed (Acts 15:1-6).

Differences of opinion between churches should be dealt with in the same way; it is important that they be so, lest the fellowship be adversely affected. They may be brought together by other churches. The only way such disputes can be impartially examined is by churches, other than the parties to the dispute, acting together in association.

H. Dangers in the Maintaining of Church Order

There are several dangers against which churches need to guard.

1. *Heresy Hunting.* There may arise a tendency for some members to regard themselves as snoopers and talebearers. When there are those in the church who pry into the affairs of others, or who are constantly on the lookout for sins and errors, an atmosphere will be created which will be deadening to the brotherly love and trust which should characterise the fellowship.

2. *Assuming a Person Guilty.* Knowing human nature for what it is may lead to a readiness to assume people guilty. Christian love, however, demands that the best is believed about a person until forced to conclude otherwise (1 Cor. 13:6, 7; 6:7). The elders should examine an accusation, to see if there is a case to answer, before it is brought before the church. The accusation must be solidly proved, and unless or until that is done, the member should be assumed to be innocent.

3. *Exploitation.* When there is a procedure for dealing with the faults of members, troublemakers have the ready machinery for bringing false accusations. Charges must be admitted and members censured only when there are two or three witnesses (2 Cor. 13:1).

Where several unproven charges are brought by a member and there is reason to suspect fabrication, the elders should discuss the matter with him and, where appropriate, warn him.

4. *Maladministrations*

(*a*) *Churches Can Make Mistakes.* No church is infallible, and it is possible that a church could wrongly censure a member. It is more likely that mistakes would be made in the administering of church order than in doctrine, since the latter is plainly laid down in Scripture and the former depends on the circumstances peculiar to each individual case. Churches may also be in error in failing to administer censures where they are due (1 Cor. 5:2).

(*b*) *The Importance of Rectifying Mistakes.* Miscarriage of justice may bring the Gospel into disrepute outside the church, or impair the authority of all censures within it.   The aim of censures is to edify both the church and the offender, but where they are wrongly applied the effect will be to destroy.   For these reasons a church guilty of such a miscarriage should rejoice at having it revealed.

(*c*) *Means of Bringing Mistakes to Notice.* There are different ways in which a church may be brought to realise a mistake has been made. Firstly, it might be by an appeal from the person censured.   Secondly, it might be by an approach in fellowship from another church, which may have discovered it from public gossip (1 Cor. 5:1), from reports from a spiritual and respected person within that church (1 Cor. 1:11), or from a direct approach by the censured person seeking membership because his conscience makes him withdraw from his church.   This approach by another church is not dictatorship but fellowship in the Gospel.   The giving of advice is not interfering with the liberty of a church, but the assisting in the right use of it.

(*d*) *Means of Rectifying Maladministrations.* The church, if it finds a miscarriage of justice has been committed, should, with all the members met together, apologise to the brother concerned, withdraw the censure made on him, destroy all record of it and rejoice in the restoration of a brother.

I. The Way Ahead

Although these practices were usually observed by Baptists and Independents in the past, this is not generally so today.   There has been a steady decline in the consideration of the importance of church order since the mid-eighteenth century and this is manifest in the Baptist histories written in recent years, which contain no reference to this subject whatsoever. The situation, however, is changing and there is an increasing realisation that contemporary practice is unscriptural and that there is a need for reformation.

A major problem facing churches today is how to return to biblical practice.   After there has been neglect for so long, the problem becomes all the more acute.   A radical change is called for and this can involve a big upheaval.

Study of this subject in detail is necessary on the part of the elders of the church.   Teaching of the members is imperative, so that all may see the importance of this matter.

A new set of articles for membership may be needed.   Full discussion on these matters will need to take place between churches and a common practice agreed in fellowship between them.   The increased mobility of people in twentieth century society make this all the more urgent.

References:

[1]This voluntary principle respects the believer's will and subjective experience. God makes the believer free and this freedom is expressed in glad alignment with the church. Seen objectively, that is from the standpoint of a redemptive act, the church is not the same as a worldy society. Having been baptised into Christ the head and into his body the church, the incorporation of the believer is final and eternal. Happily there can (objectively speaking) be no opting out, for we are kept by his power through faith unto salvation. Believers should be taught the true import of baptism. There is no such thing as resigning from the church because we do not like the colour of the curtains or because we have differences or difficulties. This is to deny the momentous nature of our having been ingrafted into Christ. Also we see at this point that infant baptism raises colossal problems. 1. Infants are regarded as ingrafted into the body. 2. As they grow up they show themselves far from having been ingrafted. 3. Eventually they are converted. 4. They now wish to express their regeneration and ingrafting into Christ, but are denied the biblical ordinance on the grounds of an unwarranted sprinkling long ago. Is it right to say they were in, opted out, but are now in again?

Editor.

Bibliography

I have referred to Garrett's *Baptist Church Discipline* (Broadman Press) and Lumpkin's *Baptist Confessions of Faith* (Judson Press). John Owen's writings can be studied with profit: *The True Nature of the Gospel Church* (Works, Goold ed., Vol. 16, p. 2); *The Administration of Church Censures* (Vol. 16, p. 222); *Instruction in the Worship of God* (Vol. 15, p. 446); *Inquiry concerning Evangelical Churches* (Vol. 15, p. 188). Thomas Goodwin also expounds the subject: *The Government of the Churches of Christ* (Works, Nichols ed., Vol. 11, p. 1); *The Government and Discipline of the Churches of Christ* (Vol. 11, p. 485).

Scripture References

References which bear directly upon the subject of church order are: Matt. 18:15-20; Acts 15:1-6; Rom. 16:17; 1 Cor. 5:1-6, 13; 6:1, 5, 7; 2 Cor. 2:6-8; 12:21; 13:1-2; Gal. 6:1; 2 Thess. 3:6, 11-15; 1 Tim. 1:20; 5:19-20; 2 Tim. 2:24-26; Tit. 1:13; 3:8-10.

Other References Indirectly Relating to the Subject are:

Acts 2:41, 42, 44; 20:17, 28; 1 Cor. 1:11; 13:6, 7; 2 Cor. 8:5; 1 Thess. 5:12; Tit. 2:1-5; Heb. 13:17; 1 Pet. 5:1-3; Rev. 2:5, 14-16, 20; 3:9.

9

The
Local Church and
Church Planting

by Keith Davies

ALTHOUGH I MUST TAKE A NUMBER OF BASIC THINGS AS UNDERSTOOD, IN seeking to deal with this subject I shall first of all attempt a brief answer to the question "What is a New Testament Church?" Secondly we shall consider New Testament patterns for church planting, thirdly we shall seek to examine certain problems, dangers and weaknesses associated with the planting of New Testament churches; fourthly I shall give some examples of attempts at church planting, and lastly I shall seek to make some practical applications. My reasons for approaching the subject in this way are two-fold—first, we as Reformed Baptists must always derive our principles for conduct and action from the Word of God, and second, we must avoid the discussion of principles apart from practice, for it simply leads to theorising and does little good to the cause of the Gospel.

1. What is a New Testament Church ?

In this paper we are interested in planting New Testament churches. It is not part of my purpose to address myself to those churches that come into being and try to combine a number of different traditions, nor do I take account of splits and schisms. We are concerned here for New Testament churches, for the pattern of true church life is discernible in the New Testament, and to that we need constantly to submit and conform.

So, what is a New Testament church? It is a true church, God's church, the Body of Christ, the Temple of the Holy Spirit. We are not left in the dark as to its basis and form. The Saviour ensured that his Word would lay out the matter clearly for his people in every age. From the earliest days, from the Day of Pentecost onwards the mind of the Lord concerning the life and work of the Church can clearly be discerned.

Although New Testament churches differed from one another in certain ways as we would expect, what was held in common was of greatest importance. An indication of the reality of this common form can be found in such verses as 1 Corinthians 7:17; 11:16; 14:33.

The basis and form of the Jerusalem Church was normative for the life of subsequent churches when they came into being. A glance at Acts 2:41-47 will reveal a number of essential features. These features are expounded in detail in the New Testament Epistles. Notice the following: "They that gladly received his (Peter's) word were baptised"—the Church was born in preaching, for the Word of God was basic. Notice also that it was a baptised Church. "They continued stedfastly in the apostles' doctrine"—it was a Church based on the teaching of truth, truth that could be systematised and defined (see Jude 3; Phil 1:27; Titus 1:9; Acts 20:27; 2 Tim. 1:13). It was truth taught by God's appointed leaders. "And fellowship"—the church had a true life expressed in practical terms (see verses 44 and 45). "And in breaking of bread and prayers"—the church was a worshipping community where the Table of the Lord had a proper place. These same marks and evidences are also to be seen in the other New Testament churches of which we have more knowledge than merely their name (e.g., Antioch and Corinth). These churches—the ones we know something about and the others—were churches which believed the truth, what we would call New Testament doctrine. They believed the great doctrines of God's grace to men—what we call the Reformed Faith; for it was New Testament Christianity that was rediscovered at the Reformation. So in this paper when we speak of Reformed Churches we mean New Testament churches, for they are one and the same.

But New Testament churches were also baptised churches organised and governed independently of one another yet living in close fellowship with one another. So we are interested here in the planting of Reformed, Free Grace or Particular Baptist churches ruled according to the patterns of God's Word by God appointed elders.

I mention all this because we need to be clear about the fundamental issues. Differences on such issues as Calvinism v. Arminianism, Presbyterianism v. Independancy, Believers' Baptism v. Infant Baptism, cannot exist happily within the same local church. To attempt to play down such differences or to ignore them will only heap up problems for later. The doctrines of salvation and the nature of the Church are basic to any thoughts of church formation and planting.

Let us now then turn to the New Testament to see how church planting occurred in New Testament times.

2. Planting a church according to the New Testament pattern

How then did such New Testament churches come into being? How did they plant new churches like themselves? We shall need to look at the Acts of the Apostles to see what happened. In so doing we shall discover the patterns for our own action today and the principles upon which we are to act. We shall deal with this matter as follows: (a) A survey of New Testament evidence, (b) Methods and patterns derived from this survey, (c) Stages in the formation of a church.

(a) *A survey of the New Testament evidence for church planting*

This is largely to be obtained from the Acts of the Apostles.

For the first seven chapters our attention is centred on Jerusalem. Large numbers of believers are mentioned (Acts 2:41; 4:4; 5:14; 6:1,7), thousands in fact; yet the Church was able to meet as one and functioned as a unity (see 2:46; 4:23,32; 5:11,12; 6:2,5). It would appear, however, that many disciples lived outside Jerusalem but were not as yet organised into separate churches (e.g., many of the priests mentioned in 6:7 would live outside Jerusalem, cf. Zachariah in Luke 1:39,65). They all looked to the Apostles in Jerusalem for leadership, however, although the break from Judaism itself was not yet complete.

Acts 8:1 marks the beginning of a new set of circumstances. With the scattering of disciples due to persecution the preaching of the Gospel came outside Jerusalem for the first time. Judaea and Samaria were affected and not least by Philip's ministry. Peter and John were sent by the Church in Jerusalem to investigate what was happening, to support Philip's work and to authenticate it. They themselves preached in many of the Samaritan villages (8:25). Philip later preached in all the cities from Azotus to Caesarea (8:40) after first ministering to the Ethiopian.

When we reach chapter 9:2 we find there were disciples in Damascus who were still meeting with the synagogues. And by 9:31 the Church was reckoned to be firmly established in Judaea, Galilee and Samaria—it had "rest". In 9:32 we read of Peter visiting the saints at Lydda. There were also disciples at Joppa (9:36,38).

Chapter 10 describes the Gentile "Pentecost" when Cornelius, his family and his friends were visited by the Spirit of God as Peter preached the Word of God to them in Caesarea. The Jerusalem church heard of it (11:1) and Peter reported to them the details. They recognised it to be of God (11:18).

The scattering due to persecution spread wider still. Phoenicea, Cyprus and Antioch all received disciples (Acts 11:19). At Antioch gentiles turned to the Lord. News reached the Church in Jerusalem, and they sent Barnabas this time (11:22), to investigate, encourage and authenticate the work. He assumed leadership in Antioch, but needing help went to fetch

Saul (Paul) (11:25). They both taught the disciples (called "the church" 11:26) for about a year.

Yet again a new set of circumstances is presented in chapter 13, where two elders of the Church in Antioch were sent out in a deliberate missionary/church planting venture. The church in Jerusalem however has been undergoing something of a change itself during this period. As churches were being formed in other places, the responsibilities of the Apostles were widening. So other leaders were appointed for the Jerusalem church—elders (11:30). James was a leader among them (12:17) as Peter was among the Apostles and Barnabas was in Antioch (cf. Gal. 2:9; Acts 15:13; 21:18). As churches were eventually formed due to the labours of the sent-out missionaries, elders were appointed over each of those churches (Acts 14:23). Reports of the work of the missionaries were given to the sending church (Antioch Acts 14:26) and other churches (15:3), notably Jerusalem (15:4). Fellowship between the churches was close and real, with a special place being given to the advice and direction of the church in Jerusalem (cf. 16:4-5).

The churches planted due to the missionary labours of the sent-out missionaries also engaged in outreach themselves. E.g., Acts 19:10—all in Asia heard the Word through the Ephesian Church, cf. 1 Thessalonians 1:8—Macedonia and Achaia heard from Thessalonica, and 2 Corinthians 1:1—from which we might imply that Achaia heard from Corinth too.

(b) *Methods and Patterns derived from the above survey.* There are three methods of planting new churches that may be derived from the brief survey we have just carried out. We may describe them as follows:

(i) Scattering (ii) Gathering (iii) Sending. We shall consider them in that order.

(i) THE SCATTERING OF BELIEVERS. In both Acts 8:1-5 and 11:19-20 the phrase "preaching the word" occurs as an activity of the ordinary believer. Believers move to new places for a variety of reasons. In both references here it is because of persecution. But what is significant is that they used the opportunity to testify of Christ. Philip's ministry was much more a proclamation of Christ (a different word is used in 8:5 from 8:4—kerusso instead of euangelizomai), although it was involved in this whole movement of believers and their spontaneous gospel work.

Yet Philip was no freelancer, nor were the other believers. The Apostles and the church in Jerusalem took a vital interest. In Philip's case, Peter and John were sent (8:14), and to Antioch Barnabas was sent (11:22). They went to investigate, encourage and authenticate. The New Testament knows nothing of individualistic freelancers of whom we have so many in 20th century evangelism.

(ii) THE GATHERING OF BELIEVERS. What is in view here is the situation which arises in various ways when a number of believers in a locality

119

meet together to serve the Lord. It will often mean seeking help from elsewhere in the matter of leadership. Sometimes it is a group of believers who are some distance from the church who establish their own identity (e.g., Acts 9:32,38—the saints at Lydda and Joppa, 25 and 35 miles from Jerusalem). At other times it is a group of believers who move into an area together with the fruit of their witness (Acts 11:26—Antioch). In both cases the encouragement and authentication of the church of which they are a part or of the wider fellowship of the churches is vital, cf Acts 9:32—Peter, Acts 11:22—Barnabas.

(iii) THE SENDING OF MISSIONARIES. Both previous methods which overlap one another to some degree may be described as unorganised and unofficial ways of planting churches, although both were and still are used by the Spirit of God in his sovereign strategy. Under this heading here we are considering the organised and official attempts on the part of a church to plant churches in other places where groups of their members do not exist, by sending representatives to engage in evangelistic work, to gather a company of believers and form a church. These representatives are variously designated in the New Testament—apostles, evangelists, and today—missionaries, church planters. They were men who were capable, gifted and fitted to lead a church as elders (Acts 13:2-3) such as Barnabas and Saul.

The New Testament makes it plain that they worked as a team, although members of the team could be drawn from different churches (cf. Acts 20:4). Each member of the team evidently maintained his links with his home or sending church (Paul and Antioch) although there was the closest possible relationship established with the new churches (Paul and Philippi, and Paul's close involvement with the church decision of the Corinthian church—1 Cor. 5:3). Teams have many advantages: effective use of the gifts of the men in the team, more manpower resources for the work, fellowship between team members overcoming that appalling sense of isolation which those engaged in the Lord's work can so often feel, training of younger and less experienced men. The support for the missionaries came from various sources (the Philippians' concern for Paul), even from their own hands (Paul's tentmaking). The sending churches evidently trusted the missionaries in the details of church life, faith and practice, not to interfere in their activity; although reports were given and visits between churches were undertaken. Their independence does not seem to have produced the problems we might imagine it would. There was constant reference back to the other churches, and the common practice of the churches was valued. No new church felt restricted, and not one appears to have isolated itself from the others.

The basic method of outreach was for the missionaries to go to the centres of population—the cities, so that the new church could then reach out to the surrounding area of towns and villages (1 Thess. 1:8; 2 Cor. 1:1; Acts 19:10). Points of contact were sought in the cities—

synagogues with their opportunities to speak, and market places where the people gathered (Acts 17:17). Sometimes a house would be a kind of base (Justus—Acts 18:7), or a semi-public place could be used (the School of Tyrannus—Acts 19:9). On other occasions it would be work done as from one house to another (Acts 20:20).

The work took time. It was not accomplished in five minutes. See Acts 18:11—one year and six months in Corinth; Acts 19:10—two years and 20:31—three years in Ephesus. It culminated, however, in a Church being formed which was led by its own elders—Acts 14:23; 20:17; Titus 1:5.

(c) *Stages in the Formation of a Church*

From all that we have seen so far it is possible to plot the progress of the formation of a church. There are discernible stages through which a work passes. We are thinking of "planting" churches; the horticultural analogy holds good in so far as the new "plant" develops and grows. Obviously this is not a rigid form that I shall lay out before you here; it is more an attempt at understanding clearly what is happening in the work. Each work is different, so I cannot say how long each stage will last, for it will vary from situation to situation.

STAGE 1. OUTREACH

Under this heading we include the work of evangelism done by both the "sent-out" missionaries and by the believers living in a particular vicinity. As opportunities arise, the Lord's people will speak of him if they have a genuine concern for the lost. Perhaps this initial witness will lead to an informal gathering of interested people who come together to consider the Christian Faith and study the Word of God from time to time.

STAGE 2. MEETING

The next stage is for a regular meeting to be held. This leads on naturally from the evangelistic activity of missionaries and from the witness of the believers. It provides a focus for the work, a temporary base from which to operate and an activity to which to invite people. So it should not be a merely informal "get-together". It should have a proper basis and form. The meeting should "get down to business" under the direction of a duly appointed teacher. The danger of isolationism or a personality-centred "holy huddle" can be overcome by the meeting being authenticated and encouraged by another church or churches (the "senders" if missionaries are involved).

STAGE 3. FELLOWSHIP

As the meeting is held regularly it will become clear that a group of people identify themselves with it and with each other. They adhere to the basis and begin to think of the group as the centre of their Christian activity and life. They have now become a recognisable "Fellowship" with an identity. At this stage the duly appointed teacher will need the help of other leaders who will share the leadership functions within the group. They should be men who fit the eldership requirements of the Pastoral Epistles for they will begin functioning as elders of the Fellowship. As yet there is probably no formal membership roll as such, although leadership and particular responsibility should be undertaken only by those who adhere to the basis and will become members of the church when it is formed. As yet the Fellowship will not meet around the Lord's Table as they have not covenanted together as a church.

STAGE 4. CHURCH

As soon as it is practicably possible the Fellowship should covenant together to form a church—with a proper doctrinal basis, a plurality of elders, pastoral oversight, meetings for worship and the preaching of God's Word, constant evangelistic activity and the administration of Baptism and the Lord's Supper.

A church should be formed only if there is a viable fellowship of believers able to function as a church independently of other churches. It should ideally have a separate identifiable meeting place. But if it is being formed from a group of members of another church, that planting church itself must remain a viable church strong enough to maintain itself when the new church comes into being. Otherwise it might just as well move its place of meeting as a whole to the new location.

There is a right time for a new church to be formed. Delay can produce frustration and resentment, but premature independence can produce weakness and ineffectiveness. Both are dishonouring to the Lord.

3. Problems, Dangers and Weaknesses

Any aspect of practical Christian living is full of problems, and the planting of new churches is no exception. On the face of it the matter seems simple enough but it can be a veritable minefield. All kinds of situations can blow up and cause a new work to founder. The devil has no love of the work we are considering here and makes it his business to make it as difficult for God's people as he possibly can. However, let us proceed, although obviously I can only touch on a few things and many other things will arise in your minds.

(a) *Independence.* At first sight it might appear that independence would be a hindrance to church planting. The idea is that an independent church does not have the resources or the will to plant new churches. It is often suggested that independence is inefficient, for it is contended that only churches that are linked connexionally can have the resources and will to plant other churches.

I firmly believe that independence is efficient and for the following reasons: one local church can take decisions and make commitments much quicker than a connexion of churches; missionaries sent out by a local church are not hampered by boards, committees, councils and all manner of petty officials; churches working together in church planting and the sending out of missionaries in a team have genuine fellowship with one another in this work as they have confidence in one another and in those they send out.

Although I believe in independence I most firmly reject isolationism and the "go-it-alone" spirit of some churches and some individuals in our age. That speaks more of suspicion and pride than a desire for the effectiveness of God's work.

But independence does undoubtedly have its problems. They are the problems such as local churches face within their own memberships. They are the problems of people. Many questions asked about church planting problems can be answered in terms of the people involved. That is, in trying to answer these questions within the sphere of human responsibility they can be answered in terms of the people involved. The kind of question I am referring to go like this: "Why do some churches, when they are formed, isolate themselves from others?" "Why do some churches leave their foundations so soon by allowing error to get in?" "Why do some weak churches resent offers of help from other churches who are in a stronger position?" These questions and others like them are asked by those who seriously doubt the wisdom and even scripturalness of the independence of the churches. We who believe in it would like to have the answers too.

I suggest to you that these questions can be answered in each separate situation in terms of the people involved. Each situation and each church is different but sometimes there is a failure to grasp the implications of the New Testament teaching on the interdependence of local churches. Sometimes it is simply pride which leads men to believe in their own self-sufficiency, or which blinds men to their own need. Churches are people —sinners saved by God's grace, but frail, imperfect people still.

(b) *Size.* It is vital that we have a church planting vision in our generation. Growth is an evidence of life, but numerical growth can bring problems. A large church can easily become complacent and often has a higher proportion of "passengers" than a relatively small church. This is still true even where a large church seems to have lots of so-called "converts" while a small church may appear to have few. "Small," however, does not necessarily mean "beautiful", for a small church can be as dead as a large church, and it certainly looks more pathetic. Small numbers do not guarantee effectiveness in a church, nor do they guarantee spirituality. Yet small companies do have many advantages where there is genuine spiritual life, namely, a greater sense of fellowship, every member knows and is known, pastoral work can become a reality.

Growth should be an outward looking thing, and a growing church should

123

seek ways of planting new churches so that new areas can be evangelised —for that is what truly local churches can do most effectively. A church planting vision is one way of preventing a growing church from becoming flabby and overloaded numerically. There is a weakness in large numbers, as there is a weakness in small.

And that brings us to consider small churches briefly. Why do some never seem to grow? How can we get such churches off the ground? The answer to these questions is often to be found with the people who are the church. Perhaps they are elderly, or have other responsibilities which preclude them from much evangelistic activity, or it may be that they are dispirited, or even lazy, or just do not know what to do. So how can others help? Other churches should offer help, and the small church should seek help from the others. It is a two-way thing. There is no loss of independence or integrity—it is a practical expression of truly biblical life and fellowship between Gospel churches. Help can be given in a variety of ways—personnel, finance, advice and so on.

The reviving of so called "dying churches" comes under this category too. A church can easily sink into low water for any of a number of reasons. It is a sign of true spiritual life if such a church recognises its state and seeks help before it is too late. In some instances it will mean that a small church will cease to exist as an independent work and will become part of another church which will then be able to treat the work as a church planting venture and act accordingly.

For a church which has fallen on hard times to resort to supplying its pulpit with itinerant preachers solves nothing, and only hastens the end. A ministry of sorts may be exercised, but the pastoral care and leadership of the Church is missing, and that does untold damage to a church. You will notice that I draw a distinction between small churches and dying churches. Not all small churches are dying. What they do about their smallness will reveal whether they are alive or not. The tragedy is that all too often dying churches will do nothing about their condition and soon become dead.

(c) *Deficiency*. There are many situations which are not ideal, and many true churches exist which are deficient of something we might consider to be essential.

(i) SINGLE-ELDER CHURCHES

It is clear that the Scriptures teach that churches should be lead, cared for and ruled by a plurality of elders, and when planting a new church this scriptural ideal should be aimed at. However, we must beware of attendant dangers. It is all too possible to lay hands on a man in haste simply to satisfy adherence to this ideal, and as a result ordain a man to a position for which he is not fitted.

I am not at all happy at denying to a church the designation "church" simply because it has a single elder. Eldership is too holy an office for men to be appointed to it simply to satisfy even scriptural scruples more to do with mathematics than suitability. However, in the matter of church planting it is better to delay the separation of a new work until there is a sufficiency in the leadership and an adequacy in the membership.

A church which has only one elder might consider seriously and prayerfully seeking a further elder from outside its membership, from another church with which it enjoys close fellowship.

(ii) BUILDINGS

A church can most certainly exist without owning property, and many do, as did the churches in New Testament times. There are many advantages however in having a regular suitable meeting place. It provides a focus for the various expressions of the fellowship of the church, and is a useful centre in which to arrange meetings to which outsiders can be invited. To meet in a home can also have attractions, up to a point; but there are draw-backs too. They are mostly to do with the home surroundings, the size of the room, and the needs of the family living there. There can be an unhealthy dependance upon the particular family concerned in the life of the church—conflicts of interest between family and church can be difficult to resolve.

So a church without a regular meeting place might consider hiring suitable premises regularly, or even purchasing a plot of ground on which to build a suitable meeting place.

In planting a new church it is important to have an identifiable meeting place before a church is separated, even though it can exist without one. My reasoning is this: the new church is going to have enough problems in its early days without having to wander from "pillar to post" to have its meetings. Since problems concerning premises can easily take up too much of a young church's time and energy, it is better to have the matter sorted out at the outset if at all possible.

(iii) CHURCH LIFE

Some will ask "Why does it sometimes not work?" "Ideals are all very well, principles are fine, but what about those situations where the whole business has come to nothing?"

There are obviously many reasons for the situations of failure we could all cite. In the realm of human responsibility it is the same answer as before—the people involved. But may I suggest to you that there is a little more to it than that? I believe it is a great deal to do with the quality of church life, seen and experienced.

It is very easy for a new Reformed church to be dull and austere in its services of worship and in its quality of life and fellowship. The ghost of "unreformed practice" haunts us. We are fearful of doing anything "unpuritan", and as a result easily become dull and repressive. A Reformed church of all churches seeking to conform its life to New Testament patterns should be vibrant and exciting! It should be a joy to meet for worship and fellowship. The Lord's Day should be the most enjoyable day of the week. Families should feel involved, and everything the Spirit of God gives to the members of the Body should have a proper place. There is nothing wrong with a proper, carefully planned and prayerfully organised "Church Programme" (as our American friends call it). It will ensure that everything necessary has its right place and proportion—including evangelism, which incredibly enough is often over-looked in many "Reformed" churches.

The quality of life of a new church is often good—it is a small, close-knit fellowship of people who have shared the birth-pangs of the young church together. But they must beware of being inward looking. The warm fellowship can only be saved from ossifying by encouraging others to join it—and they bring their own living contribution to it.

A church is a living body, and that life is to be expressed—not least in growth. Let every new church have a vision to plant others themselves.

4. Practical Illustrations

The illustrations I shall give here are all to do with the church I know best and love the most—Tuckingmill Reformed Baptist Church, Camborne, Cornwall. It is a church that has had a church planting vision and mentality during the whole of its life since it was formed on 2nd May 1970. I do not speak of it to parade it—rather that we might learn together. I also speak of it because I have been asked to speak from my own practical experience. I shall inevitably make one or two personal observations—they are entirely my own responsibility and are not to be understood as the official attitudes of the elders of the church or of the church itself. The details of the present situation are described here as they obtained in January 1978—the time of the Carey Conference at which this paper was delivered. Subsequent developments are therefore outside the scope of what I shall say here. Once the description of the state of things in a church appears in print, it is immediately out of date, for a church is a living Body, and things can change over night.

The way the church was itself formed may be of interest before we pass on to the other situations. During 1969 Redruth Baptist Church had a number of members living in Camborne (about four miles away). During this time the Tuckingmill Literary and Social Institute was offered for sale. Over the years, due to disuse and misuse the building deteriorated into a delapidated condition. It came into the hands of the local Council who offered it for sale. Members of the Redruth church living in Camborne heard of the impending auction and went to see the premises—they were in an appalling mess due to neglect and vandalism. The church considered the matter and felt it right to try to buy the building for a work in Camborne. No more than £1,500 would be offered. As one drily put it—"It will be a miracle if you get it for that price". And so it was, for at the auction no one out-bid the representative of the Church, and the Council agreed to sell, although the sum was below the reserve price.

Extensive renovations were necessary before the church could use their new acquisition for the work of the Gospel in Camborne. Members of the church in Redruth put in many hours of hard work to prepare the property sufficiently for work to commence on May 2nd 1970. It was to be an autonomous and independent church from the outset, and the Redruth church and those intending to form the new church at Tucking-mill (a part of Camborne) called two of their elders to lead the work. The new members agreed on patterns of life and work before the foundation day, so when it was formed the church had an adequacy and sufficiency although it only had 15 members (it has now—January 1978—grown to 60).

The area of Camborne and Redruth is the largest centre of population in Cornwall, and it it not without its significance that the Lord should raise

Tuckingmill—Camborne

up the Tuckingmill church in such an area, particularly as the church in Redruth would not at this time claim to be a Reformed Church.

But let us now turn to those church planting endeavours during the seven years or so of the church's existence, which illustrate what we have already considered. As no doubt you yourselves have discovered, the Lord uses various means to stir up his people in the spreading of his Gospel; so it has been with us.

We shall consider these things in the following order (the names are the places involved): (a) Falmouth I, (b) St. Agnes, (c) Illogan, (d) Newquay, (e) Hayle, (f) Falmouth II, (g) Helston, (h) Plymouth, (i) Launceston.

(a) *Falmouth I*

Having seen the commencement of the church in Tuckingmill in 1970 a group of believers in Falmouth thought it would be good if there was an evangelical church in their town too. They attended various places of worship and were members of different churches. Many travelled to Redruth on a Sunday evening because there was nothing satisfactory in Falmouth. An approach was made to the church at Tuckingmill and a weekly Bible Study meeting commenced in Falmouth. Those who led it travelled over 15 miles to it and were not really identified with the group meeting there. Also the group was made up of Christians with various backgrounds, from different traditions and with many ideas. No sense of direction was forthcoming and, local leadership did not emerge. The meeting lasted only three months, July to September 1970.

(b) *St. Agnes*

At about the same time as the church was approached by the Falmouth folk a lady in St. Agnes (a village about 12 miles North-East of Camborne) asked if we would lead a Bible Study meeting in her home. We agreed to do so. The small company that met was elderly; again they came from different churches to which they were firmly attached, no outreach was done to speak of, and eventually sickness and doctrinal differences among the regular attenders brought the meeting to an end. Even so, it lasted from July 1970 to February 1972.

(c) *Illogan*

Before the church at Tuckingmill was formed, an informal Bible Study group met in Illogan, a large village near to both Camborne and Redruth, to the north of both. It met in the home of a subsequent deacon at Tuckingmill and his family. On the formation of the church it became part of the evangelistic and outreach ministry of the church. A good number of folk attended over the couple of years or so that the meeting was held, but very few with any consistency. Some were involved in other churches fairly close by. This meant a lack of commitment to the meeting, and few had a vision for the planting of a new church in Illogan.

(d) *Newquay*

Ebenezer Baptist Church in Newquay has known times of blessing and times of leanness in its history. In April 1972 the effective membership of the church was reduced to three. They met together and agreed to appeal to the Tuckingmill church for help. We responded to their request and became responsible for the work in Newquay until May 1973. Services of Worship were maintained (the chapel is full of visitors during the summer months) and various other meetings were held, but little or no evangelism could be done.

In May of 1973 we agreed to the church becoming independent again, but it has remained in a weak state. Tuckingmill has consistently supplied the pulpit on Sunday evenings ever since. I personally believe the work became independent prematurely before an adequate church life was possible. One regret is that we did not work out and think through the relationship of the Newquay work to the church at Tuckingmill during the period of our responsibility (April 1972-May 1973). I believe this allowed us to relinquish that responsibility too easily without the work being in a proper position to exist as a fully independent and viable church. The present position (January 1978) is that the six or so members have called a man to the pastorate, but I do not know the outcome yet.

(e) *Hayle*

During 1972 and 1973 one or two folk living in Hayle (a town 10 or so miles to the west of Camborne) were converted, baptised and joined the church. They made valiant efforts at evangelising friends, relatives and neighbours; some came to Tuckingmill occasionally, and on certain

Hayle estuary

129

occasions could be gathered for Bible study in a home. It was a concern among us that something more should be done, so in May 1974 we hired the Hayle Drill Hall each Sunday evening for a preaching service and commenced a regular home Bible Study meeting in the week. We met with little or no response from the people of Hayle itself. We had a man in mind to lead the work and he did conduct the weekly home Bible Study meeting, but we could not find anywhere for him and his family to live in Hayle. He was not in a position to buy a house himself at that time, and the church was unable to purchase a house for him then.

The church subsequently considered the progress of the work and decided to stop the meetings that were held at that time. It was felt that we should wait God's time when we would be in a position to send someone to the town to work there in a full-time capacity. We have not entirely given up hope that something will be possible in the future. In fact this month (January 1978) sees the commencement of a series of informal home meetings when married couples have been invited to listen to and to discuss tape recordings of talks on the Family. It may be that these meetings will develop into something which will stand the test of time.

(f) *Falmouth II*

During 1974 some members of the church moved to Falmouth and expressed concern for the town. A regular Bible Study meeting was commenced in January 1975. A regular group began to meet and a number joined the Tuckingmill church. There were conversions and the group began to feel an identity. One of the Tuckingmill members living in Falmouth was recognised as the teacher of the group and the work grew encouragingly.

In September 1976 the Tuckingmill members in the Falmouth area petitioned the elders to consider prayerfully and earnestly the eventual formation of a new Reformed Baptist Church in the Falmouth area, and asked that a man of God's choosing should be sought to lead the work there. The elders gladly responded and the church unanimously also when it was brought to their attention.

An approach was made to "Grace Outreach to the United Kingdom" for financial help in supporting a full-time missionary/evangelist to lead the work in the Falmouth area.

In the meantime a man who had visited the church while on holiday and was known to the pastor was invited to spend a weekend among us, to minister the Word of God and to discuss the work. In fact Don Elliott visited the church twice. He was at that time an elder in Rehoboth Baptist Church Margate, Kent, and Hugh Wrigley the pastor was kept in touch with developments at every stage. Don was only called to the work after the church in Margate had given Tuckingmill consent and goodwill to approach him. They did so unanimously and with great joy. The

130

call was given and Don Elliott accepted. The Margate Church is not large, but they were willing to lose a most useful elder so that the work in Falmouth might enjoy a gain. They are to be admired for such willingness. Their sacrifice has proved to be our blessing, for the work in Falmouth has developed and grown.

There are now (January 1978) 11 Tuckingmill members forming the Falmouth and District Reformed Baptist Fellowship. They meet twice in the week and on Sundays hire the Women's Institute Hall for an evening service.

Grace Outreach—U.K. put us in touch with folk in the U.S.A. who are now helping us financially through the agency of "Aid to Independent Evangelical Baptist Churches". We praise God for their church planting vision and sacrificial giving so that the work of the Gospel might be prospered in this country.

It is anticipated that in the not too distant future the work in Falmouth will become an independent and autonomous church. Already a diligent search is being carried out for property to buy that will become a suitable meeting place for the new church.

Falmouth

(g) *Helston*

Helston is a town of some 15,000 inhabitants, about 10 miles south of Camborne, and serving a large area of Cornwall known as the Lizard peninsular.   There is virtually no Evangelical witness in the town, and in recent years the cults have made inroads.   One of the elders of the church lives there with his family, and has been holding a Bible Study meeting in his home for some time.   Various evangelistic efforts have been made with some response and interest.   Personal contact and testimony has been encouraging.   We have at present (January 1978) four members of the Tuckingmill church living in the area.   Others come to services from time to time.   Recently encouragements have been received from increased attendances at the Bible Study meeting and that on a regular basis. At present the work is still in its early stages and is somewhat hampered by certain problems which have so far proved very difficult to resolve.

(h) *Plymouth*

The Tuckingmill church produces a quarterly magazine entitled *Reformation South West* on behalf of about 10 churches in the South West of England that adhere to the 1689 Particular Baptist Confession of Faith. In 1976, as the editor of the magazine, I was sent £200 anonymously for "the beginning of a Reformed Christian witness in Plymouth".   Although the amount of money would not enable us to do anything definite—it was too small, we could not ignore it—it was too large a sum for that!   What it did however was to encourage us to think seriously about the cities of the South West which it seemed to us at that time were without Free Grace testimony.

Plymouth has a population of some 250,000 and is the largest city in the South West of England.   As far as we knew at that time there was nothing in the city that we would consider even remotely "Reformed". So we shared the matter with the leaders of the other churches linked by the magazine *Reformation South West* at our first fraternal held at Hatherleigh in Devon in March 1977.   Frank Ellis of Greenwich gave a paper on "the Local Church and Outreach", and in the light of his remarks so clearly biblical in basis, it was felt that one church should have the responsibility for doing something about Plymouth, supported by the other churches.   They all shared our burden for the city but felt that the church to bear the particular responsibility was—Tuckingmill!

It was felt wise at that meeting to spend some time investigating what was actually taking place in Plymouth already.   This we did, and our initial opinion was confirmed.   We were impressed by the appalling need of the city and felt that something should indeed be done.   It became clear however that in order to establish a Reformed testimony in the city something would have to be done from outside.

Although recently we were offered premises for our proposed work, they are far too expensive and will have to be rejected.   We are seeking at present (January 1978) the Lord's leading concerning two men to be sent as full-time missionaries to the city with a view to the eventual planting of a new Reformed Baptist church. As the Tuckingmill elders have considered this matter, it has not gone unnoticed who was actually sent out by the church in Antioch in Acts 13:1-4! However we are concentrating our efforts in looking for these men outside of our own number although each one of us is prepared to go wherever the Lord leads, should he lead us in a clear and direct manner to be directly involved in this ministry. At the moment we believe he is leading us to look elsewhere.

This proposed new work in Plymouth being too far for folk to attend at Tuckingmill on the Lord's Day, raises important questions for us concerning the character of the work. What happens when people are converted? Into which church are they baptised? What will be the exact relationship of the Plymouth work to the church at Tuckingmill? How soon should the work become a separate church? These are things for us to grapple with as a matter of urgency before ever we send anyone out as missionaries.

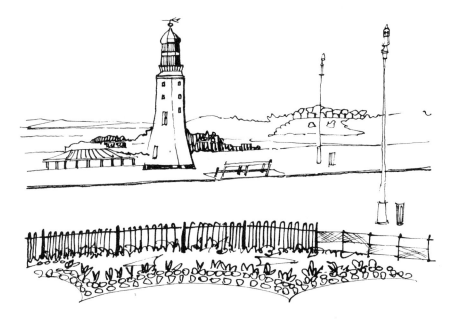

Smeaton's tower—Plymouth Hoe

133

(i) *Launceston*

For some years East Cornwall has been a "happy hunting ground" for those with "charismatic" leanings. Nothing of a Reformed nature has existed in any form at all.

In June 1977 at the Evangelical Stand at the Royal Cornwall Show for which we as a church are responsible, some Christian people from Launceston (a town on the Devon/Cornwall border) shared their concerns and burdens for something to be done about the town. They were most dissatisfied with their present situation and in further conversation and correspondence over the intervening months have expressed willingness to be involved in something to meet the need.

So we have encouraged the setting up of a Bible Study group in their home led by a man recently moved into the town who shares our convictions and has had previous pastoral experience. We are watching developments prayerfully and we are seeking to encourage the friends in Launceston as much as we can. We trust that in God's good time a strong stable work will develop and will eventually become a church with which we can have fellowship in the work of the Gospel.

All these examples are given here simply to show what one church has attempted and is involved in now. We have made mistakes, there have been failures, but we praise God for his abundant blessing and the valuable lessons we have learned. It is only doing things in a truly biblical way that really works. It is sometimes hard to discover what that way is however, especially in our age of expediency and evangelical confusion.

5. Practical Application

Let me make a plea here for churches to adopt church planting as a deliberate policy. I plead for churches to catch a church planting vision and get a church planting mentality. I will spell that out in a moment.

In all I have said I have made no distinction between "home" and "abroad". Clearly when a work is envisaged in a place too far for regular attendance at the sending or planting church the work should be done as far as possible in fellowship with and supported by like-minded churches. The work will need to have a measure of independent action from the outset, but this should present no problems where the men sent out in the team have the full confidence of the church and those in fellowship with it in supporting them.

Also, you will notice that I have given no place in church planting as we understand it to interdenominational or non-denominational missionary societies. The reason for this is simple: church planting, and that is what missionary work is in essence, is a local church matter, even when one church is working in fellowship with a number of other churches.

So let us now consider how a church can adopt church planting as a deliberate policy.

134

Firstly, if a church has a number of members living in a particular area in which it might be possible to start a work, it should be considered seriously and prayerfully, for these very members might well be God's people who will form the basis of the new church. Obviously small churches would not find this easy, but should keep the possibility in mind, for, as the Lord blesses, small churches grow into larger ones. It might be helpful to analyse the membership from time to time to see how the membership is distributed. An analysis of the 60 Tuckingmill members as at January 1978 may be of interest to you in this regard: 27 live in the Tuckingmill/Camborne area, 11 live in the Falmouth area, 6 live in the Illogan area, 4 live in Helston, 4 live in the Redruth area, 2 live in Hayle and 6 live away (training, etc.). These are identifiable areas mostly where we already have a work or have an interest in commencing one as soon as the Lord opens up the way.

Secondly, a growing church should consider seriously how large it is prepared to grow; for if a church separates off a company of members to form a new church it can often lead to more effective evangelism of the area in which the new church is planted. It also keeps the planting church alert and prevents its life from becoming flabby and complacent due to large numbers of non-working members. But how big should a church be before it does such a thing? How big should it be before it divides to multiply its effectiveness? We have a kind of rule of thumb at Tuckingmill—if we are too many to drink from one cup at the Lord's Table in our church meetings, we are too big! (I know that it all depends on the size of cup you use!) But we reckon that between 100 and 150 is the kind of size to be when you should be thinking of dividing as a matter of course. We do not want numbers just for the sake of it—we value the real fellowship we have too much for that. After all, 10 churches of 50 members can achieve far more than one church of 500 members more remote from the people.

But in the *third place,* what of the many unreached cities, inner city areas, towns and villages of our land and further afield? Is it not possible for you in fellowship with other like-minded churches not too far from you to join together in the sending of a missionary team to a needy town near you? It need not be, and indeed should not be a "go-it-alone" venture. These areas are crying out for a clear testimony to the sovereign grace of God like a thousand "men from Macedonia". Who will grasp the opportunity of our generation and go to plant New Testament churches where the glorious doctrines of God's Word are unknown?

Let me plead again for a church planting vision—resources are available—finance and people—will you do it as the Lord leads, opens doors and blesses the churches? If you hold optimistic views concerning the future, then they should be a great spur to you in these things.

May God move us all with a vision of expansion in the saving of precious souls to his honour and glory, through his Son and our Saviour the Lord Jesus Christ.

135

The
Local Church and
Missionary work

by Ian Tait

It will be helpful if we view the pathway we are about to tread by looking at the main headings as follows:

1. Missionary Outreach is the Work of God.

2. Missionary Outreach is also the Work of the Church

3. Missionary Outreach is therefore the Work of every Local Church.

4. The Missionary Call comes to the Local Church.

5. The Sending Body is the Local Church.

6. The Spirit is Lord in the Local Church.

7. A Local Church should expect great things from God.

8. A Local Church should attempt great things for God.

1. *Missionary Outreach is the Work of God*

Missionary work was born in the counsels of the Triune God where it was decreed that, by the preaching of the gospel to all people, there should be brought to eternal glory a great multitude which no man could number from every tribe, people, and language. So we read in the *Confession of Bohemia*, published in 1573—sometimes called the *Confession of the Waldenses*—of "the holy Gospel, brought to us from the Privy Council of the Holy Trinity, concerning our Lord Christ, and our whole salvation purchased by Him". That the gospel should be preached to all nations is as implicit in the new Covenant made in the blood of Christ, as it is explicit in the commands of the risen Christ. As J. H.

Bavinck has written in his *Introduction to the Science of Missions,* "If the missionary enterprise is what we have described it to be, then it can have but a single foundation: the gracious good pleasure of God in Christ Jesus".

It was the Father who sent His Son into the world that there might be a gospel to preach; it is God the Son—incarnate, crucified, dead, buried, risen, ascended, and enthroned—who is Himself the gospel. On the rock foundation of who He is, He builds the Church that is both born out of the gospel and commissioned to preach that gospel "to every creature"; and by God the Spirit, promised by the Father, sent by the Son, the disciples were empowered so that "they went forth, and preached everywhere, the Lord working with them, and confirming the Word with signs following". And the commission was to be carried out "in the Name of the Father, and of the Son, and of the Holy Spirit".

Missionary work is the gracious work of the Triune God. If there is a gospel it is the gospel of God; if there is power it is power from on high; if there is transcendent love it is the love of God; if there is grace it is the grace of the Lord Jesus Christ; if a door is opened it is—notes Paul —"opened unto me of the Lord"; if a heart is opened, it is of the Lord, as Luke writes of Lydia, "whose heart the Lord opened"; if the intellect is opened it is, as we read of the risen Christ, that "He opened their understanding that they might understand the Scriptures". History then, is His story. And evangelism is the story of the grace of God in which the Bread of Life pursues the hungry, the Fountain seeks the thirsty, Rest overtakes the weary, the Highway finds the lost traveller, the Light overcomes the darkness, Peace dismisses fear, and the Giver of Law pronounces benediction upon the guilty law-breaker! The ground of all evangelism is God Himself. It was not that Adam sought God. It was God who came saying, "Adam, where art thou?" So Paul quotes Him saying in Isaiah 65:1, "I was found of them that sought Me not; I was made manifest unto them that asked not after Me" (Rom. 10:20).

Sinners must indeed call on the Name of the Lord (Rom. 10:13-15), but before that they must believe, and before that they must have the truth, and before that a preacher must proclaim it to them, and before he does so, God must send him. And when he arrives—as a Paul to plant or an Apollos to water—only God can make him fruitful, can give the increase. In this work, therefore, men are nothing, relatively speaking. So Paul writes, "I have planted, Apollos watered; but God gave the increase. So then neither is he that planteth anything, neither he that watereth; but God who gave the fruitfulness". What then are Paul and Apollos? Just servants by whom you believed, even as the Lord gave to every man (I Cor. 3:5-7). Paul takes no credit, not even for working harder than the others! So in I Cor. 15:10, ". . . by the grace of God I am what I am: and His grace which was bestowed upon me was not in vain; but I laboured more abundantly than they all, yet not I, but the grace of God which was with me".

In the closing chapter of his *Introduction to the Science of Missions,* J. H. Bavinck points out that the first factor of missionary work is, that we know that the missionary enterprise is not a human undertaking, in which we must take into account our forces and counter-forces, but it is the work of Jesus Christ who will gather to Himself, through our instrumentality, a congregation out of every nation.

The origins of missionary outreach are found in the counsels of eternity, in which the Father said to the Son, "Ask of Me, and I shall give Thee the heathen for Thine inheritance, and the uttermost parts of the earth for Thy possession". Missionary work is the harvesting of that for which Christ died; it is the work of the Spirit, sent into the world by the Father to bring back a bride for His Son. If the Church is sent to the work it is sent "in the Name of the Father, and of the Son, and of the Holy Spirit". And the Church *is* sent to the work.

2. *Missionary Outreach is also the Work of the Church*

This is a corollary of the premise that missionary outreach is the work of God, for Christianity is "The Life of God in the Soul of Man". The Church, and every member of it, is a partaker "of the divine nature" (II Pet. 1:4) of Him who came to "seek and to save that which was lost". Missionary outreach, therefore, is the indwelling life of the Good Shepherd, driving His people out after those "other sheep" whom He "must also bring" (John 10:16). At Pentecost, where the Church as we know it was brought to birth, it was immediately manifest that missionary outreach is the nature of the Church. Whilst some aspects of Pentecost were unique and critical, the Book of Acts bears record that missionary outreach was a continuing process. Bavinck—complaining of lack of missionary interest—comments that, "people are much too busy with themselves, with questions of their own, with their own confession" This is part of the Church's sickness today. But it is more than sickness, it is disobedience, for missionary interest and outreach is commanded. That which is implicit in the nature of the Church is also commanded explicitly by the Head of the Church.

Reformation doctrine rightly stresses both divine sovereignty and human responsibility. If on the first the stress is stronger, it is no plainer than the emphasis on the second. Biblically the two concepts are often taught side by side as in Romans 10 and 11. The best of us "see through a glass darkly", but our inability to reconcile divine sovereignty and human responsibility is no excuse for our failure to give each its proper place. We are to rest in the power and comfort of the one, and assume the real responsibilities of the other.

The Scriptures do not allow any divorce between the foundation work of the gospel and the preaching of the gospel, as though one may be loved and held without the other. Rather do we read:

"Thus it is written, and thus it behoved Christ to suffer, and to rise from the dead the third day: and that repentance and remission of sins should be preached in His Name among all nations, beginning at Jerusalem."

The "death of the Cross" and the "preaching of the Cross" is as a marriage made in heaven. And what God hath joined together let no man put asunder! In the words of the Synod of Dort (1618-19) concerning *The Death of Christ, and the Redemption of Men Thereby* we read: "Moreover, the promise of the Gospel is that whosoever believes in Christ crucified shall not perish, but have eternal life. This promise, together with the command to repent and believe, ought to be declared and published to all nations, and to all persons promiscuously and without distinction, to whom God out of His good pleasure sends the Gospel".

In the agenda of a church, therefore, missionary outreach belongs to "Matters arising" out of the gospel, and not under "Any other business". It is good that in our doctrinal statements we reiterate that, beyond all human endeavour, salvation from first to last is the free and sovereign work of God by which countless myriads of people from all nations and languages, each chosen in Christ from before the foundation of the world, shall be brought from guilt through grace to glory. But no less plainly should our doctrinal statements affirm that God has bound the Church by a specific commission, by the nature of the gospel, by a compassion for the lost, and by the glory of His grace, to teach and preach the good news that Christ died for our sins according to the Scriptures and that He was buried and that He rose again the third day according to the Scriptures, and that this evangelising is to be done by the spoken and written Word, at home and abroad, in season and out of season, by all means consistent with the gospel, and that God commandeth all men everywhere to repent and to believe on the Lord Jesus Christ for the forgiveness of sins.

Paul claimed no credit for a life of missionary outreach. It was his "reasonable service", his bounden duty. "Though I preach the gospel, I have nothing to glory of," he passionately disclaims (I Cor. 9:16). This was no matter of choice—no carnal enthusiasm or activistic hobby—but of compulsion. "Necessity is laid upon me," he adds. It was a burden of responsibility from which only death or the coming of Christ could separate him, a grief which could find relief only in preaching Christ to the lost! So he feels it as he writes, "Yea, woe is me if I preach not the gospel". In the redeeming love of Christ, in the death of the Cross, his heart and mind had found a constraint there was no escaping (II Cor.

139

5:14). Here he was plunged into a debt he could never begin to repay, but yet must ever be repaying, not as a debtor to his forgiving Lord, but as "debtor both to the Greeks, and to the Barbarians; both to the wise and to the unwise . . . I am ready to preach the gospel . . . I am not ashamed of the gospel . . ." (Rom. 1:14-16). He has been put "in trust with the gospel" (I Thess. 2:4). To the Jews at Corinth—blasphemously rejecting the gospel—Paul borrowed from the Old Testament a most fearful idiom and cried, "Your blood be upon your own heads". Again we hear him as, reviewing his faithful ministry at Ephesus, he says to the elders of the Church there, "I take you to record this day, that I am pure from the blood of all men". Here are words heavy with what Dr. Oliver Buswell has described as "a solemn, even fearful responsibility".

Paul's was no thoughtless compassion. That the intellect and the heart marched together in the apostle's missionary outreach is made plain in his words that "the love of Christ contraineth us, because we thus judge that if One died for all . . . they which live should . . . live . . . unto Him who died for them, and rose again". Love and judgment went hand in hand. More than that, they went hand in hand with the Word of God. There is a thoughtful missionary compassion that is yet quite bankrupt of doctrine. With Paul the movement of heart and mind into missionary outreach sprang from doctrine. This is plain in II Corinthians 5:14, where the moving doctrine was the doctrine of the Cross, and in many other Scriptures.

Perhaps the plainest of these is Romans 8-9. In these chapters— as one ends and the other opens—his teaching of foreknowledge, predestination, calling and justification is followed, first by the comforting deductions of 8:31-39, and then, at 9:3, by the statement that "I could wish myself accursed from Christ for my brethren, my kinsmen according to the flesh". Here, having heaped up the blessings of being in Christ, the apostle to the Gentiles declares that, if it were possible he would willingly forfeit them all—be "accursed from Christ"—if only his Jewish kinsmen might be saved. Now that is missionary-mindedness! Robert Haldane—Reformed theologian and leading founder of the Scottish Baptists—comments on these verses: "In this we may discern a characteristic of a Christian. He who has no sorrow for the perishing state of sinners, and especially of his kindred, is not a Christian. No man can be a Christian who is unconcerned for the salvation of others".

3. *Missionary Outreach is therefore the Work of every Local Church*

A local church is a local manifestation of the whole Church. So Paul refers to the Church at Ephesus as "The Church of God which He has purchased with His own blood". The New Testament does not view the Church in terms of *Visible* and *Invisible*, but in terms of the *Whole* and the *Local*. For an example of the latter distinction: in Matthew 16:18, "I will build My Church" refers to the whole Church, but in 18:17, "tell

140

it unto the Church", a local church is in view, putting its own house in order. Every church has a two-fold location, spiritual and geographical, so that we find Paul addressing the saints as "in Christ . . . at Colosse", as "in Christ . . . at Philippi", and writing to "the Church of God which is at Corinth".

In the New Testament, for every reference to the *whole* Church there are more than eight references to the *local* church. As for the "visible" and "invisible" distinction, believers in heaven may be invisible to us, but we are not told that they are invisible to each other. On earth the Lord has forbidden His disciples to indulge in invisibility. Rather He has commanded them to declare themselves openly, by baptism, with the lips, and in terms of corporate fellowship. Such fellowship is to be as united as the parts of a healthy physical body, as orderly as the design of a well-planned building, as close as the bonds between the members of an affectionate, disciplined family, and as real as the relationship between a man and his bride.

The life and fellowship of the family of God is to be cultivated and demonstrated in local manifestations of that family, each one a microcosm of the whole family. So the Pastoral Epistles are written that we may know "how men ought to behave themselves in the household of God, which is the Church of the Living God . . ." (I Tim. 3:15). In the same chapter the parallel has already been drawn between the local church and a family. Paul has written of an Elder, "If a man know not how to rule his own household, how shall he take care of the Church of God?" (3:5). In the words of Psalm 68:6, "God setteth the solitary in families"; each a family into which one is welcomed, each a family bound together by incalculable blessings, conscious that it has responsibilities, secrets, resources, standards, and therefore the disciplines by which those standards are maintained. Each is a home to be guarded, so that as with its great archetype "naught that defileth shall enter therein", a home from which heresy, immorality, and a spirit of divisiveness, must be firmly excluded, that it may continue to be a home where love is to be enjoyed and cultivated, and where true rest, wholesome food, and pure fellowship are to be found. There the Father is to be loved, the presence of the Lord Jesus is to be known, and the power of the Spirit is to be demonstrated.

A local church is a local manifestation of the whole Church, and as such is to be a demonstration ground of the glory and grace of God. And this not only in the eyes of heaven (Eph. 3:10) but in the sight of the whole neighbourhood. As such it is a divine evangelistic method, heaven's continuing missionary outreach in that locality. Did not the Son say to the Father, "I pray not for the world, but for them which Thou hast given me . . . that they all may be one . . . one in Us, that the world may believe . . ."?

Missionary outreach is of the essence of the Church. That was seen plainly at Pentecost. It will be demonstrated in every healthy church fellowship. It is a token of life. Its absence is a token of deterioration. We evangelise or fossilise.

The same doctrines that spell out the darkness, death, depravity and inability of man to save himself also declare that salvation is by grace and that there is hope for the greatest sinner—even the chief of sinners—at the hands of the God of all grace. The God of election sincerely, beseechingly, even urgently invites every sinner to salvation. And He does this through the preaching of the gospel by His Church. He has foreordained *all* that comes to pass. The *all* embraces the means as well as the ends. The doctrine of election *demands* missionary outreach as surely as it guarantees that it will issue in true conversions. It is both our high privilege and our real responsibility that God has given to us "the ministry of reconciliation". Having in our hands the New Testament, we too say, "Now then we are ambassadors for Christ, as though God did beseech you by us. We pray you in Christ's stead: Be ye reconciled to God". Here, in a sentence, is the whole missionary responsibility of the Church, and therefore of the churches. It was no accident that the greater part of the New Testament was written on the "mission field". Recently a missionary, who loves the doctrines of the grace of God, wrote:

"Churches must realise that missionary work is part of their very *raison d'être*. The church which has no missionary vision is no New Testament church."

4. *The Missionary call comes to the Local Church*

In a general sense all Christians are called to speak to the unsaved, "preaching the Lord Jesus", as did those "men of Cyprus and Cyrene" who were driven by persecution to Antioch. Confronted by the starving multitudes a man who has found the Bread of Life must say, with the lepers of II Kings 7, "We do not well: this day is a day of good tidings, and we hold our peace . . ." Beyond this general call, however, Scripture shows us that there is such a thing as a special and specific call to the ministry of the Gospel. Romans 10:15 asks, "How shall they preach except they be sent?". The context will not allow that we limit this to the preaching ministry within the Church. Rather these are sent to those who "have not heard . . . into all the earth . . . unto the ends of the world . . ." (14-18). This is a call that does not originate within the heart of a man, from an imagined ability, a missionary background, a college training, or an awareness of the need. It originates from God.

Through Jeremiah, God rebuked those messengers who, unlike Jeremiah, were self-appointed, (23:21) "I have not sent these prophets, yet they ran: I have not spoken to them, yet they prophesied". The counterfeit argues the preciousness of the genuine. God called Enoch, Noah, Isaiah,

Jeremiah, Peter, Paul and a great host of others. He still calls today. In the words of the Synod of Dort (Article 3 of the heading *Divine Election and Reprobation*): "And that men may be brought to believe, God mercifully sends the messengers of these most joyful tidings to whom He will and at what time He pleases; by whose ministry men are called to repentance and faith in Christ crucified. How then shall they call on Him in whom they have not believed? And how shall they believe in Him of whom they have not heard? And how shall they hear without a preacher? And how shall they preach except they be sent?".

Our word "missionary", adapted from the Latin *missionem,* describes a "sent one". Whilst a "call" is obviously implicit in the sending, the word itself must be used with care. Scripture does use it of missionary work, as in Acts 13:2 and 16:10, but sparingly. Its more theological use is of the call to eternal life, the effective gospel call, as in Luke 5:32, John 10:3, Acts 2:39, Romans 8:30, 9:11.

The special call comes to specific people, to individuals as such. So in the Old Testament we find some sent to their own people, others, like Jonah, to the heathen. At Romans 10:15, the words "except they be sent" point to specifically called individuals, as do the Spirit's words concerning Barnabas and Saul in Acts 13:2, "I have called them".

In the New Testament the call to the individual comes also to the Church. So at Antioch comes the injunction, "Separate me Barnabas and Saul for the work whereunto I have called them". This was to the Church. The call has a duality about it. One is tempted to call it "bivocal". The call to the Church ratifies and validates the call to the missionary. The Church is to "separate" Barnabas and Saul, "prophets and teachers" though they are. The Church lays hands on them, the Church sends them away. Acts 13:3-4 reads "they . . . laid their hands on them, they sent them away. So they, being sent forth by the Holy Spirit, departed . . .". But if the Spirit is the Sender, it is by the Church that He sends. The call may come to individuals but the commission remains with the Church, with every member of it, with the whole of it.

5. *The Sending Body is the Local Church*
If the New Testament is our authoritative guide in the work of God, it is an unquestionable fact that concerning the human aspect of sending forth missionaries—sent ones—the sending body is the local church, and not a missionary society. The apostolic precedent could not be more plainly written than it is written in Acts 13:1-3, 14:26-28, 15:35-41, 18:22-23. Antioch was Paul's local church, his "spiritual home". From it he was sent out, was "recommended to the grace of God for the work". To it, to rehearse "all that God had done", he returned. Returning again, he "continued in Antioch, teaching and preaching the Word of the Lord", and on leaving for another tour was "recommended by the

143

brethren unto the grace of God". He was back again to spend "some time there" before leaving to go "all over the country of Galatia and Phrygia in order . . .". It was there, in the context of his "home church", that "when Peter was come to Antioch" he "withstood him to the face, because he was to be blamed".

The local church, the home church, is the sending body. The church, not a society! The relationship of the missionary with a society is administrative. With the church it is organic. The society is an intermediary between the churches "at home" and those seeking to establish and build up local churches "abroad". It is only too easy for a society to forget this and to regard itself as an autonomous body, independent of the churches, if not superior to the churches, and so to arrogate to itself the functions belonging to the churches. Such a society is that much less biblical. A society can so easily be a conglomerate of strong individualism, rather than a fellowship subject to the doctrine and disciplines of the New Testament. For such, much of the New Testament —such as the Pastoral epistles—is quite irrelevant. The strong individualism of the council of such a society is reflected in the practice of appointing "a friend", and not his home church, to represent the missionary in his home-land. This can add considerably to the problems of the missionary, for an individual is far more likely to suffer from doctrinal aberration than a corporate fellowship. Nor is an individual able fairly to represent the financial responsibilities which in the first instance must belong to the "family" from which the missionary has gone out. Many a missionary—young and old—has suffered grievously because of the lack of pastoral care which is owed to them by their home churches, but which is too often frustrated by an administrative body who "call in" the home church only when the situation has reached crisis point. Today's dilemma has arisen only because individuals once bravely assumed the work of missionary outreach which was being left undone by the churches. But this is no excuse for the perpetuation of that which is contrary to New Testament practice. In both church and society we need to humble ourselves before the Word of the Lord.

The rejection of societies as such is unthinkable. Rather must we thank God for those societies who have laboured to repair the churches' omissions, such as the Bible societies, the missionary societies, the publishing houses, the evangelical libraries, the translation, medical, aviation and other societies who, as hand-maids to the Church, have enormously facilitated her task of preaching the gospel to every creature. Nor would William Carey be with us in any rejection of societies as such. It was in the city of Nottingham just a hundred and eighty years ago that, after a sermon preached by Carey, it was ". . . Resolved that a plan be prepared against the next Ministers' Meeting at Kettering for forming a Baptist *Society*". In the minutes of that subsequent meeting at Kettering we read, ". . . it is agreed that this society be called 'The Particular Baptist

Society for Propagating the Gospel among the Heathen' ". No, we cannot reject societies just because they are societies, but we must view them as agencies of the churches. That Carey and his colleagues were quite clear on this point is obvious from the minutes of their meetings. Of the choice between purely "voluntary associations" and missionary councils "appointed and controlled" by the churches, the theologian Charles Hodge has a word in season:

"The people of God then, or the Church, in the wide sense of the term, are bound to do all they can to evangelise the world. One of the most important means to be employed for this purpose is the sending abroad, among the destitute and heathen, preachers of the Gospel. In conducting this work, there is a part which the Church, in her organised capacity, is alone authorised to perform, and there is a secular part which may be performed either by voluntary associations, or by Boards ecclesiastically appointed and controlled. Our decided preference is for the latter; it is a preference which every year's experience tends to confirm."

A church that has attempted to put its own house in order, as regards its missionary responsibilities, will not infrequently find that it has to discuss its relationship towards its own member missionary with a society that is not prepared to adjust its thinking to the New Testament doctrine of the Church. Such a church must be patient, firm, apt to teach, and ready to practise "longsuffering with joyfulness", remembering that the present situation has arisen largely because others arose to supply the church's missionary shortcomings.

The missionary's own church is the sending body, and as such must recognise and assume its responsibilities. This does not mean that the responsibilities will not be shared with other churches, a missionary society, or friends of the missionary, but it does mean that the responsibility, in the first instance, rests with the church of which the missionary is a member. The concept of a missionary, or any other Christian, not in membership with a church is a concept quite foreign to the New Testament. Such "lone-wolfness", being opposed to the whole idea of "fellowship", drew from John Wesley the remark that "There is nothing less Christian than a solitary Christian". By removing himself from the discipline of fellowship such a man has forfeited much of his claim to discipleship. He is less a pilgrim, and more a hobo, a spiritual gypsy. Whatever he may gain in his pursuit of imagined liberty, he loses far more in his opposition to the Word of God, and in his loss of those values that are only to be found in the real membership of a true spiritual home. This is never more apparent than when such a man participates in missionary outreach. The sending body is the local church.

The local church, recognising its responsibility as the sending body, identifies itself with the missionary by the laying-on of hands. In the person of the missionary, the church itself is going out after the lost;

part of the family is moving out to establish—on the same Rock—another spiritual home "after its own kind".

The functions of the sending body, the home church, do not end with the valedictory service. They have barely commenced. The functions are various, yet are all subject to a number of invariable principles.

Its principles must be biblical
This is a corollary of the fact that missionary outreach is the work of God. For its direction the work of God requires the Word of God.

Its principles should be approached thoughtfully
Missionary outreach is no casual hobby but a responsibility for which we must, each and all, give an account in the Day of Christ. The command to love Him with all the mind forbids a nodding thoughtlessness in His service. The need of a true thoughtfulness will seldom be more urgent than in the recognition of those called by the Lord to the ministry of the gospel. We are to "lay hands suddenly on no man" (I Tim. 5:22). When any have a sense of call to such work, their own church fellowship must consider the following.

Their Doctrine. This is at the heart of the commission. Right doctrine is a pre-requisite in the work of God (I Tim. 4:16, II Tim. 1:13, 2:2, 15, 4:1-5). A church that sends out a missionary who in the realm of doctrine is "a workman that needeth" to "be ashamed", will itself be "ashamed before Him at His coming" (I John 2:21-28). For Carey, sound theology in a missionary was fundamental. In a letter to Thomas Scott he complained, "The missionaries as they have hitherto come to me, have been pious men, but superficial theologians". Alexander Duff voiced a similar complaint. The fault lay with the sending churches. A church must be vitally concerned in the choice of seminary, college, or training school to which the would-be missionary is directed. To leave the choice entirely in the hands of a missionary society is not a discharge of stewardship, but rather an abdication of responsibility.

Their Discipline. There is no discipleship without discipline. The man who is not himself disciplined has no warrant to make disciples of others. In military thought, only the man who has learned to obey is qualified to command. Many a missionary has returned from the field prematurely simply because of failure to learn the lessons—the disciplines—of fellowship that should have been learned in his own church before he ever left for the field.

Their Development. Maturity is essential. The Scriptures say plainly, "Not a novice" (I Tim. 3:6). No missionary training nor theological degree is a substitute for maturity. Without it "Knowledge puffeth up". What appears to be "growing" may be only "swelling".

Their Demonstration. "Let these also first be proved . . ." (I Tim. 3:10) is an apostolic injunction that must be given its full weight here. If a man has no aptitude to demonstrate in the work at home, he has none to take abroad. A journey abroad does not turn a man into a missionary. Missionary work is more to do with spirituality than geography. The language problem is never as big as the love problem. The question at the threshhold of missionary outreach is always "Lovest thou Me?". And love for the Lord is not validated except there be love for His people (I John 3:14-19, 4:20-21, 5:1). Though I possess many abilities and make many sacrifices "and have not love, it profiteth me nothing". And if I possess it, it "cannot be hid", its nature demands demonstration.

Its principles can only be applied sacrificially

Giving is not an issue of primary importance, like the gospel, yet it cannot be divorced from the gospel. It is a grace that is born out of the gospel that "God so loved . . . that He gave His only begotten Son . . .". It is a response to Him who gave Himself for you, "the proof of your love" (II Cor. 8:8, 24) for Him who first loved you. It is also a means by which the gospel came to us, and a means by which we send the gospel on to others. In such passages as the eighth and ninth chapters of second Corinthians, giving is shown to be very much more than philanthropy or benevolence, and is certainly not an overflow of financial superfluity, or an extravagance born out of the excitement of a stirring missionary appeal. New Testament giving springs from the deliberate calculations of a mind that is prompted by a heart that understands "the grace of our Lord Jesus Christ who though He was rich, yet for our sakes became poor that we through His poverty might be rich". It comes from having pitched the tent of one's whole being at the foot of the Cross of Calvary. Giving is a fruit of the gospel that ripens unto "the furtherance of the gospel".

The chapters in second Corinthians show us various facets of New Testament giving. It is something holy, and Paul does not enlarge upon it until he has written many chapters dealing with unholy things in the church at Corinth. It is willing and cheerfully ready (8:3-4, 12, 19, 9:7. Comp. Exodus 25:2, 35:5, 36:6). It is real, active and business-like (8:10-11, 9:3-4), quick to keep its promises (Psalm 116:18, Eccl. 5:4). Grace does not inhibit activity, it promotes it. It is fair (8:13-15). It is openly honest (8:16-21). It is liberal (9:5-6). At times its liberality overflows into prodigality (8:1-4). Then a Mary finds the neck of an alabaster flask too narrow to express the love of her heart, and breaks the flask.

> *If the heart, at high tide, floods the brain now and then,*
> *'Tis the richer for that when the tide ebbs again.*

As the Lord Jesus pointed out, such opportunities of demonstrating one's indebtedness to Him are fleeting, and few in a lifetime. The opportunities for mere philanthropy, good as it is, are commonplace (John 12:8). As a subject, giving has a very large place in Scripture.

In the Sermon on the Mount it appears hand in hand with praying. The prohibition against ostentatious giving, "Let not thy left hand know . . ." (Matt. 6:3) has too often been used—or rather misused—to hide, not giving, but the absence of it. Paul's treatment of the subject gives no hint of such a smokescreen. The Lord's words were not condemning the *manner*, but the *motive* of the giving that was done deliberately "before men, to be seen of them . . . that they may have glory of men" (Matt. 6: 1-2). The apostolic Church laid their monies "down at the apostles' feet" openly (Acts 4:35). Barnabas gave for love of God and His children, Ananias gave for love of human applause. The difference was that between light and darkness. Motive matters. It was because motive matters that the two farthings of the widow outweighed all the ostentatious giving of the rich men.

Judas could talk glibly about giving "to the poor", but was more interested in getting! (John 12:5-6). Mary gave the costly ointment because she greatly loved the Lord who was to die for her. What Judas called wasteful, the Lord called unforgettable! Her gift is still bearing interest wherever the gospel is "preached in the whole world" as He promised (Matt. 26:6-15). Paul relates true giving to the Cross (II Cor. 8:9) as plainly as he joins it to the doctrine of the resurrection (I Cor 15:54 to 16:1). And when he writes, "Be not deceived; God is not mocked: for whatsoever a man soweth, that shall he also reap", he is dealing with failure in the realm of giving (Gal. 5:6-7. So Luther, John Brown, Lightfoot, Jamieson, Fausset and Brown, Hendriksen, Stott and others). We are to give freely because we have received freely (Matt. 10:8).

"Giving and receiving" is a marriage made in heaven (Phil. 4:15). And to return to our care of the missionary, "The Lord has ordained that they which preach the gospel should live of the gospel" (I Cor. 9:14). Even dumb animals are treated generously (I Cor. 9:9-14), how much more the man who preaches the everlasting gospel. A symptom of the sickness of the Church today is that its giving falls far short of the Old Testament standard where every ten householders kept a priest *at their own standard of living.*

New Testament giving, like that of the Old Testament, is a corporate thing. It is an act of fellowship (Acts 4:37, 11:29-30, II Cor. 8:4-5). Indeed, Paul calls it "fellowship" (II Cor. 9:13). In Malachi 3, after the question "Will a man rob God?" has been asked and answered, the command is given, "Bring ye all the tithes into the storehouse . . .". In the New Testament the storehouse is the local church. Storehouse giving is not to causes, but to God. Storehouse tithing is the only tithing in Scripture. Paul nowhere appears to individuals as such, only to individuals as members of a church (I Cor. 16:2). It is not a question of "What do I do with my tithe?". It is not *my* tithe. The tithe is *the Lord's*, even before I give it (Lev. 27:30). How impossible it is for churches to be businesslike in their missionary responsibilities, and to ensure that their own missionaries are adequately provided for, when, in their giving, "the flock" behave like lone-wolves, and "every man" does that which is "right in his own eyes". This is a mark of the absence of the Lordship of Christ in a church (Judges 17:6, 21:25).

What time, energy, and thought is wasted in the offices of societies who find it necessary to thank and often to flatter folk who send their gifts privately. What is gratifying to the flesh may add considerably to the work, and is always opposed to the Word. If the biblical pattern of corporate giving, of storehouse giving, were practised in the churches, the missionary societies—who in the final analysis are dependent on the local churches—would be among the first to gain in terms of both money and efficiency. The work must be carried out sacrificially. The sacrifice will involve a yielding of one's self as well as one's pocket as it did in the churches of Macedonia where "they first gave their own selves to the Lord, and unto us by the will of God" (II Cor. 8:5). And what willing sacrifices they were! As an old missionary saint once said in my hearing, "When a man's pocket is converted, I know he's really converted!".

Its principles must be carried out prayerfully

In spite of our emphasis on the neglected subject of financial provision, a church's care for its missionaries does not begin with giving, nor are finances its primary provision. The primary provision is prayer. Here a church begins its missionary outreach, and from this beginning the Lord of the harvest thrusts out labourers into the harvest (Matt. 9:38). No other kind of provision is a substitute for prayer. Rather is the other provision a consequence of prayer. Here, as often, we meet the antinomy between divine sovereignty and human responsibility. Both are plainly writ in Scripture. Whilst the former is the more important, neither must be diminished. Each must be given the full weight accorded to it by Scripture.

Giving is both a God-given grace (II Cor. 8:1, 6-7, 9:8, 14) and our real responsibility (Matt. 10:8, Luke 6:38, Luke 16:9, I Cor. 9:9-14, II Cor. 8:7, 11, 24, Gal. 6:6-7). That it is a grace does not lessen our responsibility. Rather does it increase it, by commanding prayer as well as giving; prayer that at the throne of grace we, and others, shall receive grace for this vital part of missionary outreach. It is written: "See that ye abound in this grace also".

Prayer is our primary provision for our missionaries, prayer in the worship, prayer in the prayer meetings, prayer in the homes, prayer in the "secret place" of personal fellowship with God. We should be ever ready to borrow Samuel's words and say to our missionaries, "God forbid that I should sin against the Lord in ceasing to pray for you" (I Sam. 12: 23). But this carries a two-way responsibility. Churches cannot pray as intelligently as they might unless missionaries write as regularly as they ought. The missionary, as well as the church, must discipline his thinking by the New Testament doctrine of the church. He is an outreach of fellowship. Between them is a love relationship. Love must be cultivated, appreciated, trusted, informed. A monthly letter to the "family" should be a minimum requirement. And it is a requirement, not a casual indulgence. The pains taken to maintain a regular correspondence—by letter, recordings, or photographs—reflect a missionary's view of the nature of the church, of the importance of prayer and, perhaps, of the spirituality of his own "spiritual home". Paul Simpson, a missionary on the Afghan border of Pakistan, is so alive to the importance of the doctrine of the church, and so conscious of his need of the prayers of his home church, that only occasionally in fifteen years has he missed sending a long and detailed weekly prayer letter.

That all aspects of missionary outreach should be carried out prayerfully is another corollary of the fact that missionary work is the work of God. The work of God requires "the supply of the Spirit of God", the power of God, the wisdom of God, the grace of God, the blessing of God, in all its outworkings.

Its principles should be handled compassionately

The missionary has gone out constrained by the love of Christ. It is to be expected that the same love should constrain our care for His servants. With our love for Him as the mainspring of our missionary concern, and His love for us as our example, we ought to be able to say to our brothers and sisters in Christ, "When we sent you forth, lacked you anything?". To ourselves the primary question should never be "How much can we spare?", but rather, "How much do they need?". In I Tim. 5:8, where Paul warns against a casual, selfish, or unrealistic attitude towards the members of one's own family, he uses words that might well be written over every church's attitude to its own missionaries:

"If any provide not for his own, and specially to those of his own household, he has denied the faith, and is worse than an infidel."

This, at least, points our priorities, and forbids any indiscriminate missionary giving until "our own" are properly cared for. Nor do such words allow us to "major" in birthday presents and other luxuries until we are providing the more basic and continuous needs of those members of our "family" who are part of our missionary outreach. The members of my own "spiritual home" at Welwyn have abolished the dichotomy between "General fund" and "Missionary fund" on the ground that our missionaries have an important place in the "general" life of the church. They are part of the main chassis, not fitted accessories!

A church's provision for its "own" is not ended with praying and giving. A missionary is more than "part of the programme", a mere project to be maintained. He is a person, a whole person, a person comprised of "body, soul, and spirit" In every part and in every way, the church should be concerned about him and his family. They need news and letters of encouragement. They need transport, sympathy with their problems, help in the realm of medical and educational requirements. They may need provision of a home for their children away from them in school, news of their aged relatives or their unsaved friends, or help with the problem of birthday presents. They will certainly need books, clothing, records, tape-recordings. On furlough they will need a home, transport, educational facilities, particular care for the family when the father is away on deputational work. Before this they will need the comfort of knowing that they will be lovingly welcomed into the life of the church, and, as their retirement comes near, of knowing that the church has provided all that is possible for the future. A compassionate church will look at all the demands that their service for the Lord shall make upon them, and share what burdens it can. As Paul could write to the folk at Corinth, "I would have you without carefulness" (I Cor. 7: 32), so should we be concerned, as far as we are able, to free our missionaries of all unnecessary concern.

6. *The Spirit is Lord in the Local Church*

It is by His Spirit that Christ—the head of the Church, enthroned in the heavenly places—rules His Church on earth.[1] In each church the Spirit is Lord, and by Him each and every church "being fitted together is growing into a holy temple in the Lord". Whilst some aspects of the Spirit's coming at Pentecost were unique, others demonstrate abiding principles of His work in the Church. To illustrate: Pentecost was the gathering of individuals into a corporate body and thus the birthday of the Church as we know it. But it was also a time of revival in which those already regenerate (Acts 1:13-15, John 13:10, 14:17, 15:19, 16:27, 17:9, 16, 22, 20:19-23) were "endued with power from on high", so that we see the main principles of revival all clearly set out in the early chapters of Acts. At the same time Pentecost was a demonstration of the fact that the church is essentially evangelistic, that the Lordship of the Spirit means the preaching of the gospel. Therefore, in its concern for missionary outreach, a church must first recognise the Lordship of the Spirit, both at home and abroad.

The Lordship of the Spirit in the home church

The sending body must have first priority here. If the spiritual life of their home church deteriorates, the missionaries will be among the first to suffer. The deterioration will be immediately reflected in terms of diminished interest, sympathy, prayer and giving. There is an even more crucial consequence.

Missionary work is the outreach of one spiritual home towards the establishing of others. It is as children growing up move out from one family to form others. Now it remains true that a body reproduces itself with its own peculiar characteristics, just as a tree brings forth fruit after its own kind (Gen. 1:11-12). It is not to be expected that a wild crab apple tree will produce the sweetness of a cultivated Cox's Orange Pippin, or that an unhealthy body will usually produce a healthy baby. Therefore the spiritual life of the sending church is of paramount importance.

It was surely not accidental that as a prelude to Paul's first missionary journey "certain prophets and teachers" in his "home church" of Antioch "ministered to the Lord, and fasted . . . fasted and prayed" (Acts 13:1-3). Not until Isaiah has first heard and acted upon the words, "Holy, holy, holy is the Lord of Hosts", does he hear the words "Whom shall I send, and who will go for Us?", and receive his commission to "Go and tell this people . . .". As an ambassador from the throne of God to proclaim the sovereignty of God and the sin of the people, a major part of his qualification lay in having seen the sovereignty of that throne, felt its judgments upon his own heart, and discovered its grace. If shepherds are to care for "the flock of God", they are before that to "take heed therefore unto" themselves (Acts 20:28). So for a church. Missionary obligations begin at home. They begin with self-examination before the Lord, in the "eternal light" that blazes from His throne through His Word.

Nor are "prayer meetings for revival" a substitute for obedience. A defeated Joshua, praying for victory, is commanded to "Get thee up; wherefore liest thou thus upon thy face? Israel hath sinned . . ." (Joshua 7:10, Psalm 66:18). It is only a holy church that will know the Holy Spirit's fulness, that will be heaven's continuing "evangelistic campaign" in its particular locality. J. H. Bavinck has written that "The success of the work of missions and the work of evangelism depends upon the ability to arouse envy". But only the grace of God can arouse this envy. Only the ripe fruit of the Spirit can arouse a hunger for the Father's table. Only the living water that Christ gives can draw the thirsty. A church that is failing to do this at home is not likely to have much part in doing it overseas. We must be concerned about ourselves. A. W. Tozer has written:

"The popular notion that the first obligation of the church is to spread the gospel to the uttermost parts of the earth is false. *Her first obligation is to be spiritually worthy to spread it . . .* To spread an effete, degenerate brand of Christianity to pagan lands is not to fulfil the commandment of Christ or discharge our obligation to the heathen. These terrible words of Jesus haunt my soul: "Ye compass sea and land to make one proselyte, and when he is made, ye make him twofold more the child of hell than yourselves".

152

A shepherd of a flock—whether a pastor or another elder—engaged in evangelistic or missionary outreach, who yet fails to "feed the flock of God" (I Pet. 5:2) committed to his care, is a man "compassionately" feeding his neighbour's children whilst leaving his own to starve. The conquests of a general who fails to consolidate his home base usually come to nothing. In his book *The Glorious Body of Christ*, R. B. Kuiper has written:

"The church that neglects the teaching of the Word of God to its members cannot long have a constituency that is zealous for Biblical missions. And the church that fails to indoctrinate its youth will soon have no missionaries to send out, most assuredly no missionaries that proclaim the only true gospel."

Only where the Spirit of Pentecost is Lord can the fruits of Pentecost be expected at home or abroad.

The Lordship of the Spirit on "the mission field"

Although for simplicity's sake we are considering the missionary as having gone out from our local church, it may be that we are sharing with another church or with a fellowship of like-minded churches the burden and privilege of supporting a missionary other than "our own". It may be that we have adopted one who had no "spiritual home" behind him, or one who, having gone out from a church of dubious doctrine, has himself come to a clearer understanding of the New Testament. The case histories may vary, and the relationships, but the basic principles of the local church and missionary outreach remain the same.

It must be clearly recognised that a missionary does not derive his mandate *from* his home church, but *from* the Spirit of Christ *through* his home church. Whilst the sending church shares with the church on the "field" a disciplinary responsibility in matters of doctrine, morality, and fellowship, in the matter of administration the direct rule of the Spirit through the church on the "field" is paramount. It must never be forgotten that whilst there is an organic "unity of the Spirit"—which must be recognised, enjoyed, and cultivated—it is a unity in diversity in which every local church is directly and immediately accountable to the Head of the Church. Whilst it is good that churches should covenant to work together in missionary outreach and in every other way possible, nothing should be allowed to impair the true autonomy of a local church. As we see in the opening chapters of Revelation, each local church is directly addressed by, and is responsible to, the Lord in the midst.

Here is no pattern for isolation. If the Head of the Church holds the members of His body directly accountable to Himself, He also holds them accountable for the maintenance of a real unity among themselves (I Cor. 1:10, Eph. 4:1-6, 13-16, 29-32, Phil. 2:1-12, I Thess. 5:12-14, II Thess. 3: 6-15, I John 4:7-21). Such a unity will mean more than an increased

153

efficiency in the proclamation of the gospel (Acts 6:1-8, Phil. 2:16). It is itself a demonstration of the gospel (John 13:35, 17: 21). It is worthy of comment that only the autonomy of a local church guarantees its right to secede from a denomination given over to apostasy.

The missionary abroad, except in a pioneer work, will of course be a member of a church "on the field". There he will be subject to all the privileges, disciplines, and responsibilities that Scripture requires of active church membership. In that church, or fellowship of churches, the direct rule of the Spirit must be recognised both by the missionary and his home church. This is not to discountenance the full and free discussion between the missionary and his home church of everything except, of course, those things that belong to the private life of the church "on the field", and have no bearing on the responsibilities of the church at home. Nothing must be allowed to impair the direct rule of the Spirit on the mission field, nor—and one is the corollary of the other—the autonomy of the church in which the missionary serves whilst abroad.

This means that, as it is important that a right relationship be sought and continually cultivated between the sending church and a missionary society, it is no less important that an intelligent and affectionate relationship should be fostered between the home and away churches to which the missionary belongs. Such a relationship must be founded upon the fact that the Spirit is the Lord in the local church.

The rule of the Spirit must still be recognised in a pioneer work where there is as yet no local church. This is not a permit to anarchy, but it is an invitation to a real reliance upon the Spirit of God, a confidence in His servants, and, for ourselves, a call to urgent prayer. In Acts 16 we see Paul, Silas, Timothy, and Luke acting decisively upon the direct guidance of the Spirit without any reference to the church at Antioch. It is also worthy of note that though the direction was given to Paul individually (16:9), the decision to recognise it as the Spirit's leading and to act upon it was taken collectively by him and his companions (16:10). Whilst the care and concern of the sending church must be ceaseless, with the missionary abroad its relationship must be moderated by these other factors. With the missionary at home on furlough the situation will be reversed. At all times our attitude to the Lord's servants should reflect the sweetness implied in Paul's words to the Church at Corinth, "Not for that we have dominion over your faith, but are helpers of your joy; for by faith ye stand" (2 Cor. 1:24).

7. *A Local Church should expect great things from God*

This is the work in which men are "labourers together with God". Here in time is the outworking of eternity. Here is a work designed in the secret place of the Most High, a work planned from before the foundation of the world, a work for which Bethlehem, Calvary, and Olivet were but preparatory, a work which is itself preparatory to ages of eternal glory. Here is the work of the Lord, the God of the impossible, who only doeth wondrous things. Here is the invincible lordship of the Spirit, the love of the Father, the grace of the Son. Here is a work which finds its values in the precious blood of the Son of God, and which shall not culminate until it gathers around His throne a great multitude which no man can number, from every nation, and from all tribes, peoples, and languages.

A not inconsiderable number of Reformed theologians believe that a majority, and not a minority of mankind shall be saved. These—who include such as Charles Hodge, Robert Dabney, and Benjamin Warfield —would ask with Augustus Toplady: "Why are Calvin's doctrines represented as gloomy? Is it gloomy, to believe that the far greater part of the human race are made for endless happiness?" or state with Loraine Boettner that they believe "that Scripture clearly teaches, that in the final analysis the great majority of the human race will be found among the saved". Such hold that the Scriptures that seem to speak of a majority lost, belong strictly to the context of the time and occasion to which they were spoken, and are no adequate foundation for what Warfield calls "the dogma that only a few are saved".[2] They hold further that there are other Scriptures, that cannot be so limited, that argue a cogent probability that there will be more saved than lost. Whatever the answer, there is an optimism that, being based upon the character of our sovereign and gracious God, knows that His Word shall not return unto Him void, but that it shall accomplish all His purposes, and that nothing can hinder His declared purpose of harvesting "a great multitude which no man could number". For this, the "joy that was set before Him", Christ died. Since "He shall see of the travail of His soul and shall be satisfied", we too shall be satisfied, and our questions ended.

The gospel that came from His first coming points us on to His second. Then, when we see the King in His glory, we too shall say that "the half was not told us". Then we shall see that missionary outreach was a movement towards the consummation of His great victory over Satan, sin, and death; a gathering of the spoils of the Cross of Calvary, in order to lay them at His feet at His appearing. On Romans 10:15 John Murray has written, "If the emphasis falls on the necessity of Christ's commission, we may not overlook the privilege and joy involved in being sent. It is the sanctity belonging to the commission that enhances its dignity when possessed".

That is true. But it is none the less true that in another sense the commission belongs to the whole Church, to every church, and to every member. So does the privilege and the joy, to those that send as well as to those that go. The latter shall one day share alike with those for whom the will of God was to stay at home (I Sam. 30:24). So should we together look to that day, and then to those to whom we send or take

155

the gospel, and say with Paul, "For what is our hope, or joy, or crown of rejoicing?   Are not even you in the presence of our Lord Jesus Christ at His coming?   For you are our glory and joy" (I Thess. 2:19-20).

8. *A Local Church should attempt great things for God*

At Nottingham, in the spring of 1792—only a few months after the completion of his famous *Enquiry into the Obligations of Christians to use Means for the Conversion of the Heathens*—William Carey "preached a sermon that was nothing short of epoch-making".   A biographer continues:

"It is probable that the young preacher made a rather strange figure as he stood in the pulpit: somewhat short of stature, rather thin, and with a decided stoop—the result of constant bending over his shoemaker's last; prematurely bald, and wearing an ill-fitting wig.   But there could be no mistaking the resolution manifest in every line of his face, the fire in his keen eye, or the earnestness of his voice.   He was a man with a message—called by God and sure of his call."

He was a Calvinist and close companion of Andrew Fuller, whose dynamic emancipation from the bondage of Hyper-Calvinism had been set forth in 1781 in his small but powerful book, *The Gospel Worthy of All Acceptation.*   Carey's sermon at Nottingham was to lead to the formation of a missionary society among a group of Calvinistic Baptist churches in the autumn of the same year at Kettering in Northampton-shire.   Through that society "the Word of the Lord" was to "have free course and be glorified" in the great sub-continent of India, and an unparalleled impetus was to be given to missionary outreach in many other parts of the world.   By 1832 the society had translated and pub-lished Bibles, New Testaments, or separate books of the Bible in forty-four languages and dialects.   "These low-born, low-bred mechanics," wrote the poet Southey, "have done more towards spreading the knowledge of the Scriptures among the heathen than has been accomplished or even attempted by all the world besides."

And this was not the whole of their missionary outreach.   Carey's text for the sermon at Nottingham was, "Enlarge the place of thy tent, and let them stretch forth the curtains of thine habitations: spare not, lengthen thy cords, and strengthen thy stakes; for thou shalt break forth on the right hand and on the left" (Isaiah 54:2-3).

Giving due place to both the sovereignty of God and to the responsibility of man, according to the Scriptures, and before expounding his text, Carey crystallised its burden with his memorable exhortation: Expect great things from God!   Attempt great things for God!

For Carey, planning the initial missionary outreach into India, the focal point was still the local churches.   The Serampore Agreement states:

". . . we think it our duty, as soon as possible, to advise the native brethren who may be formed into separate churches to choose their pastors and deacons from amongst their own countrymen, that the Word may be statedly preached, and the ordinances of Christ administered, in each church by the native minister, as much as possible without the interference of the missionary . . . Under the Divine blessing, if in the course of a few years a number of native churches be thus established, from them the Word of God may sound out even to the extremities of India; and numbers of preachers being raised up and sent forth, may form a body of native missionaries . . ."

Unless we are to deny the authority of Scripture our point of reference is still the local church, not societies or individuals. Only a hostility towards New Testament principle, or an ignorance of it, can blind us to the fact that missionary work is essentially an outreach of the church, not just an organisation of missionary-minded Christians. It is indeed a commission for the church's obedience. But more than that it is an expression of the church's life. Moses was not left to build the tabernacle without a pattern. If we have no pattern, we have New Testament principles so plainly written that a denial of them is inexcusable.

One clear principle is that in worship, fellowship, discipline, or missionary work, the basic unit is the local church. This is the New Testament norm. However great the necessity for "emergency measures", their perpetuation as "normality" is both forbidden and foolish. In missionary outreach churches have no right to abdicate those functions that are committed to them. Societies have no right to assume those functions, unless the handmaid is to oust the queen. And our King is jealous of His bride's honour. Both churches and societies must be prepared for the admonition and correction of the Word of God concerning missionary outreach today. A. W. Tozer in his *Root of the Righteous* comments:

"Churches and Christian organisations have shown a tendency to fall into the same error that destroyed Israel: inability to receive admonition. After a time of growth and successful labour comes the deadly psychology of self-congratulation. Success itself becomes the cause of later failure. The leaders come to accept themselves as the very chosen of God. They are special objects of the Divine favour; their success is proof enough that this is so. They must, therefore, be right, and anyone who tries to call them to account is instantly written off as an unauthorised meddler who should be ashamed to dare to reprove his betters.

"If anyone imagines that we are merely playing with words let him approach at random any religious leader and call attention to the weaknesses and sins of his organisation. Such a one will be sure to get the quick brush off, and if he dares to persist he will be confronted with reports and statistics to prove that he is dead wrong and completely out of order.

'We be the seed of Abraham' will be the burden of the defence. And who would dare find fault with Abraham's seed?

"Those who have already entered the state where they can no longer receive admonition are not likely to profit by this warning."

To the local church at Ephesus the Lord of the churches said, "Remember therefore from whence thou art fallen, and repent, and do the first works; or else . .".

Missionary outreach is the work of God. It is nonetheless the work of the Church, which by the Spirit of God is empowered to carry out the imperative commission of the Son of God. From Him, the Lord "in the midst of the churches", the seven-fold word peals out to us today:

He that hath an ear to hear, let him hear what the Spirit saith unto the churches.

REFERENCES

[1] The eminent and Biblical place given by Calvinism to the work of the Spirit in evangelism and missionary outreach is dealt with more fully in the book, *Calvinism, Compassion and Confidence,* by Ian Tait, due to be published in the autumn of 1972.

[2] The question of a minority or a majority saved is examined more fully, both theologically and pragmatically, in the book *Calvinism, Compassion and Confidence,* by Ian Tait. due to be published in the autumn of 1972.

11

The Glory
of the Church

by Erroll Hulse

THE FELT PRESENCE OF GOD IN THE ASSEMBLY OF BELIEVERS MET TOGETHER for worship and the preaching of the Word is any church's first and chief glory. Without this all is in vain. When our Lord threatened to remove the candlestick from Ephesus, it is certain that he did not mean that he would destroy their buildings. All that is necessary for the dissolution of a church is the removal of God's presence.

What is meant by "felt presence"? Is that not a very subjective matter —one of mere feelings? Feelings enter into it to be sure, but what is meant is the work of the Holy Spirit as he ministers to the people and as he edifies, corrects and deals with individuals in the entirety of their beings. Affected solemnity and gloomy monotone reading, praying and preaching meant to convey the fear of God, or a feeling of his presence, are no guarantee whatever of God's presence or blessing. Indeed it can be mere humbug. On the other hand the most fervent and lively expressions of joy do not spell the presence of God. It is possible to work-up or stimulate by artificial means the most ardent expressions of worship. Yet not one soul will afterwards retain any serious or lasting impression of sin or repentance.

A church may seem to be very ordinary—the preaching faithful but not outstanding and the worship straightforward but certainly not awe-inspiring, yet a tremendous amount of positive spiritual work may be going on within that body of people. Even though she may be dressed in the garments of mediocrity God is in the midst of her. That is her glory!

For the Israelites in the wilderness the ark of the covenant was a visible sign of God's presence as he guided them along. The details of the ark as they relate to the truth of God should not escape our attention. The inspired craftsman Bezaleel constructed the ark of acacia wood and covered it with gold. It was a simple box construction and contained the tables of stone upon which God himself had inscribed the moral law. The lid was made of pure gold and was called "the mercy seat". This word is very expressive because the Greek word (*hilasterion*) translated "mercy seat" literally means "propitiatory". It denotes the place where propitiation has been made by the sacrifice of a life, the blood of which has been sprinkled over the very place where the law demands that justice be satisfied. The God who gave that law and who is the administrator of it is satisfied that justice has been vindicated. Therefore he is able to come and occupy the seat where mercy can be dispensed. It is indeed a seat of mercy, one which can now be approached by every person who puts belief in Jesus Christ for salvation. If for any reason the law and Gospel are not preached in a local church we can be sure that the glory of God will depart. He will not be present to bless if salvation is not proclaimed. If Christ in his atoning death is not lifted up then we cannot expect the people to be drawn to him? The glory is gone because the very heart, the Gospel itself, has been cut away.

That the Israelites valued the presence of the ark as essential is seen in the defeat of Israel during the time of Eli's priesthood recorded in 1 Samuel 4. News of the death of his sons was traumatic enough but Eli, upon hearing that the ark of God was captured, was overwhelmed. We read that he was so shocked that he fell off his seat backward beside the gate, his neck was broken and he died, because he was old and heavy.

Eli's daughter-in-law, Phinehas' wife was pregnant at that time and about to give birth. When she heard that her father-in-law and her husband had died and that the ark of God was taken she gave birth. The shock took its toll and she expired, but not before she had given a name to the child she had borne. "Call his name *Ichabod*," she said, "for the glory has departed from Israel, for the ark of God was taken."

The glory of Israel was the personal approbation and presence of the Lord. His presence with his people marked them as the people of God, separate and distinguished from all other peoples. They were the people of his choice, of all his love, as Amos put it: "You only have I known of all the families of the earth" (Amos 3:2).

The displeasure and departure of the Lord were signified in the capture by the Philistines of the ark. Defeat in battle signified national disaster. If God be for us and with us, who can be against us? If God leave us and actually fight against us of what magnitude is such a disaster? Little wonder that the shock of such a thing killed both Eli and his daughter-in-law!

This brings us to the ark and the local church. As has already been asserted the glory of the local church is the presence and blessing of the Lord. In normal circumstances he is always present to edify, nourish, teach, correct, comfort and add to his people. In exceptional times he comes in great power and glory to multiply and strengthen his people and work just as at exceptional times the Lord came down in a cloud of glory in the tabernacle (Num. 11:25, 12:5, Exod. 34:5, Ps. 99:7).

Care should be taken not to confuse the term "Ichabod". I have known people to run around crying "Ichabod" because reformation has removed cherished but unwarranted or unscriptural traditions from a church. The glory of God is not dependent upon old architecture, a favourite hymn book or archaic expressions. The glory or worth of anything must be tested by the truth.

God has nowhere restricted his glory to any one culture or form of service. Sometimes believers spend their time contending for their opinions or peculiar prophetic viewpoints as though the glory of God's presence depended on that! In contrast to those who strain at gnats and swallow camels, Spurgeon in the Downgrade Controversy contended for the great central Gospel doctrines. One great truth upon which the Gospel depends and for which he strove was the inspiration of the Scriptures. Where Modernism enters, the glory departs.

This brings us to a closer examination of the word "glory". As we have seen in the case of 1 Samuel 4:21—glory is put for the ark of the covenant. That was glory. God's presence is glory! But the actual Hebrew word *kabod* means weight, heaviness or honour. It stands for that which is worthy. By Scripture usage we can deduce that glory means that which is full of value or worth. Christ is infinitely glorious in his person. We read, "And we beheld his glory, the glory as of the only begotten of the Father, full of grace and truth" (John 1:14). Believers are being made like him "being changed into the same image from glory to glory" (2 Cor. 3:18). The New International Version translates the text, "And we, who with unveiled faces all reflect the Lord's glory, are being transformed into his likeness with ever-increasing glory, which comes from the Lord, who is the Spirit".

Now let us examine in more detail the glory of the local church proceeding as follows:

1. What constitutes a church's glory?

(a) basic and essential glory.

(b) heightened glory.

2. A few observations on ways in which churches are deprived of their glory.

161

3. The preservation of a church's glory.

(a) The importance of doctrinal instruction.
(b) The necessity of constant and genuine evangelistic enterprise.
(c) Heresy and the glory of a church.
(d) Building according to the Scriptural principle of 1 Corinthians 3:11-15.

1. What constitutes a church's glory?

As we have seen the Lord's presence unquestionably constitutes the glory of a church, but in what way precisely do we determine that? I would answer the question by referring to two aspects of this glory: firstly, basic and essential glory; and secondly, heightened glory.

(a) *Basic and essential glory*

If we review the average local church today we might easily conclude that there is very little deserving the adjective "glorious". In fact painful features such as luke-warmness among some members, the necessity for discipline, sluggishness in readiness to serve, restriction in giving and sometimes lethargy in the worship services are just some contributory factors which compel the conclusion that the church is anything but glorious.

Outwardly the average local church may be very much like that burning bush which Moses saw. In wilderness conditions a bush is dry, feeble and brittle. A burning bush could be reduced to ash in a few minutes. The whole thing looks worthless. Outwardly the local church can look like a bush in the wilderness. The members are hardly illustrious. "Not many wise men after the flesh, not many mighty, not many noble, are called" (1 Cor. 1:26). If one noble or mighty is present it is not unlikely that we discover sooner or later that that same person has a problem or shortcoming such as propensity to worldliness, or a weakness such as a very real lack of discernment. We do not talk about it (Jas. 4:11) but pray about it (Eph. 6:18). If anything is to be done it should be done by those ordained to oversight in the spirit of meekness (Gal. 6:1).

Moreover as we view most of the churches today we must confess that there is little conviction of sin, no extraordinary appreciation of the great and deep truths of God and little witness of the kind that draws many people in to hear the Gospel. The prayer meeting is supposed to be the gauge or indicator of spiritual life. In most cases attendance is lower than it should be and often much of the prayer is repetitive and un-inspiring. In too many cases it reveals a lack of that prior spiritual preparation of heart and mind which public utterance deserves.

The overall picture in most cases is not one of shining glory.

This being so, you always find some individuals in the churches who imagine that things used to be very different. They hark back to the time when they were converted and baptized. How wonderful it all was then! Nothing like those good old days! The pastor preached so well then, it was so uncompromising, so powerful, so evangelistic, so doctrinal! But now things have taken a backward step! There have been problems and disappointments in the church. Discipline has had to be administered. The pastor does not seem to have the same vitality; he fails to speak out as he should. In contrast to this critical judgment there are other members who feel that the preaching has matured. It has more depth and is richer, revealing more compassion and feeling than those earlier utterances which, while they were flashy and impressive, were often hardhearted and unwise. Despite the difficulties and setbacks the church has grown, even though in a spasmodic kind of way. Some have come, matured and gone off to enrich other churches or have become involved in church planting elsewhere. Most have grown and advanced in the Christian life and continue to do so. Cases of discipline have been essential and, as always, very unpleasant. In most cases they have been greatly owned and blessed of God to the overall life of the church. There have been discouraging patches with little conversion work and even less conviction of sin.

Few would deny that the picture just painted is a common one.

Now I contend that in the everyday humdrum work of the local church there is *a basic and essential glory*. Christ is made sanctification to us (1 Cor. 1:30). He is in the local church just as he was in the burning bush. He is in the worship services, in the sermon preparation, in the prayers, in the visiting, correspondence and daily communication. To belittle the daily round of church work is to overlook the fact that the members of the body of Christ are progressing in sanctification. It is true that activity or service can be superficial but when rightly motivated with God's glory in view the Lord guarantees that not even the giving of one cup of cold water will go without reward (Matt. 10:42). Sanctification cannot be separated from expositions assimilated, spiritual books studied and experience gained in outreach or work done in the name of the Lord. Obviously some grow more quickly than others and for a while a few may seem to be going backward rather than forward. But so it was in the wilderness journey, which is in itself a vivid illustration of sanctification. How can we explain the fact that despite a truly terrible chronicle of rebellion, complaint, setback, reversal and failure, the people were refined and in the end reflected the highest qualities? When they entered Canaan they were described as "holiness to the Lord" (Jer. 2:2,3), and in Joshua we read that "Israel served the Lord all the days of Joshua, and all the days of the elders that overlived Joshua" (Josh. 24:31). That is a commendable record.

We should not allow ourselves to become discouraged by entertaining falsely romantic ideas about the church. We must not think of the church as being like one of those paddle-boat pleasure steamers sailing down the Mississippi—one great big happy party! That is not so. The church through history has passed through stormy seas and fiery trials. Tribulations, afflictions and mortifications are all to be understood and interpreted within the context of the local church, which is the centre where these matters are prayed about.

We do well to enhance our outlook toward the week by week activities of the church, never allowing them to be anything less than the wonderful privileges that they are. Worship and prayer together, teaching the young, visiting the fatherless and the widows in their affliction—is that not glorious? If God is in it, as he is, then it is glorious! We are the losers if we ever take these privileges for granted. "What," says someone, "visiting some old feeble shut-in on a cold winter night! Do you call that glorious? You must be joking!" "Inasmuch" says Christ, "inasmuch as you did it unto one of the least of these, you did it unto me." In other words if you were going out into adverse weather to visit the Lord himself you would think that glorious, but because it is old granny Jones you don't think so!

By and large the general affairs of an average evangelical church possess the basic and essential glory of God's work in sanctification. Father, Son and Holy Spirit are involved in the overall gradual conformity of all the true members to Christ's likeness.

This is well illustrated by the church of Smyrna described in Revelation. Tried, poor, suffering and hounded by bloodthirsty persecutors—what glory here? None, except in the eyes of those who can see a shining crown of life laid up for those harassed, humble, unglamorous believers. Many churches in Communist countries today seem to bear a close resemblance to Smyrna. Poor in this world's goods, restricted, harassed and handicapped! What glory here? Again it is a case of the burning bush. These believers are joined to Christ. "In all their affliction he is afflicted" (Isa. 63:1). This is a difficult verse. E. J. Young points to the rendering, "In all their afflictions, there was affliction to him". Says Calvin, "God accommodates himself to the manner of men, by attributing to himself all the affection, love and compassion which a father can have". In all their privations he cares. He will never leave them nor forsake them. Their glory is this that Christ is in them—the hope of glory and among them.

(b) *Heightened glory*

We turn now from that which is basic but nevertheless glorious in its own right to consider times of revival, when what has been going on steadily or very slowly breaks out like a fire well laid over burning embers. A survey of revivals in the history of the church reveals that essential elements are always present such as repentance toward God and subsequent reformation of life. The word "revival" requires protection just as do some rare forms of wild life which are threatened by extinction. This is because many talk today about "arranging revivals" and actually announce them before the time. Revival is that repentance or change of life which God sends down from heaven in his own way and at his own time (Acts 5:31, 11:18).

In America particularly, techniques have been designed and refined at great ingenuity and expense to produce an initial response by way of people coming forward to register their feelings. This has resulted in what *Time* magazine terms as an "evangelical boom". One of the evangelical leaders, the founder of the organisation called "Campus Crusade" has spoken about raising one billion dollars (1,000,000,000 dollars!) by 1982 for soul winning! The superficiality of the Campus approach is sad. It is the antithesis of revival. The huge organised evangelical movements of our generation bear no resemblance to revival and exercise no notable influence on the secular mind and culture of society. The manufactured efforts of today are like a bright fireworks display in the sky at night rather than the day by day, week after week ploughing, planting and tilling of land which is needed for the production of a harvest. The collection of dead ashes the morning after the fireworks display is very different from the harvesting of the great grain loads of wheat from the lands of the earth.

Revivals differ much in character. The sixteenth century reformation consisted of an immense upheaval. The expounded Word of God was the instrument that turned multitudes from superstition and ignorance to Christ and a new life which was all embracing for home, church and civil life. The Reformation was a time of heightened glory.

The Puritan age in England also represented a time of heightened glory when many preachers enjoyed great authority and power in preaching. We only need think of such men as Samuel Fairclough, Richard Rogers, William Gouge and Richard Baxter.

Every revival has its own stamp and character. We can see this in the revivals recorded in Scripture such as the Judges revival (Judg. 2:1-4), that under Samuel, the restoration under Nehemiah, the call to repentance by John the Baptist, the movement of the Spirit at Pentecost and the growth of the Church revivals recorded in the travels of Peter and Paul. Revival can be linked with reformation when the underlying foundations of church and civil life are thought out and relaid. That happened in the sixteenth century and occurs on the mission fields today when whole tribes reform their way of thinking and life because of the transforming power of the Gospel. There is no area of man's thought or practice which does not come under the searching and refining power of the Gospel. "Every thought is made captive" (2 Cor. 10:5).

Revival mostly emanates from powerful preaching without trappings. No elaborate stagework, lights, make-up, fan-fare, orchestra, acoustic adjustments, microphone or platform artists assisted John the Baptist! A loin cloth formed his covering and the sky was his sounding board. The power of the Holy Spirit and a burning message of repentance were the chief characteristics of that revival in the wilderness. Such a prospect should be yearned after and earnestly sought by every preacher of every local church. There is something unique in preaching which comes in the power of the Spirit. This surely is the central issue because the Scriptures emphasise the primacy of preaching. When the hearts of the people burn within them they will not only be enthusiastic to return but will persuade their friends to accompany them.

Powerful effective preaching is evidenced when the Holy Spirit fills the preacher and descends upon the assembled company. The coming down of God is very much associated with revival. It is the very essence of heightened glory. The term used to describe it is the shekinah glory. The Hebrew word (*Shechaniah*) does not appear in our translations. It means "dweller of Jehovah" or "Jehovah's friends". The name occurred among some of the priests and Levites. The idea is that of God coming down in power and great glory as the one who dwells among his people. The scenes of sorrow for sin and of bursting joy because of justification by faith which occur in revivals result mostly from the concurrent effects of the preaching and the Holy Spirit working in the hearts of the people. Such heightened glory is what we urgently need and what we long for in our local churches.

The revivals in Ruanda and Korea in this century were accompanied by much confession of sin. That was a distinguishing feature, revealing deep conviction of evil within and sorrow for offence toward God. Efforts to transplant such movements fail because God is absolutely sovereign in revival. We must not imagine that our favourite revival preacher in history did not know what it was to battle with stony ground and arid pastures. Whoever in our English speaking world spoke with the power of George Whitefield? Yet it has been said that although he visited Scotland fourteen times during twenty-seven years of his ministry, it was only twice that his visits there were distinguished by special displays of Divine power. The revival at Cambuslang, in 1842, under Whitefield's preaching scarce has an equal in Church history. Such an occasion described by Arthur Fawcett in *The Cambuslang Revival* (2) was one of heightened glory when compared to the rest of Whitefield's profitable and edifying ministry in Scotland.

The eighteenth century awakening, of which the Cambuslang revival was a part, has its unique character expressed in its hymnology. Uninhibited, unfettered confession of the Gospel and salvation mark out that time as one of glorious increase and joy. It is a sheer pleasure to sing their songs and be refreshed by celebrating that time of ingathering. We wish we could be like that but somehow cannot manufacture or repeat that time of heightened glory when unusual unction was given to the preachers and most important, a willingness among the people to listen and receive the message.

Heightened glory is seen not only in evangelical fervour and intense zeal

166

for the Gospel to be effective at home but also in missionary fervour and desire to evangelize the world. Such was the outcome of the 1859 revival. A local church can be wonderfully used in missionary work as elders from that church go abroad being supported by the faithful prayers of the membership at home.

The prospect of increased numbers brought in by means of a heaven-sent revival is almost too good to be true. Such a time of heightened glory would be timely today when the faith of many wavers. We have seen somewhat of a reformation in doctrine and practice which could hardly have been brought about by human agency alone. Some have seen a few conversions here and there and a gradual increase ebbing and flowing over the years. But none of my generation and acquaintance, as far as I know, has experienced a season of revival or heightened glory which could in any way compare to the time of refreshing to which reference has just been made.

That our Lord should view numbers coming to himself with unmingled satisfaction we have no doubt. That the angels have royal feasts of joy in revival times we also do not doubt. That the Scriptures encourage us by means of so many promises of prosperity to pray for revival we know to be true—yet how few of us really believe revival to be a possibility and how many of us seek it truly and earnestly? Too often our hopes grow feeble. Disappointments cool our prayers and efforts. Spiritual battles weary us and often reduce our faith and expectation.

Whatever happens let us keep the prospect in mind. Let us read of former revivals and be in touch with areas of genuine blessing today. Let us resist the temptation to view the subject of revival as a phenomenon which occurs so seldom that it is very unlikely to happen in our churches. To combat such thoughts we should encourage ourselves by reading accounts of former awakenings. I have often been refreshed by turning to Sprague's *Lectures on Revivals*.

By way of conclusion to this part of our subject note this typical description of heightened glory:

The subscriber was settled as pastor of this congregation December 1804. In August 1807, a powerful and extensive revival commenced. The first decisive evidence of the special presence and power of the Holy Spirit, was on the Sabbath, under a powerful sermon on Prayer, by the Rev. Dr. Gideon Blackburn. A number were awakened that day; and new cases of conviction, and hopeful conversion were for a considerable time occurring at almost every religious meeting. The special attention continued for about 18 months, and the number added to the communion of the church as the fruits of this gracious work, was about 120. The subjects of it were generally deeply exercised; and most of them continued for a considerable time in a state of distress, before they enjoyed the comforts of the hope of the gospel.

This revival was the first I had ever seen; and it was a solemn situation, for a young man, totally inexperienced in such scenes. It was general through the congregation, and in a few weeks extended into neighbouring congregations, and passed from one to another, until in the course of the year, almost every congregation in what was then the Presbytery of Jersey, was visited.

The next revival with which the Lord favoured my ministry, visibly commenced in December 1812. It was on a communion Sabbath. There was nothing peculiarly arousing in the preaching. I was not expecting such an event; neither as far as I have ever discovered, was there any peculiar engagedness in prayer, or special desire or expectation on the part of Christians. I saw nothing unusual in the appearance of the congregation; and it was not until after the services of the day were ended, when several called in deep distress to ask me what they should do to be saved, that I knew that the Lord was specially in this place. This was a day of such power (though I knew it not at the time), that as many as *thirty* who afterwards joined the church, were then first awakened. And it is a remarkable circumstance that the same powerful influence was experienced, on the same day, in both of the Presbyterian churches in the neighbouring town of Newark. It was also communion season in both those churches.

This revival continued about a year; and the number of persons added to the communion of this church as its fruits was about one hundred and ten. The subjects of this revival generally were deeply and long distressed, and in many instances, their distress affected their bodily frames. Frequently sobbing aloud was heard in our meetings, and in some instances, there was a universal trembling, and in others a privation of bodily strength, so that the subjects were not able to get home without help. In this respect this revival was different from any others which I have witnessed. I never dared to speak against this bodily agitation, lest I should be found speaking against the Holy Ghost; but I never did any thing to encourage it.

This description reminds us once more that revival can come suddenly and unexpectedly. The manifestations always seem to differ. The danger of excess and abuse is always present. The intensity and volume of work involved in attending to people's needs increases dramatically. Problems multiply as people multiply. Revival is not all glory but it is increased and heightened glory. Such a prospect should always be earnestly sought.

2. A few observations on ways in which churches are deprived of their glory

Before tackling the question of practical ways in which we should guard the glory of a local church we need to recall the wide variety of ways in which that glory is impaired or destroyed. The adversary is always endeavouring to create error or heresy, tempting believers into sin or stirring up disunity. It was so in the Apostolic era and has been so ever since. The New Testament scene is far from idyllic. The church at Corinth was torn with schism, plagued with immorality and distressed by those who were engaged in worldly lawsuits against each other. The churches of Galatia were threatened with a deadly heresy as were the churches at Colosse. The seven letters to the seven churches of Asia reveal a variety of deficiencies all of which deprived the churches of their glory in one way or another. Many are the lines of attack to bring about sin, shame, disorder, division or schism.

3. The Preservation of a Church's Glory

While it is an ever present responsibility to pray for revival it is obvious that it cannot be created. The preservation of values precious in the sight of God belongs very much to the realm of human responsibility. Christ acknowledged the orthodoxy and zeal for good works exemplified by the church at Ephesus but was grieved that they had lost their first love. Ephesus was described by him as *a fallen* church! The letters to the churches show that the maintenance of orthodox belief and practice as well as love for God pertain to the basic glory of a church.

With hindsight we are able to observe the way in which churches which were once glorious have declined and eventually disappeared. The two factors of soundness of heart and mind are inseparable. When the heart is cold, orthodox faith can become rigid and dead, but spiritual declension seems to result mostly in doctrinal indifference. This leaves the door open for all kinds of error to enter, which undermine and then destroy the glory of the churches. There are innumerable responsibilities involved in church life, but I would like to refer to four in particular.

a. *The importance of doctrinal instruction*
b. *The necessity of constant and genuine evangelistic enterprise*
c. *Heresy and the glory of a church*
d. *Building according to the Scriptural principle 1 Corinthians 3:11-15*

a. *The importance of doctrinal instruction*

When Paul refers to the whole armour of God (Eph. 6:10-18) he uses the language of the military warfare of his time to illustrate the reality of spiritual conflict. When we think of modern military combat we think in terms of highly sophisticated weaponry—aircraft carriers, polaris-submarines, tank-destroying missiles carried by helicopters, and now neutron bombs. Nations spend huge sums of money on defence. The leaders know that while there is much talk about peace and "détente", as it is called, it would be fatal to reduce military capability to resist the ambitions of forces basically hostile to our way of life. Total incompatibility of political doctrines dictates that there will always be warfare whether cold or hot. While a balance of military power is sustained it is likely to remain cold which is infinitely better than the holocaust of a hot-war. Holocaust is a word meaning burning whole and is something of overwhelming proportions.

The spiritual parallel is obvious. We are engaged in a relentless war. Forces opposed to Biblical Christianity are the same now as they have ever been. The cults have not changed their doctrines nor have the major religions of the world.   Included in the major religions is pseudo-Christianity.   For many years liberal Church leaders have been saying that Christianity is not doctrine but life.   By this means resistance to their liberal anti-supernatural and humanistic ideas is broken down.   Those evangelical churches which scorn the idea of Confessions and Creeds using the slogan "No creed but Christ" play into the hands of the liberal theologians who have infiltrated most of the major denominations.

A recent example of non-doctrinal Christianity is seen in the call of the Archbishop of Canterbury, Dr. Coggan, for intercommunion between the Anglican and Roman Churches.   We have not heard of any opposition to this from evangelical Anglican leaders but the proposal has been rejected in a variety of places by Roman Catholics.   They declare that they cannot compromise the doctrine of transubstantiation which means that they insist on believing that the bread and wine of the communion are changed literally into the body and blood and divinity of Christ.

This is just one example in which it is necessary to know our doctrine. What do we believe the communion to be?   We are required to know what the Bible teaches on that matter, where the relevant passages are and how they relate to each other.   This involves doctrinal instruction.   A confession of faith such as the Westminster Confession of Faith (or the 1689 Baptist Confession which is modelled on it) shows just how much is involved by way of doctrine.

We have thought of military preparedness and note that powerful forces are at work in the Western world to reduce seriousness, alertness and readiness on the military front.   While not equating the two subjects it is interesting to observe the forces at work in evangelical circles which regard doctrine as unimportant.   It is true that it is possible to cause damage by contending for the truth in a hateful and ugly way rather than pleading the cause of truth in love.   Today the emphasis is on experience. So long as Christians have a common experience some feel that they can omit doctrinal issues because of the many difficulties that arise when doctrinal details and implications are discussed.

What does the New Testament say about this subject?   I believe it is possible to show that there is an emphasis throughout on believing and confessing truth clearly and in detail in a way which is gracious and which reveals genuine love for the people who oppose the saving truths of the Gospel.

The Judgement to come and the Gospel of justification by faith must be declared with power and clarity.   And when disciples are made they are to be taught *all things* which Christ has commanded (Matt. 28:18-20).

The book of Acts records the Gospel preaching of the apostles in which the most relevant truths were proclaimed in the plainest and clearest terms. The epistles follow the same pattern.   Maximum clarity is evidenced on every front whether it has to do with the resurrection, with eternal punishment, with marriage or with the divinity of Christ.

Ephesians 4:7-16 is an important passage because it reveals the centrality of the teaching ministry and tells us the purpose of it, namely stability and strength in the Christian life.

The pastoral epistles likewise show the importance of doctrine. William Hendriksen in his commentary suggests an outline on 2 Timothy which provides an excellent illustration of this subject. He says, as regards sound doctrine, "*hold on to it* (ch. 1), *teach it* (ch. 2), *abide in it* (ch. 3), *preach it* (ch. 4)". Hold on to it, not being ashamed of it (1:12,16); teach it to trustworthy men who will teach others and thus preserve it (2:1), abide in it, because grievous times will come (3:1), preach it because your office requires that you discharge your responsibilities (4:5). The church is described as the pillar and ground (foundation) of the truth. Therefore if the glory of a local church is to be preserved then it is important that a consistent doctrinal preaching ministry be maintained. If the preaching is allowed to degenerate into mere talk which is obscure, flabby, non-definitive and sentimental, then it will not be long before the sheep and lambs are carried off in all directions by wolves who have been awaiting the advantage of weak shepherds and a defenceless flock. Our Lord charged Peter to feed the flock (John 21:16). Paul exhorted the Ephesian elders to do likewise (Acts 20:25). Peter addressing all elders commands that they feed the flock of God (1 Pet. 5:2). Influenced by the spirit of the age there are Christians who disparage Christian doctrine. In so doing they are guilty of compromise. Unwittingly they are betraying the cause of Christ. We can be certain of this when the members of a church are hardly able to say what they believe and are unwilling to defend the Gospel, then the glory is fading. When the elders of a church no longer care about doctrine we can be sure that it will not be long before the light of that church is extinguished.

b. *The necessity of constant and genuine evangelistic enterprise*

Evangelism is a necessity as far as the glory of a local church is concerned because without it the wonder of salvation is nullified. If believers are endued with a sense of the surpassing greatness of God's power toward them in opening their eyes and turning them from darkness to light and from the power of Satan to God, and forgiving their sins by the sacrifice of Christ's blood, then they will express appreciation of such amazing grace by concern for others. Absence of such concern in prayer and effort reveals absence of appreciation of the magnitude of salvation in the heart. A church lukewarm in evangelism is a lukewarm church, and a church lukewarm is a church less than glorious.

The church described in the New Testament is one which was constantly expanding. When the believers were scattered because of persecution they went everywhere preaching the word (Acts 8:4). When a time of

171

peace followed the church throughout all Judea and Galilee was built up and continued to increase (Acts 9:31).

Unlike the situation today we observe no special organisations for evangelism. Nor is there so much as one exhortation to the Christians to evangelise. We do see tremendous efforts by the unbelieving Jews to stop the witness of the Christians who filled Jerusalem with their doctrine. The truth is that if the church is filled with the life of Christ then the love and compassion of Christ in evangelism will flow out. Nothing will be able to quench that life. The aim then should be for a virile, healthy and spiritual church without which the evangelism will be artificial in character.

Having asserted that it is nevertheless important to add that evangelism needs direction. It should constantly be the subject of prayer. We see these principles in operation in Acts 13:1-4. Through prayer and fasting direction was given as to the delegation and nature of the work. In other words those specially gifted for the task need to be sent out by the church in the work of evangelism from house to house and in the market or concourse places of the towns round about.

Someone might say that these assertions seem to contradict what was stated formerly about the absence of organisations in the New Testament. In answer to that it needs to be stressed that the local church is the agent of evangelism not fly-by-night organisations. One brother pastor known to us was sentenced to prison in the Communist country where he lives through the activity of an organisation which copied his evangelistic literature without his permission and spread it in an unwise and impersonal manner which aroused the civil authorities to apply the law. Evangelism is to be done with the background of holy Christian living as exemplified in the body of Christ, the local churches. Evangelism is not machinery. Evangelism is not merely dropping books and tracts from the sky. If evangelism were simply a matter of making knowledge known apart from the personal outworking of that knowledge the work could well be passed over to technocrats and high powered organisations consisting of business organisers. For this reason the word "genuine" has been employed. Evangelism ought to be the expression of the life of Christ flowing out of his body and not artificial in the sense that it is merely organised activity by private organisations.

Evangelism should also be constant. It should be the same all the year round and in all seasons—winter, summer, autumn and spring. Too often evangelism is thought of as a seasonal effort. At no point in the year should there be any lack of concern or prayer for all the unsaved people around who are at all times receiving the witness of the Gospel personally from the members of the church. If in addition to that special times of organised visitation can be embarked upon all the better so long as the tendency is resisted to think that at any point in time our responsibility to evangelise is diminished.

172

c. *Heresy and the glory of the church*

This is very common.   Hence it is practical.   It is relevant.   How does a church deal with it.

Paul suggested that the heresies at Corinth were permitted by God in order that the church might be purified.   The word (*hairesis*) means a self-chosen opinion (1 Cor. 11:19).   The root of the word is *I choose*. The emphasis is on self-disposition or self-choice—pleasing oneself rather than the body.   One's opinions are given the priority and the result is refusal to submit to the common interest.   The word is not used very often in the New Testament but the way Peter employs the term (1 Pet. 2:1) has disposed the view that heresy is that self-opinion which denies the Gospel in a fatal way whereas error while being wrong does not actually destroy the Gospel.   A heretic is an opinionative or factious person.   After two admonitions such a person is to be rejected (Titus 3:10), and Paul exhorts that those who cause divisions should be marked and avoided (Rom. 16:17).

The glory of a local church is affected in an adverse way by heresies particularly when espoused by groups within churches who then operate within the body in the interests of their self-chosen opinions.   Yet we are to understand that God has expressly permitted such a thing in order that the body may be purified either by the repentance or the removal of those who cause the schism.

Heresy is often thought of as something external to the churches— Jehovah's Witnesses, Mormons etcetera.   But Paul warned the elders of Ephesus of heresies arising from within (Acts 20:30).   The testing occurs within the churches and the answer is clearly provided as to why God permits that which can cause much pain to a local church.   "That those who are approved may be manifest."   Faithfulness to the truth is tested. The temptation to follow a persuasive person (it may even be a close blood relation) can be tremendous.   Not only is faithfulness to the truth put to the test but character is also subjected to trial.   Someone who nurses grudges, discontents or resentments may be tempted to join hands with those who may be agitating and disturbing the church with their special views or opinions.   They may join the heretics (I use the word as I have defined it from 1 Cor. 11:19) not because they agree with those views but because this gives them the opportunity of expressing their dissatisfaction because of their resentments.   They may be sympathetic only with some points stressed by the heretics and side with them for personal reasons more than anything else.   Nevertheless they are being weighed in God's balances and will be judged by him.

The time arrives when God in his providence provides an opportunity for true loyalty to be tested.   Those who are not really in harmony with the church of which they are members are carried away.   On the other hand those who may seem to lack strength of personality or mind, whom some

173

would think to be the easiest prey to the factious party which in the hour of trial looks for as much support as possible, often surprise everyone by being faithful, true and firm. Their loyalty to the body of Christ and thus to Christ himself is gloriously manifested.

Faithfulness to the truth is put to the test as well as loyalty. But there is a further test for which we need to be approved. That test is the test of humility and submission. Church membership involves this aspect which is of major importance. It is all very well talking about serving God but all service involves submission to the Master. If we do not see submission within the body of God's people then where can we expect to see it? An enormous amount of activity goes on today which is totally devoid of any discipline by way of submission to gathered churches. It would seem that there are some characters who in this earthly life are completely unable to submit to others. They operate therefore in their own right and create their own following. There are so many agencies run by autocrats who use *their own* prestige or *their own* finance to operate *their own* work independent of any local church. This is important to note because sometimes the heresy or self-chosen opinion may not be of damning character. It may be a distortion merely of some practice, or some truth exaggerated or pressed out of proportion. It is made a matter of contention and used as an issue by which a group leader is able to carry off some of the malcontents in a church. Thus a new following is formed around the group leader who himself has never been able to submit to others.

In all this it would seem that the important lesson is that one should encourage and strengthen loyalty within our own hearts—loyalty to God's people and to God's church. It cannot be stressed enough that the testing that God allows is not a testing merely of assent to correct doctrines, but a testing of the whole person, a testing of obedience, of submission, of love to Christ and to his people. Those who love their own self-made opinions or emphases more than what God requires will fail. They will be disapproved. Unless they repent they will be found false in the day of judgment. Those who hold fast and are not carried away will be approved in this life and in the next.

Such testings are real and relevant today. During the last two or three years the writer has come across instances of this. Some can be cited as examples. In one case 29 went out of a church for charismatic opinions and in another case 10 for similar reasons, in another 25 because of hyper-Calvinistic opinions and in another 10 for similar ideas—in another five families with self-formed opinions accompanied by discontent and resistance to much needed reformation. In one traumatic case about half the membership (70) departed because of self-chosen views insisted upon. In the last named instance all have been replaced in a most remarkable fashion mostly by conversions. The pastor and people have been wonderfully vindicated for their firm stand. In most cases the churches are strengthened and emerge humbled, purified and more ready to rely upon God than upon their own abilities and gifts. It is only right to say however that in some (albeit rare instances) there is terrible tragedy which simply cannot be explained. One church known to us of over 60 members has been utterly shattered and now no longer exists. It is likely that the name of Christ and the cause of the Gospel in that town will not be recovered for a generation.

Those scattered abroad by such a devastating affair may through the lessons learned be used and contribute helpfully in other churches.

The main lesson learned from 1 Corinthians 11:19 and from the out-working of that express declaration of God's permissive will, is that the glory of any local church is enhanced when those who resist the heresy in question emerge approved and strengthened. Because all things are possible with God individuals who have been carried away may be retrieved and in their recovery they may live to serve God and enhance the glory of Christ their redeemer by humble and submissive service in his body called the church local.

d. *Building according to the Scriptural principle of 1 Corinthians 3:11-15*

In the first chapter on the subject of the ideal church, reference was made to the composition of a church but with one aspect in mind, namely, that of children growing up into the ranks who while living outwardly respectable lives turn out to be unspiritual. But apart from that aspect, if due care is not exercised, unruly or carnal elements can gain entrance into a church from outside and soon acquire such a measure of influence or control that the church is adversely affected. Discipline which is exercised in a spiritual and discerning manner is then essential if the glory of a church is to be preserved. It is such discipline that our Lord was calling for at Thyatira. The false prophetess, Jezebel, had to be dealt with but it seemed that the church was reluctant to act. Perhaps it was too hot an issue to be faced at that time. It cannot be denied that immorality and other disorders have been left to persist in churches because of fear of the reactions that would follow.

Wise, competent and united elders in a church are essential when there is schism in a body such as existed at Corinth. The glory of any church will soon be destroyed where contention and division go on unchecked.

What is the best way of trying to maintain the unity of a church? What is the best foundation for preserving her as a united body which will reflect the glory of God and be like that beautiful figure in the Song of Solomon, "fair as the morn, bright as the sun, and terrible as an army with banners" (S. of S. 6:4)? I believe Paul's answer to this question is found in his letters to the divided church at Corinth and I refer now to 1 Corinthians 3:11-15.

In this passage the Church is likened to a building and the officers of the

Church to labourers. Jesus Christ is the foundation of the building. Upon that foundation can be built incombustible materials, gold, silver or precious stones, or combustible, wood, hay, stubble. We are told that every man's work will be tried. If his work comes through the fire he will receive a reward. If his work is burned up he will suffer loss. It is added that he himself will be saved as one coming through the fire.

Now the point at issue is whether the gold, silver and precious stones represent true believers who are built on Christ and joined to him or are these materials representative of true doctrines. In contrast to that does the hay, wood and stubble represent those who made a profession of faith and yet were not truly part of Christ's body? Will they be burned up?— or are we to understand the hay, wood and stubble to be false doctrines that will be burned up.

It should be immediately apparent that there is little or no ordeal involved in a conflagration of false doctrines like the bonfire made at Ephesus of spurious books (Acts 10:19). There might be shame felt by those who may have preached some of those false doctrines but with the shame much joy that all pestilential errors should now be consumed once and for all.

However the idea that it is false doctrines that will go up in smoke cannot be the correct one because the text explicitly declares that a man's work will be tested. The fiery testing of God's perfect judgment and assessment will be applied to the Gospel labourer's work as it applies to people. It is they who will have to stand the test. The doctrines will have done their work one way or another and those same doctrines will have produced a harvest. The work concerns living people. Therein lies the ordeal. Will they survive? Will they come through? Many Gospel ministers with whom I correspond are scrupulous about the doctrines they preach and have little fear about that matter because they know they have not compromised the Gospel. But most of us have very great concern about the people harvested through our preaching. Some have already gone to be with the Lord and we are confident that they were, and are now truly in Christ. There are others who fill us with deep concern. Sometimes we are filled with dire forebodings as far as they personally are concerned because their works are not consistent with the faith they profess (Jas. 2:24). I say this to show that it is always people we are concerned with. A pastor or an elder is concerned with the people—that is their work and that is what will be subject to the test. A surgeon's primary concern is for the survival of his patient. His surgical instruments are important. If they are the cause of infection and death he will be grieved by the negligence involved. The sorrow concerns the dead patient not the punishment of or destruction of the instruments.

Let us view the context of 1 Corinthians 3:1-15. In verse nine Paul actually says that *we are* God's building. In verse sixteen he declares that we are the temple of God. It is not doctrine but people that make up the temple. Two New Testament passages confirm that it is people that make up God's building, namely, Ephesians 2:20-22 and 1 Peter 2: 4,5. *We* are builded together (Eph. 2:22) and we are lively stones built up in a spiritual house (1 Pet. 2:5).

We should observe that all the descriptions of coming judgment concern people who will all be put without exception to the most vigorous trial. In the sermon on the mount our Lord likens the ordeal to a terrifying storm and flood which test the foundation of every personal structure. In Revelation 20:13 the testing is one of utmost scrutiny. Every work is examined of what kind it is. This is confirmed by Christ's description of the Great Judgment in Matthew 25. The day referred to by Paul—the day shall declare it (1 Cor. 3:13) is the day of judgment. That to be declared is the total outcome of a man's work and teaching in terms of that which is ultimate and final—namely, eternal salvation or eternal perdition!

The Church of Rome has made much of this passage in an attempt to bolster up the utterly unscriptural notion of purgatory. But the ordeal through which the workman passes is not a purgatory in which his own soul is purified and refined but an ordeal in which his work is tested. He is compelled to observe the results of his work as it respects people. This is what the author of the Hebrews epistle means when he says that those who are entrusted with rule "must give account" and then adds that joy or grief is involved (Heb. 13:17).

There is surely no better way of assimilating the solemn meaning of what this means than viewing present day examples. The Gospel minister who cuts the corners, lowers Scriptural requirements and admits those into the membership of the church who do not bear the marks of regeneration is harming the church. He may be praised as a successful preacher but he is deceiving people in the worst possible way. If his church is made up of false converts there awaits him in the day of assessment the most awful ordeal of seeing most of what he thought he had accomplished relegated to perdition. So serious is his error in allowing this to happen that he may wonder about his own salvation. Yet Paul says that though he suffers so great a loss he himself may pass the test being proved a true Christian even though a deplorably deficient workman.

And what are we to say of our modern evangelists, some of whom pass on false converts by the tens of thousands? Since I am dealing with the local church and her glory all I will do in answering that question is to say that local churches should examine the basis on which they cooperate in evangelistic campaigns and also exercise the sound Scriptural standards for testing the repentance and faith of those who respond to calls for decisions. The discernment required to avoid quenching the smoking flax or breaking bruised reeds, in bringing in lambs but shutting out wolves, is one of the most exacting tasks committed to the elders of churches. The composition of a church has a radical effect on her worth or glory.

Of course mistakes are made. Some may be delayed unduly, others may be admitted and then prove unsound. When such absent themselves or cause trouble or division then loving, firm, patient and determined discipline must be applied for the wellbeing and glory of the church.

Despite the fact that our spiritual warfare is often intense, the demands upon our limited resources are relentless. The malice of Satan is persistent. Therefore we must take heed to the whole counsel of God and preserve as best we are able all that constitutes the basic worth or glory of the church to which we have been joined. If then the Lord is pleased to send heightened glory, his will be the praise and ours will be the joy (Ps. 126).

12

The Architecture
of the Local Church

by John Davison

DURING THE LAST FEW CAREY CONFERENCES A TRADITION HAS BEEN established of visiting some Puritan Meeting House in the vicinity of the Conference centre. These visits have created considerable interest in the question of the type of accommodation used by churches and the layout most suitable to the needs of Reformed worship. It is clear that many would welcome a consideration of this subject since it affects every church and, rightly or wrongly, frequently involves the church in its greatest financial outlay.

It has become normal among evangelicals, in contrast to those holding ritualistic views, not to be too particular about the building in which the local church worships. Quite correctly, the emphasis has been placed on the presence of Christ in the midst of his people wherever two or three are gathered in his name. "God can bless us in a tin shed" has become the attitude of many, and it appears normal that the more spirited the church, the less attention is paid to the environment of worship, as if there is something very worldly in desiring a well designed place of worship. From a superficial reading of the Bible many would claim that there is nothing laid down in Scripture to dictate the form of such a place.

The results of this attitude are too obvious to require attention and comment, and are not only a barrier to outsiders whom we seek to reach, and an inconvenience to our worship but are dishonouring to God in failing to present a correct, biblically-based expression of our faith. In *Christ and Architecture*, which is perhaps the only book on the subject of relating Reformed worship to its architectural expression, Donald I. Bruggink states: "Architecture for Churches is a matter of Gospel. A church that is interested in proclaiming the gospel must also be interested in architecture, for year after year the architecture of the Church proclaims a message that either augments the preached Word or conflicts with it . . . if the gospel of Christ is worthy of accurate verbal proclamation week by week, it is also worthy of faithful architectural proclamation, where its message speaks year by year."[1]

Historical Retrospect

The rich legacy of church buildings which we possess in Britain shows clearly in concrete terms the various beliefs and practices of the worshippers over the centuries. In the medieval Gothic structures the long nave was designed for the ceremonial processions and the chancel, cut off by a rood-screen from the remainder of the building, was the province of the priests, where they performed the superstitious rites of the Roman Church. The columned nave with its mysterious lighting from (idolatrous) stained glass windows was not designed for the hearing of sermons. At the Reformation this was all changed. The preaching of the gospel was so important that the Reformers could not allow the churches to remain as they were. The stone altars which spoke so forcibly of the blasphemies of the mass and denied the finished work of Christ were broken up. A wooden communion table was set up in the chancel. The rood-screen was torn down and the faithful welcomed into the chancel to sit around the table in primitive apostolic simplicity. Out went the stained glass and in its place was substituted plain glass to let in more light so that the common people could open their Bibles and follow the sermon. A prominent place was assigned to the pulpit on the long side of the nave to allow as many as possible to gather within sound of the Word of life. A large sounding board would be constructed over the pulpit to emphasise its importance and to prevent the words of the preacher being lost in the high vaulted roof. To the Reformers these matters were not things indifferent, they were vital to the proper functioning and expression of the church. However, like Stephen, they believed that "God dwelleth not in temples made with hands", and in a time of crisis, such as that experienced by the 17th century Scottish Covenanters, men of this stamp were prepared to forsake their buildings and continue to worship in the open air or in barns. So we must avoid regarding the place of worship as a peculiarly holy place consecrated in some mysterious manner and in which alone God is to be found but must also avoid the opposite view that anything will do for the worship of God. In the Old Testament the prophet Haggai took the people to task for looking after the building of their own houses when they should have given due attention to the temple.

Is it not, therefore, unscriptural of us today to be so particular about arranging our own homes, while giving little or no attention to the ordering of the house of God?

At the heart of the Reformed faith is the doctrine of justification by faith alone in the finished work of Christ. The Bible declares that "faith cometh by hearing, and hearing by the Word of God" (Rom. 10:17). To the Reformers this meant that the one over-riding factor in all their thinking was the preaching of this Word. Only by the means of "the foolishness of preaching" (1 Cor. 1:21) had it pleased God to save men. Now preaching affects the intellect—it is not primarily a matter of the emotions. In the medieval period men were taught to worship God through their emotions. In preaching the emphasis is upon the understanding—the rational part of man. The Reformers found the perfect vehicle for the expression of this rational (not rationalistic) approach in the new style of architecture introduced at the Renaissance. The Renaissance movement in learning and the arts took place simultaneously with the Reformation, and its clear logical approach to architecture commended itself to the Protestant churches. Instead of striving to impress the congregation with mysterious and dramatic effects the whole object was to enlighten men and women by the proclamation of divine truth and everything in the house of God was geared to this end. Consequently, new places of worship (designated "meeting houses", rather than the term "chapel" which is likely to be confused with Romanist places of worship or "church" which applies to the company of believers) represented a totally new concept. The shape of the building tended to become more square so as to ensure that the maximum number of hearers were gathered as near as possible to the preacher, to hear the Word proclaimed. Columns were eliminated or reduced in size by the use of cast iron so that the congregation could see the preacher. A flat ceiling was introduced to eliminate echo and to distribute the preacher's voice throughout the building.[2] The pulpit was given emphasis by its size and prominence and was fitted with a sounding board—a device over the head of the preacher to deflect his voice to all sections of the assembled congregation. Large clear windows were provided to give light to those who could follow the preacher as he read and expounded the Word. Galleries were provided to increase the number of people who were within good hearing distance of the preacher. The whole effect was at once simple, dignified and highly meaningful. Everything was in its correct place— right down to the precentor's box immediately below the pulpit from which the singing was led, and the large communion table around which the believers would literally sit in imitation of the example of the disciples at the institution of the Lord's supper.

Governing Factors

All buildings are erected to fulfil some particular requirement and it is axiomatic that architecture begins with the solution of the functional

181

The Reformed Church, Bant, Holland
Homeliness, dignity and economy achieved through simplicity

needs. Therefore it is essential when planning a new meeting house, or
re-arranging one which exists, that thinking must start with the inside,
where the activity goes on. Creating an external "impression" is secondary. In this respect the Victorians started the wrong way round.
Protestants with an inferiority complex built their meeting houses to look
"ecclesiastical" by use of the Gothic style[3] and these were indistinguishable
from what Bunyan called the "Steeple houses" of the establishment or the
"Mass houses" of the Papists. The resulting interiors were frequently
much less suitable for Reformed worship than the old fashioned "preaching boxes" of the 17th and 18th centuries. When the young Spurgeon
burst upon the London scene it was at the very height of the theological
movement back to ritualism. He decisively entered his theological
protest against this movement and backed home his doctrinal orthodoxy
by stipulating that the new Metropolitan Tabernacle be erected in the old
fashioned classical "Grecian" style.[4] In essence this building was nothing
more than an outsize Puritan meeting house with the people gathered
round the preacher's rostrum in circular form rather than in the square
shape. What then are the basic factors which should govern the design
of our meeting houses?

(1) *The centrality of the preaching of the Word*
The pulpit must be prominent above everything else. I would go so far

as to say that it should be overpowering. The first impression received by an outsider on entering should be that this is the very *raison d'être* of the place. No pulpit—no meeting house. The Romanists do this with their altars. They raise them up on a platform, they make them large and build with enduring stone. They decorate them in elaborate fashion. They erect a huge baldachino (covering) over them and pour down mysterious sources of light to highlight them. The whole plan of the sanctuary is subordinated to and made to focus on the altar. So should we do with the pulpit. Build it large. Use solid construction— why should it consist of 1 inch square steel legs supporting a flimsy lectern? One good thump on such a contraption from a modern Whitefield would be its end! If you must, paint it brightly! Make it high, but beware of placing the front row of pews too near. Give the preacher enough room to move round in it. Do not trap him. Make sure that the pulpit is highlighted, if need be with spotlights concealed in the ceiling. Above all place it in the most prominent focal position which in most plans is central on the end wall. Studiously avoid all temptation to put it off-centre and give prominence to the table or baptistry—this is a sign of sacramentalism! Better still, why not place it central on the (long) side wall and gather the pews around it facing towards it from three directions? This was normal practice in Scottish meeting houses for over 200 years. It could save you the capital and maintenance costs (to say nothing of the distorted sounds) of an amplifier system, or, alternatively, preserve the pastor's voice for a few years longer. The use of an amplifier system in a new building is quite unnecessary if it is designed properly and quite undesirable in view of the inevitable distortion and "remoteness of the preacher" which it produces. Furthermore, there is a direct link between the eye and the ear.[5] Again, Spurgeon realised this, and ensured that children from the Orphanage sat as near the pulpit as possible so that they could *see* him and thus be enabled to *hear* him. It is a fact that if the eye cannot see the preacher, the mind tends to wander. The preacher can tell you much with his hands and if he can be seen comfortably without strain upon the vertebrae of the hearers it will produce better listening. The use of a sounding board above the pulpit will greatly aid the distribution of the preacher's voice and will add tremendous emphasis, and thus importance, to the exposition of the Scripture.

(2) *The Significance of the Sacraments*

There is no ground in Scripture for ignoring the importance of baptism and the Lord's supper. In fact because they were so clearly ordained by our Lord himself in his earthly ministry, we must pay due attention to their recognition and expression in our meeting houses. However, it is clear from Acts chapter 2 verse 42 that the "Apostles' doctrine" (i.e., preaching) took precedence over the breaking of bread. This gives us the clue to the relationship of preaching and the sacraments in the life of the local church, and hence in all honesty our meeting houses should express

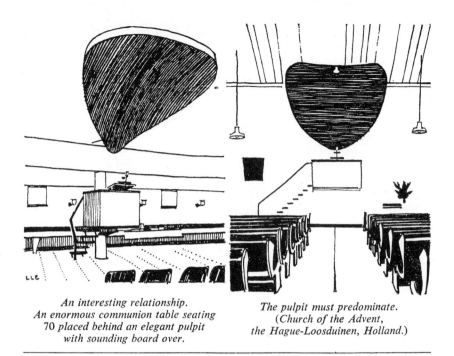

An interesting relationship.
An enormous communion table seating
70 placed behind an elegant pulpit
with sounding board over.

The pulpit must predominate.
(Church of the Advent,
the Hague-Loosduinen, Holland.)

this.   The Word is paramount, but the sacraments are still obvious and important.   The solution generally adopted in the past has been to place a large pulpit behind and above the table.   But regrettably the baptistry has been almost forgotten; in fact stowed away under the floor as if Baptists have an embarrassment hidden below the deck of which they are ashamed.   We do not need to place it half way up the end wall, nor situate it immediately inside the entrance to the meeting house, like some subterranean public convenience down which worshippers are prone to fall.   I am not exaggerating—it is not unknown for paedo-baptists to mistake such baptistries (especially when tiled) for the church toilets! Surely there is a better method of impressing upon our friends the serious nature of the ordinance.   If the congregation is located on a flat floor the baptistry will need to be raised up to the view of all and this will make it necessary to raise the pulpit still higher.   However, if the congregation can be seated on a sloping floor (and how few sites are flat) then a "grand-stand" effect, (like the slopes of Jordan where John's activities could be clearly watched) is obtained, and the baptistry can be located at floor level with the pulpit above, but not too high.   Other solutions can be devised providing the *evidence* of the baptistry is to be seen at all times, not only to remind believers of their obligations (a reason frequently brought forward for the paedo-baptist arrangement where the font is placed near the main entrance door) but also as a challenge and testimony to un-believers.   For too long we have preached a lop-sided Gospel of repentance

184

and faith and have ignored the other part of the great commission—to command converts to be baptised as a sign of their union with Christ in his death, burial, and resurrection. We are apt to preach the "repent" part of Peter's exhortation, but omit the "and be baptised every one of you!" (Acts 2:38). A properly displayed baptistry speaks eloquently of this union.

The Lord's table, as can be seen from Acts chapter 2, verses 42 and 46, played a prominent part in the apostolic Church where the practice was to hold the communion service weekly, or even daily at times. In Holland, Scotland, and other countries the Reformed practice has been to literally sit down at a large table in marked contrast to the unreformed practice of Rome and others to bring communicants to kneel at an altar rail. This alone is reason enough for adopting this practice, but when one studies the New Testament and early Church practice the whole idea of regarding this as a memorial supper becomes even more meaningful.

In some churches today there tends to be quite a problem regarding unbelievers coming and sitting down in the main body of the congregation, thus creating difficulties for the elders in the distribution of the elements during the communion service. To avoid this there is much to be said for the communicants, at least in small churches of under 100 members, coming forward to sit around a long table or a series of tables. One new church has six linked tables accommodating 80 communicants at each sitting. In Holland, some churches have a "communion room" attached to and open to, the main body of the meeting house, but nevertheless recognisable as a separate space. This can also be used to seat overflow congregations or for other special functions. It has even been suggested that a high level "upper room" might be constructed off the main auditorium, but, beware! To keep pace with this exaggerated literalism, it might be necessary to turn the baptistry into a section of the river Jordan!

The table should look like a table as well as be used as one. If the Scriptural significance of the supper is to be retained by the use of the common cup and the one loaf symbolising the one body (no concessions made to modern hygienic "medicinal glass" theology!) then it would seem logical to leave the cup and the plate on the table at all times, even when not in use, as a reminder of the significance of the table. If it is objected that the church's silver plate is far too precious to leave lying around, it needs to be asked why the church doesn't use something more domestic (as would have been used by our Lord at the institution of the ordinance). Stainless steel is more practical and far cheaper, not to mention the endless possibilities presented in the realm of pottery. In fact, this point of domestic family atmosphere should be reflected in the table itself. No elaborately carved affair covered with texts is required. If a text is needed to show its function then its basic design has failed to demonstrate its use. A solid, plain wooden table or one constructed of tubular steel

*The Church gathered around
the Word.
(The Cornerstone Church,
Santpoort, Holland.)*

and plastic laminate would be ideal to convey the appropriate character. It might further be worth considering doing away with the idea of special high backed and padded chairs for the elders.   Surely the Lord's table isn't the place for status symbols.   Why not domestic chairs for all?

Great care should be taken to avoid misuse of the table.   Its function is to serve the purpose of a family remembrance feast.   It is not a flower pedestal or a resting place for offering plates.   When some foreigners enter our sanctuaries, they get the impression that we worship flowers, or perhaps the organ pipes!   The focal point of the meeting house must be reformed according to the Word of God and all other items, however pleasant or necessary, must be relocated.   Is the offering plate system essentially biblical?   When our Perth church re-adopted the traditional Scottish "box or plate at the door" system, the offerings actually increased, much to the amazement of the sceptics!   By all means let our meeting houses be places of beauty and flowers have an important part to play in this, but we do not eat them at the Lord's supper, nor is it helpful to have to spend the service viewing the precentor or presiding elder peering at the congregation from behind the undergrowth, first one side, then t'other!   It is even more ludicrous if he himself is bearded!   In one Scottish example the worshippers cross a well planted and enclosed courtyard before entering the meeting house, but once inside their whole attention is focused upon the pulpit, table, or baptistry (whichever is in use).   When they turn round to leave they are again confronted with the beauty of the flowers in the courtyard through a large picture window in the rear wall of the meeting house.   Apart from serving as a place of pleasantness and beauty, such a courtyard could administer to the communion and friendship of the gatherers, which issue we now take up for discussion.

(3) *The Concept of the Gathered Church*

As Baptists, we hold firmly to the biblical concept of the local church as a fellowship of believers who have all been born (spiritually) into, and adopted into, the family of God. The members of this fellowship are not to be merely on nodding terms, but are to live the common life of a set-apart community, though in the world they are not of the world. They have a vital corporate life. They are not just a loose conglomeration of worshippers but have a common love for each other. This unity is fundamental and is why so many of the older churches, and some of the newly founded ones, tie their members one to another by means of a church covenant.[6] Surely this vital principle must not be overlooked in the design of our meeting houses. It is not enough just to provide an adequate number of comfortable seats. Expression must be given to this oneness.

There are several ways in which this can be achieved. In an open air meeting or in medieval days before seats were introduced into ecclesiastical buildings the natural tendency is for people to gather around the preacher in a half circle. This is the most economic way in which to accommodate people around a focal point. Such a plan is eminently suitable for expressing the oneness of the local church gathered around the Word and ordinances. However, as the use of chairs tends to emphasise individualism and the cost of curved pews is prohibitive, it may be necessary to modify the idea by straightening out the seating lines. In the old Puritan meeting houses and throughout the 18th century the general arrangement was to have the pews arranged in three blocks facing inwards on three sides of a square or rectangle with the pulpit on the fourth. This involves the preacher in extra work in preaching through an arc of 180 degrees. But it has the advantage of causing him to look specifically at the different groups rather than staring into space in the general direction of the congregation, most of whom are sheltering behind the people in front of them. With the three-sided arrangement many more people are brought within a short range of the preacher. The use of balconies on one, two or three sides can further add to the expression of the gathered church and bring the congregation nearer to the preacher. Another method is to place the congregation in a "pit" or sunken area below the general floor level of the perimeter circulation spaces. The congregation thus becomes an entity in its own right. Every attempt to divide the congregational seating in two by a central aisle must be stoutly resisted. There is nothing worse practically than to preach to an aisle in a church divided into two groups without any logical explanation for such a division. However, the use of a two or three sided seating arrangement can be used effectively to subdivide the total sanctuary so that when small meetings are required

Toxteth Chapel, Liverpool
an example of a dignified and functional interior

(e.g., weddings, etc.) it is possible to fill only one section of the seating and thus to avoid the sparsely inhabited "prairie effect" when a few people place themselves everywhere in a large building. This disintegrated effect makes it appear as though each surviving member was suffering from an infectious disease and needed to be separated by a maximum distance from the other victims.

It is a strange fact that in recent years some Baptist churches have followed the unreformed churches in introducing choirs into their building without any New Testament justification. If it is thought that the God ordained system of congregational singing is impossible to implement in a given church and the singing is so bad that something has to be done, why not place the best singers in the rear pews to sing *with* and assist the congregation rather than locate them in the same situation as entertainers at the front facing the congregation and singing *to* them. The whole problem of entertainment in our meetings is outside the scope of this article, but it must be acknowledged that some older buildings would appear to be so ill suited to such entertainment that one wonders if their designers went out of their way to ensure that such an activity was impossible in the church. In this connection the use of a "platform" instead of a pulpit for the preaching of the Word is very open to abuse. Only one preacher is needed at one time in the pulpit and although the pulpit should be designed as visually dominating, it need not be so large as to accommodate a group of entertainers who have no scriptural place in the church anyway. Also, it should be recorded at this point that it is very distracting for a preacher when members of the congregation are intent on studying the reaction to the preaching registered on the faces of the choir members, or organist or deacon. It is always better for all platformers to sit with the congregation during the preaching. It has been well pointed out that the best position musically for all aids to singing is from the rear and hence the positioning of the organ in the rear gallery of the older Lutheran meeting houses. It also avoids the organist being under the unnecessary gaze of the entire congregation.

However, having stressed the importance of expressing the unity of the local body of believers gathered at the Lord's table, there is something to be said for the *architectural* recognition of those whom the church has *spiritually* recognised as shepherds of the flock. In Holland the elders often have special pews near the pulpit for their exclusive use. It then immediately becomes apparent who, in human terms, runs the church and visitors who want spiritual help are able to know whom to approach. The old Scottish custom was (and still is in some areas) to lock up the elders, complete with communion table, in their own box pew. The church is then *seen* to be under discipline. One delightful feature in the Dutch churches is that space is often provided for the elders own copy of the Confession of Faith to be placed alongside the Bible in the elders' pew, symbolising the adherence of the church, through its elders, to its doctrinal basis. Woe to any visiting preacher who sees an elder reach for his copy of the Confession during the exposition!

Conclusions

The primary object of this article has been to stimulate thought rather than propose specific solutions. It will never be possible to include everything which might be desirable in a meeting house, especially if this consists of the conversion of a building originally designed for some other use. However, the principles set down provide a framework to direct thought and design. The most important matter is to obtain the right approach to the ordering of the meeting house: details will then follow naturally.

To summarise, three important factors must be kept in mind:

The Building Matters

It can either honour or dishonour our God who is worshipped in it. The Scripture exhorts us to "let all things be done decently and in order". If we are rightly concerned to return to a New Testament structure for the local church, let us ensure, so far as is possible, that this is given adequate visual expression in our meeting houses.

Buildings matter because they involve the expenditure of large sums of money given for the work of the Lord. Good design is a matter of good stewardship.

Buildings matter because, if badly designed, they can hinder the activities of the local church. Convenience and beauty must go along together.

Freedom from Bondage

One of our primary prerequisites in the realm of reformation is liberation from the rule of erroneous traditions. Generally speaking, most of what has been introduced into Christianity in the past hundred years or more is suspect or positively detrimental to true New Testament Christianity, and nowhere is this more evident than in the realm of church architecture. The sacramentalist longitudinal plan with emphasis all on the table (or altar) is now almost universal. Nearly every book dealing with the design of places of worship advocates this arrangement. Radical thinking is urgently required on the part of the Lord's people if their buildings are to avoid a direct denial in permanent visual terms of the verbal message which is proclaimed from the pulpit.

Function not Style

Lastly, attention must be concentrated primarily on the functional aspect of the design concept. This is not to say that a merely functional solution in itself is adequate, but that any solution to the design of a meeting house without an adequate functional synthesis is unsatisfactory. Basic aesthetic values arise out of imaginative functional solutions to basic functional problems, and should not be regarded as in opposition to them.[7]

May the Lord grant to his people boldness, imagination and understanding that all things might be ordered according to the New Testament pattern.

REFERENCES

[1] *Christ and Architecture* by Donald J. Bruggink and Carl H. Drappers, Eerdmans Publishing Company, 1965. This book is an absolute "must" in the reading of every elder and deacon. Every church should have a copy in its library.

[2] See *Preaching and Preachers*, by Dr. D. M. Lloyd-Jones, pages 162 and 163. "The first essential in a church building is that it should have good acoustic properties. . . . The one great rule, the essential rule in that respect, is a flat ceiling. . . . Flat ceilings should be compulsory. Our forefathers knew this. They built square buildings with flat ceilings, and the result was, and is, that however big they might be, they are acoustically almost perfect. It is not the size of the building that matters; the acoustics are mainly determined by the ceiling."

[3] Ibid., page 162.

[4] *The Full Harvest;* C. H. Spurgeon's Autobiography, pages 11-12. Spurgeon says that the reason for the Tabernacle being designed in the Grecian style was that "We have a great part of our Scriptures in the Grecian language". He also proposed, "Every Baptist place should be Grecian, never Gothic. . . . God give us the power and life of that master of the Grecian tongue, the apostle Paul, that here like wonders may be done by the preaching of the Word as were wrought by his ministry". While agreeing heartily with the latter part of Spurgeon's statement, it must be acknowledged that the former part was very much the expression of a Victorian.

[5] See *Preaching and Preachers* pages 82-83. "effective speaking involves action."

[6] 2 Cor. 8:5.

[7] It is accepted that there is no such thing as a standard plan. The needs of each church must inevitably differ in varying degrees.

Also by Carey Publications

THE WAY AHEAD

96 pages
60 pence